Praise for *Cyber Crime Fighters: Tales from the Trenches*

"*Cyber Crime Fighters: Tales from the Trenches* offers one of the most insightful views of the latest criminal threats to the public: cyber crime. This book provides a good primer on how your personal information can be easily obtained by some of the folks you least want to have it."
—Maureen Boyle, crime reporter,
The Enterprise of Brockton, MA

"Experts Felicia Donovan and Kristyn Bernier pull no punches in explaining the dangers lurking on the Web, from identity appropriation and theft to using new technology and the Internet to facilitate real-life stalking. Parents especially will be shocked at how easy it is for predators to target and solicit children online.

"By clearly explaining the dangers that lurk online and highlighting practical tips to minimize your risk, the authors have created a book that not only educates but empowers readers to protect themselves."
—Jennifer Hemmingsen, columnist and former public safety reporter,
The (Cedar Rapids, Iowa) Gazette

"*Cyber Crime Fighters* provides a thorough and frank look at the dangerous, ever-evolving world of crime on the Net. A sobering, informative read all the way through."
—David Gambacorta, crime reporter,
Philadelphia Daily News

"Excellent book with a lot of real-world examples and prevention tips. Highly recommended for everyone who wants to be armed against online threats."
—Dr. Vladimir Golubev, Director,
Computer Crime Research Center

"A great resource for both technophiles and technophobes in the brave new world of cyber crime."
—Jana G. Pruden, court and crime reporter,
Regina Leader-Post

"In times where education in cyber crime or new-age crime is a must, this book is the answer. With elaborate case studies and apt examples, it is interesting for professionals and the public alike. A hearty thanks to Felicia and Kristyn for an excellent read."
—Sunny Vaghela, CTO, TechDefence Security Consulting,
Cyber Crime Investigator, Cyber Crime Cell,
Ahmedabad, Gujarat, India

DATE DUE

NOV 0 2 2010	
NOV 1 6 2010	
DEC 0 3 2012	

CYBER CRIME FIGHTERS

TALES FROM THE TRENCHES

FELICIA DONOVAN AND
KRISTYN BERNIER

800 East 96th Street,
Indianapolis, Indiana 46240 USA

Cyber Crime Fighters: Tales from the Trenches

ISBN-13: 978-0-7897-3922-3
ISBN-10: 0-7897-3922-4

Library of Congress Cataloging-in-Publication Data:

Donovan, Felicia.

 Cyber crime fighters : tales from the trenches / Felicia Donovan and Kristyn Bernier.

  p. cm.

 ISBN 978-0-7897-3922-3

 1. Computer crimes. 2. Computer crimes--Investigation 3. Internet.

 I. Bernier, Kristyn. II. Title.

 HV6773.D66 2009

 363.25'968--dc22

                                2008043878

Printed in the United States of America

First Printing: December 2008

Trademarks

All terms mentioned in this book that are known to be trademarks or service marks have been appropriately capitalized. Que Publishing cannot attest to the accuracy of this information. Use of a term in this book should not be regarded as affecting the validity of any trademark or service mark.

Warning and Disclaimer

Bulk Sales

Que Publishing offers excellent discounts on this book when ordered in quantity for bulk purchases or special sales. For more information, please contact

U.S. Corporate and Government Sales
1-800-382-3419
corpsales@pearsontechgroup.com

For sales outside of the U.S., please contact

International Sales
international@pearson.com

Associate Publisher
Greg Wiegand

Acquisitions Editor
Michelle Newcomb

Development Editor
Craig Leonard

Managing Editor
Kristy Hart

Project Editor
Anne Goebel

Copy Editor
Bart Reed

Permissions Editor
Marcy Lunetta

Indexer
Lisa Stumpf

Proofreader
Water Crest Publishing

Publishing Coordinator
Cindy Teeters

Book Designer
Anne Jones

Compositor
TnT Design

Contents at a Glance

Table of Contents

List of Cases

Foreword

When I entered law enforcement in 1983, there were no personal computers and therefore no type of cyber crime. Had anyone said the name "cyber crime" back then, we would have thought they were talking about a movie involving superheroes! Fast forward to today, and law enforcement along with the rest of the world comes to a grinding halt when computers malfunction or are otherwise interrupted.

We often joke about how were we able to get along before we had computers and cell phones. But if there is one crime that has changed how we do business, it is indeed cyber crime. It has revolutionized the field of law enforcement. Child predators in particular are now able to trade images worldwide of real children being sexually exploited and tortured from the comfort of their own homes. These crimes defy jurisdictional and political boundaries. Adults who are sexually attracted to children can easily find and manipulate children online. These are the worst of the cyber crimes, and there are simply not enough trained police officers in the world to stop them.

As history shows, where there is a new way to commit crimes, criminals will find it. Computers and the associated technology that comes with them is the proverbial double-edged sword. It is an avenue that opens up all possibilities for good and for evil. We live in a unique time when children are growing up in what can best be described as an Internet society. Their parents (my generation) know far less about the Internet than they do. But the criminals are right there with them.

There is no better time than now for *Cyber Crime Fighters: Tales from the Trenches* to be written and published. Both authors bring their own unique perspective and firsthand experience to this subject. This book should be mandatory reading for every rookie officer attending the police academy, as well as every seasoned officer, and for all citizens who want to protect themselves and their families. We may never have enough trained officers to defeat these crimes, but through education, we can enable the public to defend themselves so that they never become victims in the first place.

—Janet Champlin

Retired Captain Janet Champlin is the 2008 recipient of the Women in Law Enforcement Excellence in Performance Award. As Captain of Detectives, she oversaw the Internet Crimes Against Children Task Force. A graduate of the FBI National Academy, she now operates the Black Dog Investigative Agency LLC.

A Message from the Authors

"The only thing necessary for the triumph of evil is for good men to do nothing."

—Edmund Burke

Cyber Crime Fighters: Tales from the Trenches is an important part of your personal safety arsenal. The reality these days is that you are far more likely to become a victim of a cyber crime than a physical crime. Preventing victimization online can translate into preventing yourself from being vulnerable offline as well. Studies show a significant correlation between stalking and physical abuse, sexual assault, and even homicide; therefore, every step toward education, awareness, and prevention can make a huge difference in regard to your safety.

Many books are now available about cyber crime and online safety, but few are written from the perspective of two women with over 25 years of combined law-enforcement experience who understand both the limitations of law enforcement and the court system in prosecuting cyber crime—as investigators, experts, and victims of cyber crime.

For example, the reality of the legal system today is that prosecuting a cyber stalker, even if a guilty verdict is obtained, does not mean the offender will necessarily spend a great deal of time behind bars—if they're even sent to prison at all. This does not take into account that only a fraction of these incidences are ever reported, let alone prosecuted. It is estimated that 1.4 *million* people are stalked in America every year. Only 42% actually report their stalker to the police, with 57% saying that they did not initially report for fear of being ignored or laughed at (University of Leicester, 2005). It is estimated that over 80% of stalking incidences on college campuses are not reported to the police (National Victimization of College Women, Fisher, Cullen, & Turner, 2000). That's the painful reality we see day in and day out in our real jobs.

Cyber Crime Fighters chronicles the real-life stories of fighting cyber crime, how it can be prevented, and the human component of victimization—putting a face on the issues and telling the stories of victims that are never told.

We'll show you the shocking tools readily available to cyber stalkers and identity thieves. This book becomes an important tool in your personal safety arsenal by providing information in an easy-to-understand format with resources for further investigation.

We'll reveal tools available to track someone's whereabouts—both in person and online—including many that can be installed in under 5 minutes! We'll cover important issues such as whether it's legal for someone to covertly take your picture with a digital camera and post it online. We'll provide specific websites for you to get a better idea of how much of your personal information is already available online, plus teach you how to limit your information from getting out there in the first place. These are the tools of cyber stalkers, but we want you to be aware of them so you know exactly how a cyber stalker thinks. For a cyber stalker, information is dominance and power, and we show you the websites they use and the lengths they'll go to obtain that power. *Cyber Crime Fighters* shows how a few simple steps can reduce your web whereabouts from being tracked. We introduce the concept of online voyeurism while explaining the laws about digital privacy, and we give you easy steps to follow to shore up your computer's defenses to prevent identity theft. *Cyber Crime Fighters* covers the most recent stories and technologies to ensure your personal online safety. We even share our own personal experiences, including becoming victims of cyber crime and trying to "catch our own predators." We also give you and your children important safety tools to use.

Cyber Crime Fighters covers the impact of social networks, the migration of cyber crime to the cell phone platform, the Adam Walsh Act, legislation to stiffen penalties against sex offenders, voyeurism, YouTube as a virtual ground for all kinds of criminal activity, and the horror of online dating gone bad.

If you were to install a security system in your house, does it guarantee you'll never get burglarized? Of course not, but it can significantly reduce the chances of someone breaking into your house. You still need to be vigilant and mindful. Consider this book an adjunct to your personal safety system. It is the flashing red alert to advise you that the email that sounds too good to be true, is. It is the caution flag that let's you know someone's demeanor could easily lead them to becoming an online stalker. It is the resource that shows you what tools are available that make it easy for someone to track your whereabouts, read your email, and steal your identity. We even show you ways to protect your iPod and laptop from getting stolen.

The purpose of this book is not to scare anyone away from going online, but rather to educate readers on how to go online and be safe. The Internet can be a very safe place with some basic knowledge of what is *not* safe and how to avoid it.

Stay safe.

—Felicia and Kristyn

---

note

Whenever possible, we have used actual cases that have been publicly disseminated. In many cases, we have identified offenders by name. We do not, however, identify victims by name, even if their names were publicly released. We have changed the names of victims in order to protect their identity. We feel very strongly about not revictimizing anyone for the sake of this book.

About the Authors

Felicia Donovan is a law-enforcement technology and cyber crime expert, having spent the last 10 years at a New England–based police department as the Information Systems Manager. She delivers keynote addresses and frequently lectures on cyber crime–related issues, including online safety. Her experience in computer forensics was recognized by the FBI, in particular her work in enhancing digital images of child victims of a pedophile. She is the author of *The Black Widow Agency* series of books and has been featured in many articles, including articles in *Law Enforcement Technology Magazine*. She has been a victim of identity theft and of caller ID spoofing—a cyber crime that caused her to become unwittingly involved in a homicide investigation. She is a member of the International Association of Chiefs of Police, New Hampshire Police Association, Sisters in Crime, and Mystery Writers of America. For more information, visit her website at www.feliciadonovan.com.

Kristyn Bernier is a detective and 15-year veteran of a New England–based police department whose current specialization is undercover Internet crimes and special investigations, which includes narcotics and other vice crimes. In addition to fighting cyber crime, she spent 5 years as an undercover narcotics investigator, and she also specializes in the areas of domestic violence, stalking, sexual assault, and sexual offenders. Kristyn is an investigator with the Northern New England Internet Crimes Against Children Task Force and has received recognition for that work from the New Hampshire Department of Justice. She is the recipient of the New Hampshire Attorney General's award for her contributions to narcotics cases and is a member of the Sex Offender Monitoring and Tracking committee. She is also a certified crisis negotiator with her jurisdiction's regional tactical Emergency Response Team. She has addressed legislative sessions in an attempt to modify and strengthen sexual predator laws and frequently addresses the public regarding online safety for children, parents, and teachers.

Acknowledgments

Once again, Kristyn had a great idea. Amazing what comes out of your head. I owe you, Partner. To my agent, Jill Grosjean, for her continued hard work and support, thank you. To everyone at Que, we made a great team.

To my siblings, John, Allison, and Vi, for always being there.

And always, to my friends and family, especially Jess and John, with all my love. You make all the work worthwhile.

—Felicia

This is for the officers, investigators, prosecutors, advocates, social workers, and health professionals who fight for justice every day; who give 110% of themselves when the call comes in; who come armed with patience, understanding, passion, compassion, and creativity in their efforts to end the nightmare and put the bad guy away. This includes the incredible cops and support staff I work with every day.

To four of the finest supervisors I have ever served under, who are also four of the finest people I have ever worked alongside of: Captain Janet Champlin of the Portsmouth Police Department, Commander James Norris of the NH Attorney General's Drug Task Force, Sergeant Richard Farrell of the NH State Police, and the late Lieutenant Steven Demo of the Portsmouth Police/NHDTF. From each of you I have learned so much; from each of you I have received support, guidance, acceptance, and encouragement; from each of you I have collected special things that have contributed to who I am today.

To my mom, the most amazing woman I know, and my dad (who is looking down from heaven and thanking God that my expensive private education wasn't wasted) for everything. To my one and a half men, Shawn and Jagger, both of whom keep me grounded, keep things in perspective, and remind me that there is more to life than my job (xoxo). To my wonderful family and friends (Felicia, you know this includes you). All of my love to all of you.

—Kristyn

We Want to Hear from You!

As the reader of this book, *you* are our most important critic and commentator. We value your opinion and want to know what we're doing right, what we could do better, what areas you'd like to see us publish in, and any other words of wisdom you're willing to pass our way.

As an associate publisher for Que Publishing, I welcome your comments. You can email or write me directly to let me know what you did or didn't like about this book—as well as what we can do to make our books better.

Please note that I cannot help you with technical problems related to the topic of this book. We do have a User Services group, however, where I will forward specific technical questions related to the book.

When you write, please be sure to include this book's title and authors, as well as your name, email address, and phone number. I will carefully review your comments and share them with the authors and editors who worked on the book.

Email: feedback@quepublishing.com

Mail: Greg Wiegand
            Associate Publisher
            Que Publishing
            800 East 96th Street
            Indianapolis, IN 46240 USA

Reader Services

Visit our website and register this book at www.informit.com/title/ 9780789739223 for convenient access to any updates, downloads, or errata that might be available for this book.

1

Cyber Stalking

Toni emerged from her hairdressing appointment to find her ex-boyfriend, Frank, a violent young man who once put her in the emergency room with a broken rib, sitting across the street on a bench. Walking quickly to her car, Toni, hands shaking, fumbled to find the release lock. Once inside, she locked all the doors and sped off. This was the fourth time in the last week that Frank had found out where she was going. She headed toward her friend Claire's house, checking in the rearview mirror the whole way to see if she spotted Frank's car. She deliberately made several wrong turns and circled the block three times to ensure no one was following her. Two hours later and feeling much better from her visit with her friend, Toni stepped out of Claire's house only to find Frank sitting across the street again.

How did Frank always know where Toni was? Just prior to their breakup, Frank had installed a small receiver inside Toni's car that he had purchased on the Internet for $500 (see Figure 1.1). This GPS Snitch device is no bigger than a set of keys and can be hidden in just about anything—a bag, a car—to give a stalker instantaneous knowledge of someone's whereabouts. It runs on batteries but can be hard-wired into a vehicle to eliminate the need for batteries. It was hidden behind the dashboard. The receiver, which was hard-wired into the vehicle, was feeding Toni's whereabouts to Frank 24 hours a day, 7 days a week. All Frank had to do was dial up his cell phone or access a computer to find out exactly where Toni's car was (see Figure 1.2). The map overlay shows the path of a vehicle equipped with GPS Snitch. The path and location can be retrieved via an Internet browser or a web-enabled cell phone. If the cell phone is not web-enabled (meaning it cannot display an Internet page), the location can be sent via text message ("123 Main Street @ 10:05AM") at regular intervals.

(Courtesy Max Borges Agency)

FIGURE 1.1

GPS Snitch device

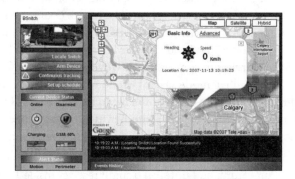

(Courtesy Max Borges Agency)

FIGURE 1.2

Map overlay that shows the path of a vehicle equipped with GPS Snitch

High-Tech Stalkers

Many people are familiar with the term *stalking*, but few understand the concept of *cyber stalking*, which is stalking with a technology component to it. Whether someone is stalking via the Internet or stalking using the many tech tools available for purchase for tracking and snooping on another person, it is cyber stalking.

Many stalkers consider finding and tracking someone a personal challenge, a way of proving that they are smarter than their target. Other times, stalkers' efforts are aimed at trying to upset and provoke their victims by constantly reminding them of their presence. Combine that warped mentality with a little technical knowledge, and it's like leaving a car unlocked with the keys in the ignition. Unfortunately, many people (both men and women) lack the knowledge to understand *how* someone is tracking them.

In this book, we provide numerous examples of cases from both the media and our own experiences in law enforcement with one goal in mind—to make you aware of all the dangers of cyber crime. The more you know, the better your chances are of never becoming a victim.

We not only want to share the tools of cyber criminals, but in the case of cyber stalkers, we explain how they think. We'll put you inside the head of someone who derives devious pleasure in proving he is smarter than his victim and controlling his victim.

GPS FOR THE EX-SPOUSE

Sonya could not understand how her ex-husband always managed to find her. Their marriage had ended rather amicably, or so she thought, so it seemed like more of a coincidence than anything that Peter always seemed to know where she'd been.

"How was the new restaurant?" he asked her one day on the phone.

Sonya knew she hadn't told him about going to the newly opened restaurant with her date, a man she had just begun seeing. But Peter seemed to know everywhere she'd been—whether she'd walked there or had driven. Peter knew when Sonya was at the public library, when she'd taken their son to the pediatrician, and when she went out with Hank, the new man in her life.

How did Peter know Sonya's whereabouts? One day, while Peter came to pick up their son, Sonya left her cell phone on the counter. When Peter insisted that their son would need warmer clothes, Sonya went with her son up into his bedroom to pack more clothing. In the 3 minutes that Sonya was upstairs, Peter had managed to enable GPS (Global Positioning System) tracking on Sonya's cell phone (see Figure 1.3).

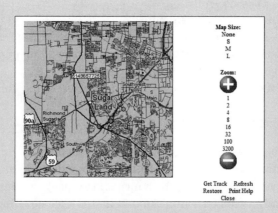

FIGURE 1.3

GPS cell phone tracking

The genesis of GPS was to try and track fleets of trucks making deliveries. By tracking fleets, companies could find the most cost-effective routes to send the trucks on. The technology later emerged on cell phones, whereby a person's location could be determined if ever they had an emergency. When you purchase a cell phone these days, it likely has a feature that can be turned on or off to broadcast the general area you're calling from. But this same feature can easily be used to determine your whereabouts at all times to someone who wants to track you.

"How I Stalked My Girlfriend"

In his February 1, 2006 blog, "How I Stalked My Girlfriend," appearing in *The Guardian* (London), columnist Ben Goldacre writes about how easy it was to set up GPS tracking on his girlfriend's cell phone. He did so with her permission, of course, but even so, he was astounded at how quick and easy it was to do:

I unplugged her phone and took it upstairs to register it on a website I had been told about.... I ticked the website's terms and conditions without reading them, put in my debit card details, and bought 25 GPS Credits for £5.

Almost immediately, my girlfriend's phone vibrated with a new text message. "Ben Goldacre has requested to add you to their Buddy List! To accept, simply reply to this message with 'LOCATE.'" I sent the requested reply. The phone vibrated again. A second text arrived: "WARNING: [this service] allows other people to know where you are. For your own safety make sure that you know who is locating you." I deleted both these text messages.

On the website, I see the familiar number in my list of "GPS devices" and I click "locate." A map appears of the area in which we live, with a person-shaped blob in the middle, roughly 100 yards from our home. The phone doesn't go off at all. There is no trace of what I'm doing on her phone. I can't quite believe my eyes: I knew that the police could do this, and telecommunications companies, but not any old random person with five minutes access to someone else's phone. I can't find anything in her mobile that could possibly let her know that I'm checking her location. As devious systems go, it's foolproof. I set up the website to track her at regular intervals, take a snapshot of her whereabouts automatically, every half hour, and plot her path on the map, so that I can view it at my leisure. It felt, I have to say, exceedingly wrong." (Source: http://www.guardian.co.uk/technology/2006/feb/01/news.g2)

COMPUTER KEY STROKE STALKING

When Annette ended her relationship with her partner, Deborah, she immediately changed her email address, advising only those she most closely trusted of what her new address was. But Deborah seemed to always be able to find out what Annette's new address was. Annette switched from Yahoo! to Google Mail thinking it would make a difference, but it did not. Annette knew her closest friends and family would not divulge her new address, yet within a day or two, she would receive another email from Deborah.

Unbeknownst to Annette, prior to the end of their relationship, Deborah had installed a keylogging program, one of dozens available on the Internet, on Annette's computer (see Figure 1.4). This keystroke-logging program, many types of which are available for free, was not only recording every keystroke Annette made, but was also recording the passwords to every account Annette had. Annette frequently checked her bank balance and paid her bills online. When Annette continued to reject Deborah's efforts to renew their relationship, Annette discovered that her credit cards had been used for unauthorized online purchases.

(Courtesy of SolidOak.com)

FIGURE 1.4

The SnoopStick is a computer thumb drive (USB drive) that, within 60 seconds, launches a secret program that allows someone to view everything typed on the target computer from any other computer in the world.

The keystroke-logging program is not easily detected, and it can monitor websites visited, online chatting, instant messaging programs, and email messages, both incoming and outgoing. It is marketed as a parental control tool and has the ability to block access to websites or restrict access to the target computer during certain hours. It is readily available from www.snoopstick.com for $60.

A TALE OF TECHNOLOGICAL TERROR

In the summer of 2005, Sherri Peak, a mom in the suburbs of Seattle, Washington, needed to separate from her husband's overbearing behavior. He was obsessive, jealous, and insisted on knowing everything she did and everywhere she went. He even demanded to see shopping receipts to match up the timeframes in which she was gone. Things escalated to the point of physical altercations. He repeatedly called her coworkers to determine where she was, ultimately causing Sherri to fear for her safety. Sherri sought a restraining order in October of 2005; however, the judge only granted a mutual order telling the two to stay away from each other. Robert Peak somehow always knew where Sherri was and what she was doing, and he repeatedly violated the order. At one point, he even found out when Sherri was planning to go to the police station to report that he had violated the restraining order. Imagine her surprise when he arrived at the police department ahead of her and had already advised the police that nothing was going on.

Robert's behavior had Sherri fearing for her life. She told *Women's eNews*, "This is a case of 'watch him come kill me...'" and told *Dateline NBC* in an interview, "I lived like a hostage."

Sherri got a new job but did not tell Robert where she was working; however, she spotted him near her new office park. Robert also found his way outside a restaurant where she was attending a birthday party and one day appeared behind her vehicle at the airport. Robert had no reason to know where she was going. Robert sometimes left letters and coffee for her in her car in the morning, always letting her know he was close by.

Sherri changed her locks, but when the installer came to put them in, she realized the seals had been broken on the boxes and that a set of keys was missing. Robert even located a coworker of Sherri's whose house was on the market and showed up at his home pretending to be a homebuyer. He then began asking questions about the women in the office. The coworker later realized it had been Sherri's ex when Sherri showed coworkers a photo of him and asked them to be aware that he might show up at work looking for her.

Sherri Peak knew that Robert had to be using surveillance technology to stalk her; however, when she couldn't find any evidence, she sought help from the Bellevue Police Department, who took her case very seriously. Sherri's vehicle was searched from one end to the other. Police, as well as customs and immigration officers, spent 2 hours going through her car. Frustrated, they went so far as to remove the vehicle's dashboard, and it was there they realized Robert Peak had rigged a cellular telephone with a Global Positioning System into the vehicle. Without Sherri suspecting, Robert had connected the phone to the car battery and had enabled the device to answer without ringing when he called its number. Robert could monitor any conversation going on in Sherri's vehicle at the dial of a number.

Eventually, cellular phone records were obtained, which revealed 99 hours of documented calls placed between August of 2005 and February of 2006, when the device was discovered. There were calls of 1-minute duration and others lasted for more than 45 minutes.

Robert Peak was arrested, and he admitted to installing the cell phone/tracking system. A search of his home netted the missing keys to Sherri's new locks, night-vision goggles, computer spyware, printouts of emails Sherri had written to other people, as well as her bank account numbers and passwords. Police also discovered an application for a pistol permit. Peak was convicted of felony stalking and was sentenced 8 months in jail. Sherri obtained a 10-year restraining order.

note

It should be noted that Sherri Peak went public regarding her case, and to this day, her experience is being used in training across the country for law-enforcement officers, social workers, domestic violence advocates, and prosecutors. This woman turned terror into triumph, and her strength, bravery, and tenacity should be recognized.

The Victim's Side

It is important for victims to work with law enforcement and advocacy groups to develop a safety plan and then methodically build a case. Keeping the victim safe and obtaining the best evidence to prosecute the criminal are priorities. A stalker's behavior is obsessive and can escalate suddenly at any time, making deterrence and criminal apprehension difficult. Often the most dangerous time for a victim is when he or she tries to leave to get help, because a stalker feels threatened by the notion of the victim being inaccessible and this can trigger an escalation in violent behavior.

The good news is that law enforcement agencies are more sensitive these days to victim needs and the dynamics of these dangerous relationships. Laws are changing to reflect the seriousness of these violent crimes. Responding officers and investigators are better trained to build these cases from a behavioral approach as well as a technological approach.

Prosecutors are on board as well, but the reality is that these types of cases are still difficult to prosecute. Typically, these infractions occur over time and in various jurisdictions. Each single incident can initially appear to be benign. A single occurrence of behavior does not often constitute a crime, and even when a pattern of behavior is established, the crime is often a lower-level misdemeanor, which results in very little jail time, if any at all. It is not uncommon for these cases to take months and sometimes years to prosecute, and when a conviction is won, the jail time is not necessarily significant given what terror the victim has endured.

One of our goals in writing *Cyber Crime Fighters: Tales from the Trenches* is that by detailing cases, we help readers recognize specific behavior patterns and steer clear of the person exhibiting them *before* the situation escalates into a dangerous one. We want you to understand that other educated, level-headed, intelligent people have fallen victim to cyber stalkers and predators because they did not recognize those patterns. History, as the saying goes, repeats itself. By sharing all these stories, it is our sincere hope that you will never become part of the history of victimization.

> It is our sincere hope that you will never become part of the history of victimization.

COPS USE GPS, TOO

As a side note, we'd like to point out that the bad guys aren't the only ones using GPS tracking. In June of 2008, the Manchester, Connecticut Police Department made quite a bit of news in their use of a tiny GPS tracking device they placed inside a bottle of Vicodin.

According to news sources, Manchester Police Detective Jim Graham came up with the idea of placing the device in a large pill bottle following a string of bold robberies—including one in which a 16-year-old clerk was held at knifepoint—that had area pharmacies on edge. The GPS device could be set up via a transmitter to notify authorities if it was moved from a designated area.

Police arrested 41-year-old Frederick Faunce of Connecticut for the robberies following his latest break-in in which he scooped up the GPS-enabled bottle. The device was easily tracked via computer to Faunce's truck, which was parked outside his workplace.

This case was widely publicized for law enforcement's efforts to "think outside the box," or in this case "outside the pill bottle."

Identity Assumption

Unlike identity theft, which is usually focused on perpetrating fraud, *identity assumption* is more commonly used to destroy someone's reputation.

An Easy Way to Tarnish a Reputation

Consider the case of Margaret, who ended a 3-year relationship with a man and did not resume dating for over a year until she met the man of her life, Andrew, at a Catholic Singles meeting. Imagine Andrew's shock when he Googled Margaret's name only to find comment after comment that she had posted on pro-abortion websites in favor of abortion. Andrew, a devout Catholic, ended the relationship. It was only after Margaret begged for an explanation that Andrew mentioned the comments he had found. Margaret was shocked.

Falsely posting comments in a public forum that specifically digresses from someone's known beliefs is identity assumption in its mildest form. Imagine someone's picture getting uploaded to the tens of thousands of pornography websites. Imagine having a pornographic website created in your own name along with compromising pictures of yourself. And by the way, those pictures can easily be created using image-editing programs such as Photoshop. This is the same software used by magazine and print editors to make teeth whiter, remove an inch or two from waistlines, and so on. A face from one photo can easily be placed on another or edited using commonly available software.

The Wild, Wild Web

Much of the Internet is still the "Wild, Wild Web" and remains largely unregulated. There is very little authentication of email accounts, websites, and blogs. Anyone can establish them. In an effort to lure pedophiles, law enforcement routinely establishes false identities as young adolescents. There is no validation of age, gender, sex, or location on most free email programs; hence, it is very easy for anyone to create a false identity.

Websites are easy to create with just a bit of technical knowledge. Remember all the phony websites established to accept donations in the wake of Hurricane Katrina? Imagine if a website was created using your name and image with links to such nefarious activities as pornography or even worse, child pornography. This is the modern day equivalent of scrawling "For a good time, call Jane Doe" on the bathroom wall. Someone with an axe to grind can do much damage in little time.

THE DEAN ISENBERG CASE

This is exactly what happened to a female realtor in Florida. This woman, who is married with young children, received more than 700 phone calls, day and night, some of which were answered by her 11-year-old daughter, asking for sexual favors. Her phone was swamped with text messages propositioning her. Finally, when the victim broke down on the phone in tears to one of the callers, the man revealed that he had seen her ad on Craigslist.com.

Craigslist is a nationwide website that allows people to post ads for free. We'll discuss some of our personal experiences with Craigslist and other social networking sites in more detail later on, but in this case, someone posted the victim's phone numbers in more than 20 raunchy personal ads on Craigslist. One ad reads, "Are you looking for a little afternoon delight? Stop by me and you'll leave with a smile." It also included detailed fees for "services," the victim's personal cell phone number, and stated she was operating "in or around Miami downtown."

The female victim hired a private investigator, who was able to trace the postings to a Yahoo! account created falsely in her name. The victim contacted Craigslist and advised them of what was happening. The ads were removed but continued to appear as fast as they were removed. The victim suspected another realtor was behind the efforts because of a real-estate deal that had gone sour between them. Armed with all the information she and her private investigator had gathered, she went to the police.

Many of the ads were resolved back to the personal computers of a 42-year-old rival Florida realtor, Dean Isenberg. By "resolved back," we mean that there is a clearly identifiable way to trace most, if not all, of a person's computer activity when they are on the Internet. We'll get into this further later on, but this is a clear case where it was traceable enough to meet the definition of "probable cause" to obtain a search warrant. Armed with their search warrant, police raided Isenberg's home and seized four computer towers, two laptops, and three BlackBerry smartphones. When forensic investigators searched Isenberg's computer hard drives, they allegedly found evidence connecting him to the ads, along with several photos of scantily clad women, which he purportedly used in the ads.

On January 2, 2008, Isenberg, who, up until then had maintained his innocence, was sentenced to 4 years of probation. As part of a plea deal, Isenberg pleaded guilty to four counts of misdemeanor stalking. Along with the probation, Isenberg was sentenced to 300 hours of community service and ordered to pay $12,500 to the victim to cover investigative costs.

With no regulations whatsoever, people can put together a website for just about anything. Websites can be used for professional reasons. They can be used to sell cars, share recipes, or list team stats. They can provide critical medical information or archive history that would otherwise be lost, but they can also be built to completely damage a person's reputation, promote child sexual exploitation, or to perpetuate a dangerous infatuation.

THE AMY BOYER STORY

In a tragic story that took place not far from where the authors work, Amy Boyer (shown in Figure 1.5) a young woman from Nashua, New Hampshire, was murdered on October 15, 1999, by a young man who claimed to have fallen in love with her while in the eighth grade. What makes this story even more horrendous is that the young man, Liam Youens, 21, had set up not one but two websites professing his love for Amy and his plan to murder her. He made his move one afternoon as Amy left her job at a dentist's office, pulled up beside her, put his gun to the window, and called her name. Seconds after killing Amy, he killed himself.

(© AP Photo/Jim Cole)

FIGURE 1.5

Amy Boyer's parents holding her photo

Detectives investigating this awful tragedy were shocked to find a website with Amy Boyer's name that Youens had built proclaiming his love for Amy. On it, he described how he had been stalking her for years. It also described the killing in detail, exactly as it eventually happened. "When she gets in, I'll drive up to the car blocking her in, window to window," the website read. "I'll shoot her with my Glock."

The website had existed for almost two and a half years. It should be noted that there are millions of web pages are out there, even today, that few people stumble upon unless they have a specific reason to go to them. No regulatory authority can oversee the billions of pages that change each and every day. Websites are coded with "metadata" that lets them be located by search engines. For example, if you type in "Cyber Crime Fighters," you'll likely be taken to the "official" website of www.cybercrimefighters.biz. That is because the website contains "metadata" to tell the search engines where to find it. However, if someone doesn't search for it in the first place, a website could be out on the Web for years and never receive any visitors. That's why no one ever stumbled upon the site Youens created.

The websites were immediately taken down after the murder. According to authorities, Youens had also used the Internet to buy Amy Boyer's social security number from an online company called DocuSearch. He paid $45 for this information. Using false pretenses, he was able to find out Amy's employer address and phone number.

In 2000, as part of the Violence Against Women Act, Congress extended the federal interstate stalking statute to include cyber stalking and adopted Amy Boyer's Law (42 U.S.C. Section 1320 B-23 P.L 106-553), which prohibits the sale or display of an individual's social security number to the public, including sales over the Internet, without prior consent.

Sticks and Stones

Cyber stalking is a unique form of cyber crime because it has the potential to move from a web address to a real address—from the virtual to the actual. Our experience has proven that, too often, cyber stalking is not taken seriously by authorities because it may not involve physical contact or because the victim and stalker do not live in close proximity to each other. This needs to change.

When a victim in New Hampshire complains of being cyber stalked by someone from California, her complaint needs to be taken just as seriously as if the offender lived in the same town and posed a physical threat. It is not acceptable to tell a victim to "turn off your computer" or "change your email address" if she needs that email address for professional purposes.

Even if the cyber stalking never crosses over to a physical threat (and we sincerely hope it doesn't), it is still as frightening, real, and distressing as in-person threats. Words *will* hurt you—being terrified has both psychological and physical manifestations.

The retail giant Wal-Mart was recently taken to task for selling t-shirts that read, "Some call it Stalking. I call it Love" (see a similar t-shirt in Figure 1.6). Women's groups and victim advocacy groups across the country were outraged. Wal-Mart quickly pulled the t-shirts off their shelves and stated, "It is not our desire to encourage or make light of such a serious issue through the sale of any products we carry."

(© CafePress.com)

FIGURE 1.6

A stalking t-shirt similar to the one once carried at Wal-Mart

The "Stalker" E-Card

Imagine you are checking your email and receive notification that you have received an electronic greeting, or "e-card." You click the link and are taken to a site with a black background upon which the following letters appear, one by one, as if they are being typed to you in real time:

Does it bother you to know that I am thinking of your beautiful green eyes and soft brown hair? You can turn this off, you know, and I'll be gone. Or will I? Maybe I'm nearby. Where is that again? That's right, Washington Road. I'm watching you.

How frightening this would be to anyone, but especially to a victim of a stalker, cyber stalker, or domestic violence. And yet the example we've given here is very similar to the eerie stalker e-card message created by a well-known, major greeting card company just a few years ago. The card's design centered around allowing the sender to "customize" it with very specific details, such as hair and eyes, location, and so on.

Just like websites, electronic cards can be created by anyone. There is no validation of who created them or where they came from without a detailed forensic investigation, and that is not likely to occur unless the e-card was somehow connected to a major crime.

Needless to say, this e-card was pulled from the site and is no longer accessible, but we mention it to point out that cyber stalking can come from many technologies. Even major corporations with millions of customers and big public relations departments sometimes lack oversight of their products or the insight that stalking is not a joke. Just ask anyone who has ever been a victim.

The anonymity of the Internet lends itself to people expressing themselves in ways they might not ordinarily express during face-to-face communications. As a result, people may say things that offend or outrage others.

Bestselling author Patricia Cornwell recently appealed to her readers to counter negative reviews of her novel *Book of the Dead*. It wasn't just one bad review, but a sudden onslaught of hundreds of negative reviews appearing on sites such as Amazon and eBay. Cornwell suspected an organized group was behind the effort and appealed to her readers to counter these negative reviews with positive ones. The negative reviews did not stop the book from becoming a bestseller, but it points out just how easy it is to use a very public and largely unregulated medium to wreak havoc on someone's reputation. Just like the female realtor who became a victim of identity assumption, a person's reputation can very quickly plummet using the power of the Internet.

Cyber Stalking and the Law

The general legal definition of stalking includes five parts (or elements) that are necessary to prosecute the crime in most states:

1. A "willful course of conduct"...

2. ...of repeated or continued harassment, without permission,...

3. ...of another individual...

4. ...that would cause a *reasonable person* to feel terrorized, frightened, intimidated, threatened, or harassed...

5. ...and that actually causes the victim to feel terrorized, frightened, intimidated, threatened, or harassed.

The term *reasonable person* refers to the average, everyday person and how he or she might respond to a situation where they are exposed to repeated harassment or other stalking behavior. The response to such a situation would be based upon all of the information available to the person at the time. Essentially, we can simplify the concept by generalizing that a "reasonable person" would respond to a situation in a manner similar to the response of a majority of people exposed to the same set of circumstances. For instance, if a message is left on an answering machine by an ex-spouse stating that he or she is going to come smash all your car windows, and that ex-spouse has damaged your property before, it is likely that if 10 people hear that message, the majority will respond that the threat should be taken seriously. It is reasonable to believe that the ex-spouse will follow through on the threat.

Acts that qualify as stalking include following or appearing within the sight of someone; approaching or confronting someone in a public or private place; appearing at the workplace or home of another; entering the person's property (trespassing); contacting someone repeatedly via phone, mail, or email; getting other friends or family to harass a person on the stalker's behalf; leaving notes, presents, or other items for the victim.

Although stalking is a crime in and of itself, it is important to remember that stalking often occurs along with other crimes, such as trespassing, assault, criminal threatening, sexual assault, vandalism, criminal mischief, and prowling. Although stalking does not require that a person know his or her stalker, more often than not, the stalker is someone the victim knows or has been involved with.

Most states have stalking statutes with corresponding requirements and sentences. Many states also offer the protection of a *stalking order*, an order very similar to the civil domestic violence petition or order. The requirements can vary, but essentially a course of conduct, including two or more behaviors, must occur that makes the victim afraid for his or her personal safety. Your local law-enforcement agency or family court can guide you as to the steps that can be taken to obtain a stalking order.

The Violence Against Women Act of 2000 made cyber stalking a part of the Federal Interstate Stalking Statute, but federal legislation is still lacking. Therefore, the bulk of legislation still falls at the state level.

In 2006, President Bush signed federal anti-cyber stalking legislation. At the time of this writing, 45 states currently have cyber stalking-related laws. Several states have pending laws, and the four remaining states (Idaho, New Jersey, Utah, and Nebraska) have no legislation. It should be noted that in some states, laws that are aimed at preventing cyber stalking are really meant to protect victims under the age of 18.

Cyber Stalking Facts

The following statistics shed some light on who the stalker is and who the stalker targets:

- Sixty-six percent of stalkers pursue their victim at least once per week.
- Seventy-eight percent of stalkers use more than one approach.
- Eighty-one percent of victims stalked by an intimate partner reported that they had previously been assaulted.
- Eighty-seven percent of stalkers are men.
- Ninety-four percent of female victims are stalked by men.
- Sixty percent of male victims are stalked by other men.
- Just over 13% of college students reported being stalked.
- Sixty-two percent of cyber stalking victims are female, primarily ages 18–24.

  (Source: www.wiredsafety.org/resources/powerpoint/cyberstalking_study.ppt)

Just like domestic violence, stalking and cyber stalking at the hands of a former intimate partner can escalate and result in danger to a victim. Factors used in threat assessment include looking at the stalker's level of motive, means, ability, intent, and experience. A rise in these things, in combination with one another, can determine the level of threat facing a victim. The danger potential is often seen in "dramatic moments" such as the arrest of the perpetrator, the issuance of a restraining or stalking order, court hearings, custody hearings, anniversary dates, and any family-oriented holiday. The threat level is greater to a victim during these times.

Lethality Assessment Tools

Many law-enforcement agencies are now using *lethality assessment tools*, including the model used by most agencies in the State of Maryland. The Maryland Lethality Assessment Program for First Responders was instituted in the State of Maryland through the Maryland Network Against Domestic Violence and was recently recognized as one of the Harvard Kennedy School's Ash Institute's "Top 50 Programs" of the 2008 Innovations in American Government competition. The Lethality Assessment Program (LAP) is based on 25 years of research by Dr. Jacquelyn Campbell, of the John Hopkins University School of Nursing, and is a result of the following bodies of research:

- Only 4% of domestic violence–related homicide victims ever take advantage of domestic violence program services.

- In 50% of domestic-related homicides, officers had previously responded to a call at the scene.

- The re-assault of a high-danger victim is reduced by 60% if a domestic violence shelter is utilized.

The goal of the LAP is to prevent serious injury, re-assault, and domestic-related homicides by encouraging victims to seek out support and services provided by domestic violence programs. It includes a screening tool for first-responding law-enforcement officers and a protocol referral so that officers can initiate appropriate resources, with the goal of facilitating a conversation between the victim and a domestic violence hotline counselor.

These assessment tools primarily ask questions of victims in the form of checklists and look at factors such as prior victimization and abuse, any prior drug or alcohol abuse on behalf of the perpetrator, the perpetrator's threats toward the victim or her children, the perpetrator's access and degree of interest in weapons, violence outside the home, stalking behavior, history of suicide attempts, history of the relationship including prior breakups, the perpetrator's physical access to the victim and her family and/or relatives, and violence against family pets.

At this time, the Maryland Lethality Assessment Program may be the only system in the country that utilizes a research-based screening tool and an accompanying referral protocol that facilitates a cooperative effort between law enforcement and domestic violence programs in helping high-risk victims seek support services and domestic violence intervention programs.

The lethality assessment tool results in a score that assists law enforcement in understanding the potential threat toward a victim. It's a valuable tool from a law-enforcement perspective, but one that victims don't have available to them. Therefore, we'll add perhaps the most important tool you always have with you—*your gut instinct*. Listen to it. We've seen hundreds of cases where victims said they heard "a tiny voice" or had a "funny feeling" telling them not to respond to that email or that someone seems to violating their personal space or is overly friendly, and so on. Your gut instinct is there. Listen to it!

CYBER STALKING PREVENTION TIPS

Here are some suggestions to incorporate into your daily computer routine that will decrease the likelihood that you will become a stalker's target:

- Use a gender-neutral screen name.
- Avoid giving your online passwords out to anyone else. Most companies do *not* require your password to assist you on account matters.
- Establish your primary email address for friends and family whom you trust and set up a secondary email account for other activities, such as online groups and posts. Most free email providers such as Yahoo! and Google allow you to have more than one account. It is even possible to run two sessions with two separate logons at the same time for ease of message retrieval. Consider setting up the "public" account with limited information and a gender-neutral name such as "BookFan," which does not give away your sex. There is no validation on most free-email sites, and although everyone wants to be honest, it is in the interest of your own personal safety not to reveal your true address, city, date of birth, and gender.
- Learn to "lurk" online before posting actual messages to online groups. This will give you a chance to get more familiar with how the online group operates and to read the posts of its members to see if you feel comfortable participating.

If You Think You Are Being Cyber Stalked

If you find that you have caught the eye of a cyber stalker, these are some valuable suggestions to stop the unwanted intrusion of the stalker:

- Make it clear to the other person you do not want any further contact with him or her through *one* message and save that message. If you send it by email, use the Blind Copy (BC:) feature of your email program and send a copy to yourself for your records.

- Save everything! Do not delete any emails or text messages. If you can, print out any emails and save them. Do not alter them in any-way. Save the original emails online because they may contain important routing information that can help law enforcement determine the sender.

- Once you advise the person you want no further contact, do *not* reply to him or her! Better yet, do not even open the emails or attachments from a suspected stalker. Stalkers often derive pleasure out of provoking someone. If you continue to reply, you continue to provoke.

- Have your own personal safety network of friends, family, and resources. Always let someone know where you will be and when you are expected to return.

- Take security measures at home, in your vehicle, and at work in conjunction with your cyber safety measures. Memorize emergency numbers and have them on speed dial on your cell phone. Keep your cell phone charged and with you at all times. Block outgoing Caller ID and do not accept private calls.

- Do not be afraid to seek counseling if necessary for your well-being.

- Contact your local law-enforcement agency. Oftentimes, the laws regarding cyber crime and cyber stalking are murky. Only a professional police officer can advise you about the law. Follow the advice and direction you are given. Unfortunately, many victims do not follow through with law-enforcement advice.

- If it is determined that no law has been broken and the person persists in contacting you, consider notifying his or her Internet service provider and advising them. They may take action depending on their internal policies.

- Make certain that if the abuser/stalker is an "ex," there is no chance he or she had the opportunity to download any programs that aid in monitoring your online activity. Be aware of spyware and how it can give a stalker the ability to monitor *all* of your computer use.

- Seek information on obtaining a stalking order or restraining order. Laws and procedures vary from state to state. However, your local law-enforcement agency can guide you toward the process that best meets your needs.

- If you find a website that is focused on harassing you, it may violate local harassment laws. Furthermore, becoming familiar with search engines such as www.whois.net can assist you in determining the owner of any malicious website. Again, assistance can be found with your local police department or victim advocacy group.

- If you can, create a new email account or an additional email account using a free web-based email site. Do *not* provide detailed information about yourself in the profile.

- Change your passwords and PIN numbers because email addresses are often used by abusers and stalkers to impersonate their victims or cause them harm. Change your passwords frequently.

- Search for your name on the Internet on major search engines such as Google and Yahoo!. You will be amazed at what you may find about yourself online. This may show that your contact information is easily accessible. Be sure to search for your full name in quotation marks, as this will give search engine results for your name in its entirety and condense results. If you do not use quotes around your full name, you will likely end up with many results that include your first name and last name somewhere in an article or blog, but not together or even referring to you. For example, searching for Jane Smith (without quotes) could result in an article where Jane Doe and Charlie Smith are mentioned together. Also check out sites that specialize in telephone number, address, or name searches to see what is out there. (See Chapter 2, "Two Bedrooms Up, One Bedroom Down—What Someone Can Find Out About You on the Internet," for more information.)

Teen/Tech Stalking

Anyone with teenagers knows how comfortable teens are with technology, but this has led to a new form of cyber stalking dubbed "teen/tech stalking" in which cell phones and text messages—the staples of many teens nowadays—are used to harass, dominate, and/or humiliate young people, in most cases teen girls.

Teen Study

Teenage Research Unlimited recently conducted a nationwide survey of 615 teens between the ages of 13 and 18. The results are alarming:

- Thirty percent admit they've been text-messaged or emailed up to *30 times an hour* by a boyfriend or girlfriend checking up on them.

- Eighteen percent said their partner has used a social-networking site to harass them.

- Seventeen percent said their partner made them "afraid not to respond to a cell phone call, email, IM, or text message."
- Ten percent said they had been threatened in calls or messages.
- Fifty-eight percent of parents whose teens were physically assaulted by their partner did not know it had happened.

Online Games—The New Stalker's Ground

We're seeing an alarming trend in cases connected to online games being used as a playground for cyber stalkers, pedophiles, and other forms of cyber crime. Here are a few interesting cases:

- A 31-year-old Australian woman was arrested when she traveled to North Carolina to lure a 16-year-old boy she encountered playing *World of Warcraft*.
- A 26-year-old Florida resident is under investigation for allegedly coaxing a 15-year-old girl he played *World of Warcraft* with to run away with him.
- In China, a *Legend of Mir 3* player is spending the rest of his life behind bars for fatally stabbing another for the "theft" of a virtual sword.

Online gaming has evolved considerably in the last few years, from static games where a player competed against the computer, to "virtual communities" in which one player is virtually pitted against another.

Popular online games such as *World of Warcraft*, *Second Life*, and *Halo* are known as *massively multiplayer online games*, or *MMOGs*. They allow players to interact and chat with each other in real time.

Players adopt virtual personas in the form of characters or "avatars" when playing. Unlike social networking sites where participants might try to be polite, these gaming sites pit player against player in a highly competitive, and often "virtually violent" atmosphere. Because they include socialization opportunities via web chats and instant messaging, they also provide fertile ground for pedophiles.

Just recently, a 20-year-old man from Saratoga Springs, New York, was arrested for allegedly stalking a 15-year-old girl he met while playing the online game *Halo*. This man drove 40 hours from New York to Spokane, Washington, a trip of almost 2,600 miles, to meet her and then sent her a threatening text message when she rejected him. The girl's parents watched the man drive by their house, noted his license plate, and called the police. His case is pending.

Online Gaming and Malware

Of the 137 million computer users, it is estimated that a quarter of them play some form of online game. In addition to the opportunities this opens up for cyber stalkers, it also creates a fertile ground for *malware*— malicious software that can do nasty things to your computer, including stealing your account information. We will discuss malware in greater depth in Chapter 11, "Phishing, Pharming, Spam, and Scams," but it is interesting that the majority of malware is found in China, where passwords are stolen surreptitiously to aid in identity theft and fraud. China has become a breeding ground for skilled programmers and code writers who cross the line from "hackers" to "crackers" (criminal hackers). The more sophisticated online gaming becomes, the more opportunities it presents for cyber crime to be committed.

Would You Say It to My Face?

The Internet can be a very safe place to travel if you know how to protect yourself online. The most important line of defense to your online personal safety arsenal is to ask yourself one thing: Would I tell a stranger who looks suspicious to me, someone I have just met for the very first time in person, what I'm about to say online?

It is easy—due to the supposed "anonymity" of the Internet—to say things you would never dream of saying to a stranger you've just met on a bus or in a bar. The Internet is not anonymous, not by any means. The perception that what you say online to a stranger 3,000 miles away won't come back to haunt you is a dangerous one to have. Always act under the premise that the person you're communicating with online is sitting next to you just a few feet away before sending that email or posting that blog. We're not trying to limit anyone's freedom of speech; we're just suggesting that you think about what the potential reaction of what you say online could be before you post—for your own personal safety.

National School Board Survey

A recent National School Boards Association survey reports that more than 25% of the educators polled report they are aware of false websites and/or pages being created for the purposes of exacting revenge on an educator.

TEACHERS—THE NEW CYBER STALKER'S TARGET

In February of 2008, a North Carolina high school student, along with four other students, was charged with cyber stalking after creating an online message board that accused one of their teachers of being a pedophile.

The students went as far as to create a fictitious website called www.teacherpedofiles.com and listed the teacher's name on it. Teacher rating websites such as www.ratemyteacher.com already exist. These fall within the bounds of "free speech" and are legal. What made the North Carolina case illegal was that the students falsely accused the teacher of criminal behavior. North Carolina law makes it illegal to electronically communicate false statements about "indecent conduct or criminal conduct...with the intent to abuse, annoy, threaten, harass, or embarrass."

The student who created the website has been charged with a misdemeanor offense of cyber stalking. The school will impose further sanctions on that student and the others.

In another case in March of 2007, two North Carolina students were accused of impersonating two assistant principals by creating false MySpace accounts. One was portrayed as a pedophile, whereas the other was portrayed as a racist.

TEACHERS FIGHT BACK: THE ERIK TROSCH STORY

In Philadelphia, a high school senior used his grandmother's computer to create a fake MySpace account impersonating his school principal, Eric Trosch. In fact, several students were involved in creating multiple fake MySpace account pages with Trosch's profile, picture, and title, along with allegations that he was a pornography enthusiast who enjoyed urinating in women's mouths and considered Michael Jackson to be his hero (see Figure 1.7).

In a case that will test First Amendment rights, the principal has sued the students he accused of creating these pages. In his civil lawsuit, he stated that the online postings damaged his reputation and left him embarrassed and humiliated. His attorney stated that "the profiles went far and beyond what you would see on a bathroom wall in a school." The principal alleges that another profile created by a student said his favorite movie was pornographic, and a third created by two brothers said he had had intimate relationships with students and brutalized women.

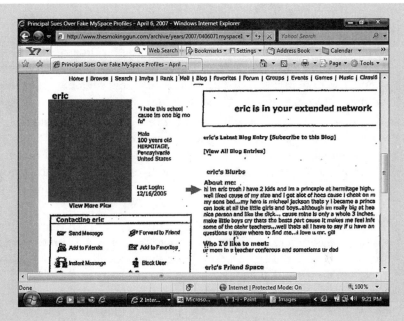

FIGURE 1.7

MySpace prank page profiling a high school principal in Pennsylvania

This will be an interesting test to see how far the online lampooning and degrading can go.

Interestingly and disturbingly enough, this practice is fairly common, and teens often find it humorous to set up MySpace pages for a principal or teacher they are not particularly fond of. We have seen this with at least two local educators who had been targeted for this type of degradation. The MySpace pages contained their photos, address info, and even phone numbers. The fake profiles were mean and humiliating. Ironically, we stumbled upon one of the pages in the course of an investigation. The other was discovered because the kids were bragging about it at the local high school. For one of the victims, we found three separate prank pages.

THE ANNA DRAKER CASE

In another interesting case, assistant principal Anna Draker of the Clark High School in San Antonio, Texas, is suing two students for putting up a MySpace website that depicted her as a lesbian and contained "obscene comments, pictures, and graphics," according to the court filing.

What makes this case unusual is that Draker is also suing the students' parents for "negligence by failing to supervise their children." The police were able to determine that the computers used to create the site were located in the students' homes, and Draker's lawsuit says that the parents have a duty to know what their children are up to—especially in light of both students' past run-ins with Draker at school.

"Allowing access to the Internet, unsupervised and without restraint, poses an obvious and unreasonable danger that such children would utilize the Internet for illicit purposes such as the ones alleged above," says the suit in accusing the parents of "negligent supervision."

Women as Perpetrators

In February of 2008, a 50-year-old Oregon tax attorney was arrested and charged with trying to frame her ex-boyfriend by sending explicit pictures of him to his boss. What we find interesting about this case—in addition to the fact that a woman was doing the cyber stalking—was the elaborate methods she used to try and cover her trail, including the use of prepaid cell phones to make harassing phone calls and phony email accounts, as well as regular mail to stalk and harass. This was also the first case to invoke Washington State's cyber stalking law from 2004, the state where the offense was alleged to have occurred.

CYBER STALKING PREVENTION RESOURCES

- The Stalking Resource Center at The National Center for Victims of Crime (www.ncvc.org, or call 1-800-FYI-CALL)
- CyberAngels (www.cyberangels.org)
- Safety Ed International (www.safetyed.org)
- End It Now (www.enditnow.gov, or call 1-800-799-SAFE)
- Love Is Respect (www.loveisrespect.com, or call the National Teen Dating Abuse Hotline at 866-331-9474)
- National Domestic Violence Hotline (www.ndvh.org, or call 1-800-799-SAFE [7233], 1-800-787-3224 [TTY])

2

Two Bedrooms Up, One Bedroom Down—What Someone Can Find Out About You on the Internet

In the course of doing research for this book, we stumbled across someone who claimed to be an expert on cyber crime. We are always willing to share information about cyber crime with other professionals, but by our nature, we're also very cautious about sharing too much information until we are certain of that person's credentials.

As a matter of routine, we used public tools and websites to learn more about this person's background. Her impetus for getting involved in cyber crime came from her claim of once having been a victim of a cyber stalker. We have worked with victims of both stalking and cyber stalking. People who have been through the horrors of being stalked are usually very careful afterward about revealing any personal details about themselves in public or online. This person, who we'll call "Tanya," was not. We started digging further by looking at the details Tanya was putting out on her personal and professional blogs.

Within an hour and with only web-accessible records, we were able to piece together an excruciatingly detailed background dossier about Tanya's life. We knew her maiden name, the names of her family members and their email addresses, her previous married name, her maiden name, what brand of beer her current boyfriend preferred, and on and on. We were shocked at how much personal information she had put out on the Internet despite her claim to have once been a victim of a cyber stalker. It was frightening to see.

We're not sure why Tanya put her private life on public view, but we hope that she, as well as everyone reading this book, understands that each bit of personal information one puts out on the Internet is like a puzzle piece. For example, if you use your email address to leave a note at an online obituary site that reads, "Uncle Joe, we will miss you," you've provided another piece of the puzzle for a potential stalker who now knows your family name and can use that to reach out to other family members.

If you write on a blog that your boyfriend, Henry, is applying for a job at a specific location in a certain town, what's to prevent a stalker from going to that location to befriend Henry?

Our point is this: There are numerous ways people can find out about you on the Internet (read on). Why make it any easier by providing such specific details about yourself that anyone with a head on their shoulders can use to find or stalk you? Use common sense!

> There are numerous ways people can find out about you on the Internet. Why make it any easier by providing such specific details about yourself that anyone with a head on their shoulders can use to find or stalk you?

Your Digital Footprint

Internet users are becoming more aware of their "digital footprint," meaning their presence online. According to recent reports, 47% of those surveyed have searched for information about themselves online, up from just 22% just 5 years ago. However, few monitor their online presence with great regularity. Just 3% of self-searchers report that they make a regular habit of it, and 74% have checked up on their digital footprint only once or twice (source: Pew Internet & American Life Project, 2007).

The Best Sources to Find Out About People

Take it from us, the more personal information you reveal about yourself on the Internet—whether intentionally or unintentionally—the easier it is to profile you. Whenever we are investigating someone, one of the first places we look for information is Google (www.google.com). This "engine of all search engines" provides a quick source of any existing reference on the Internet. Through its Advanced Search feature, it is easy to customize searches for specific phrases, including names, email addresses, screen names, and so on.

If your name is publicly listed in the phone book, Google also produces a convenient map showing your exact address and location. How much easier can it get for a stalker?

We not only Google a suspect's name, but variants of the name as well as the suspect's email address. If the suspect has ever posted anywhere using his email address, we can usually follow that link back through a browser to see where and what he has been posting. Many postings on Usenet groups or online interest groups can be displayed by searching for the email address of the poster. Try entering your own email address in Google and see what comes up.

"Tracking Teresa"

The online safety group NetSmartz (www.netsmartz.org) has developed Internet safety presentations for students of all ages and their parents. One of the videos we often show to middle school and high school students, called "Tracking Teresa," illustrates how much information the "bad guy" can garner from what appears to be a benign advertisement online in a matter of minutes.

This presentation has had an eye-opening impact on students, teachers, and parents alike, because it illustrates just how easy it is to find out about that unsuspecting potential victim. If you or your children have an opportunity to attend one of these presentations, we highly recommend you do so. As we will continue to say throughout this book, awareness and education are of the upmost importance in arming yourself against cyber crime.

Town and City Websites

Most major cities have put their property and tax assessment information online. Many smaller municipalities have done so as well. The level of detail that some of these websites provide is most disconcerting. Figure 2.1 shows what we found on a simple search of a major city's website. (Note: In an effort to protect the owner's privacy, we are not providing any specific location or owner information.)

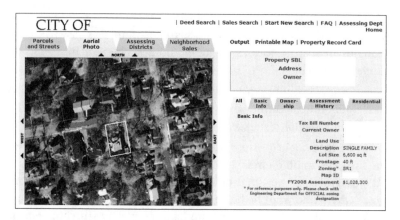

FIGURE 2.1

A U.S. city tax assessor's listing for a residence that shows the amount of detail these databases often hold and are accessible to anyone online

In this publicly accessible tax assessor's database, we were able to tell the owner's name and address, the value of their house, and how many bedrooms it has and on which floor; see a detailed map of where the house is located, view an aerial photo of the house, and see a floor map describing each room. We also had access to the prior owner's name, the type of heating system the house has, any outbuildings or other structures (including whether or not the garage was attached), plus a host of other details that would provide those with criminal intent plenty of information to make their efforts easy.

In this publicly accessible tax assessor's database, we were able to tell the owner's name and address, the value of their house, and how many bedrooms it has and on which floor; see a detailed map of where the house is located, view an aerial photo of the house, and see a floor map describing each room.

Unfortunately, this kind of information is considered in the public domain and is difficult to keep off the Internet. Real-estate transactions are often printed in local papers with the owner and seller's name.

If having your name and address appear on public tax assessment or real-estate transaction records is a concern for you, you may be able to work with your realtor and attorney to stay anonymous. It may be possible to place the property in the name of a trust. The trust name could be the name of the location, such as "123 Main Street Trust," so your name never appears on any of the tax records.

If this a personal safety issue for you, contact your attorney and ask prior to transacting the closing to explain what your options are. Most realtors are very cooperative and will work with you on this.

Zillow—We Know Your Neighborhood

Oftentimes we come across tools that, from one perspective, serve a valuable purpose, but from our perspective, give criminals an edge. For example, the website Zillow (www.zillow.com) is a useful real-estate tool that provides quick information on neighborhoods. We put it to the test and, sure enough, within minutes we were able to view aerial photos of neighborhoods displaying the overhead view of houses and could quickly flag where the more valuable houses were located.

We understand that perspective buyers would want this information and see the value in its ease of use, but we're trained to think like the bad guys. What a tremendous tool this would be for burglars who were looking to target specific neighborhoods and houses. Burglars often stay in their own areas because this is the kind of information they gather intelligence about—which houses are in upscale neighborhoods, which houses are surrounded by fences, which houses are on streets with easy access, and which areas to hide in. With tools like these, criminals could easily expand their territory.

We Know Your Dog's Name

Dog license registration information is considered in the "public domain," so many cities are now including this information online as well. Think about the ramifications of a total stranger with less-than-honest intent, knowing not only your dog's name but its breed. A burglar would certainly love to know that you have a toy dachshund in the house and not a pit bull.

Online Memorials

In dealing with the death of a loved one, it's only natural to want to express your memories of the dearly departed. As sick as it sounds, this is a treasure trove for cyber stalkers. Many times the loved ones of the deceased not only will pay tribute to the deceased online, but give their full names, their relationship to the departed, and often provide an email contact.

Preying on those who are grieving is a heinous thing, but that's just the kind of information that would empower a stalker. Remember that a stalker equates information with power.

Recall the supposed "cyber crime expert" we mentioned earlier? In the course of reviewing this person's blog, she mentioned that a family member had recently passed away. Given that small tidbit of information, we were able to quickly locate the obituary in an online paper. That obituary had a link to the online memorial provided by the funeral home. These online memorials are quite common, and with good intent they allow everyone to express their feelings about a dearly departed friend or family member. However, by reading the obituary and the online memorial, we were able to piece together an extremely detailed family tree of this individual. The obituary provided her maiden name, meaning we now had the means to track her history prior to her marriage. More importantly, we were able to obtain the email addresses of most of her immediate family members. Were our intentions unscrupulous, we could have easily delved further into her family history and even contacted family members under false pretenses to gain their confidence and trust.

It is difficult in times of mourning and grief to think about the potential danger this information could present, but it needs to be said: Provide limited personal information in online memorials. "Aunt Kate" is better than "Kate Jones of Podunk, New York." Do not include your email address. Assume that close family members already have it.

Political Contributions

Politicians are obligated under law to report all contributions made to their campaign. This information must be disclosed to whomever requests it and is usually published somewhere, often on the Internet or in news stories. We are not trying to discourage anyone from contributing to a politician's campaign, but be aware that if you use your home address, it becomes public information. Better to use a P.O. box or business address if at all possible.

People Search Sites

Many search sites on the Internet can be used to quickly return records about people. Many of these sites charge a fee, depending on the level of information sought, including background checks, criminal history checks, property owned, civil actions, and so on. However, many also allow a "free" check with a limited return of information. Just running the free check may surprise you by how much information is returned. We ran such a check without paying any fees and were able to determine what town a person had lived in previously, other names associated with this person, the name of this person's ex, previous neighbors' names, as well as this person's maiden name and age.

We recently demonstrated the level of information available through a paid subscription to a "people" database site to an author doing research on a book. Granted, law enforcement has greater access to some parts of this information, but to give a more realistic view, we did a generic, non–law enforcement

How much easier it would be to taunt a victim by describing the old apartment they lived in or to mention an ex-neighbor's name.

search. The author was amazed to find names of former neighbors, clubs she had been a member of, every address she had ever lived at, cars she owned or had previously owned, the status of loans and judgments, and so forth. Much of this information can be purchased by anyone online for a fee, and if someone was trying to build a dossier of someone, this is exactly the type of information they'd be willing to pay for. How much easier it would be to taunt a victim by describing the old apartment they lived in or to mention an ex-neighbor's name. The cyber stalker, at the very least, is going after an emotional reaction to inflict psychological trauma and power.

Search Your Own Name

We encourage you to search for your own name and see what comes up at the following sites:

- Intelius (http://find.intelius.com/)
- People Finders (www.peoplefinders.com)
- U.S. Search (www.ussearch.com)

- ZabaSearch (www.zabasearch.com)
- Pipl (www.pipl.com)
- Wink (www.wink.com)
- Spock (www.spock.com)
- LinkedIn (www.linkedin.com)

Is there a way around this information being made public? Unfortunately, public records are just that—public. However, in this day of greater awareness of online privacy concerns, if you can document through a police report that you are, in fact, a victim of cyber crime or cyber stalking, it is possible to try and work with some of the reporting companies to restrict your information. We're not saying it's easy to do, because once the information is on the Internet, it's out there, but short of legally changing your name (which some victims have done), it's very hard to completely remove all trails.

The Wayback Machine

The Wayback Machine, located at www.archive.org, is a nonprofit site that makes it possible to go back and visit websites that have long since been removed from the Internet.

The founders of this project, which include the Library of Congress and the Smithsonian, have a legitimate purpose. Like any other historical collection, the Internet mirrors societal and language changes and is ever-evolving. The founders of this project are attempting to catalog those changes so future historians can look back and see what the Internet looked like a hundred years ago. Unfortunately, this also means that many sites with your personal information may be permanently archived and still available.

Website Registration Records

Believe it or not, privately registered websites can lead to a trough of information about someone. When a website is registered, certain information has to be provided, including the owner's name as well as billing and administration information. Many web hosting companies make this information public. There are numerous online tools for looking at website registration information. One we use quite frequently is www.betterwhois.com, shown in Figure 2.2.

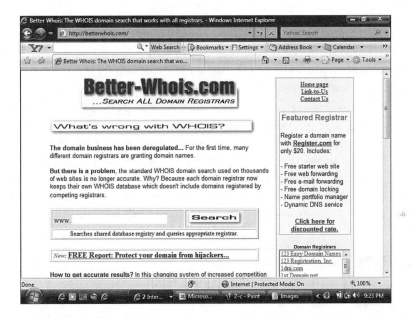

FIGURE 2.2

The front page of www.betterwhois.com

If you are going to register a website, see if the hosting company allows for private or "domain discreet" registrations; otherwise, your personal registration information can be quite public. If you were to design a family website, for example, we might be able to go to the domain registry and access your home address, home phone, alternative email address, alternative phone, and how long the site has been up. We recently showed someone who, for professional purposes, had her own domain name, just how much information we could find out about her. She was shocked. Using a "discreet registration" is a much safer way to register and will restrict any personal information from being revealed. The betterwhois.com entry will go back to the hosting site with a note about the information being private or restricted.

E-Venge

In an interesting twist, several new sites have sprung up that allow the public to exact revenge on those they feel have done them wrong. This electronic revenge (or "e-venge") is wide open and, in our opinion, borders on the libelous in many cases.

DontDateHimGirl.com

For example, there's the Don't Date Him Girl website. Here's a recent posting about a profiled man. The actual posting includes his real name, his picture, and his screen name.

> *Beware! This is the worst of the worst. He does it all. Lies. Cheats. Steals your money. All while being sweet as pie to your face. I didn't find out until the end, but for the entire 2 years we were together, he cheated on me. Even while we were living together. Even while I was in surgery. After 26 years of dating, I can honestly say he is the most despicable dirtbag I ever had the misfortune to come across. There's much much more so if you run across him and want to know more, contact me and I'll tell you all about it.*

Lessons Learned

If there is one lesson to be learned here, it is this: Although you may not be able to control the fact that your city puts your homeowner information on the World Wide Web where anyone can find it, you *do* have control over what you put out about yourself. Consider every detail of what you reveal about yourself when posting to that jewelry exchange forum. Did you just let someone know you love expensive rubies? When putting that rare book up for auction on a site such as eBay, are you letting someone know that you might have an even larger collection? When you post pictures of your Rottweiler on the dog lover's forum and say, "King is a gentle giant," consider how a thief would react to that. Take control and limit personal details. You're not talking to another person in the same room. You're talking to millions of people who could potentially stumble on these details you've just provided.

3

Cyber Crime Tools You Won't Believe

In Chapter 1, "Cyber Stalking," we showed you how a GPS (Global Positioning System) can be used for tracking people, but there are many other techniques and devices that can aid an avid stalker.

Wi-Fi Tracking

Would it surprise you to know that your own computer could provide a means of tracking you? Most newer computers, especially laptops, are Wi-Fi (wireless) enabled, meaning you do not need any cables to connect to the Internet. If someone has had access to your computer and knows your computer's name ("Mary Smith's Laptop," for example), they can easily listen for your broadcast signal within a few hundred meters to ascertain your whereabouts.

Packet Sniffers

Beyond locating you via your computer, someone with a program such as a packet sniffer can actually grab the data you type and read it if it is unencrypted, within proximity. When you type on a wireless Internet connection, the computer sends the information through the air in small groups of data, called "packets."

A packet sniffer program sniffs the air much like a dog lifts its snout to find a scent. Such programs are readily available on the Internet, often for free. Packet sniffers can be fine-tuned to listen for keywords such as "login" and "password" to gain access to account information. In fact, packet sniffers have become quite specialized and can be used for sniffing specific types of traffic, such as MSN messages and live chats (see Figure 3.1).

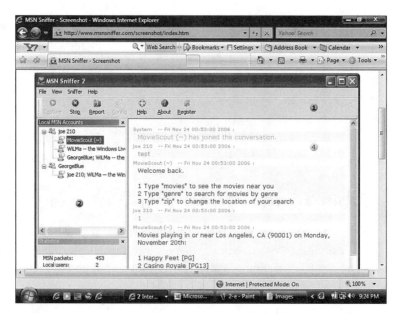

FIGURE 3.1

A sample screen from a packet sniffer used to sniff out traffic from an MSN live chat

It should be noted that packet sniffers have a legitimate use in information technology—to determine network traffic—but too often they are used for illegitimate purposes. They can also be used on a hard-wired network to sniff out data. (Read more about wireless networks in Chapter 16, "Your Online Safety Checkup.")

Bluetooth Locating

Bluetooth is another means of connecting devices wirelessly. Your cell phone and laptop may be "Bluetooth enabled." Bluetooth differs from Wi-Fi in that it broadcasts a stronger signal covering greater distances and is more expensive. Most Bluetooth applications have default security settings. If someone knows your device name, they can sniff for your device location to within 50 to 100 meters.

What Is an IP Address?

Given the millions of computers in use and online at any given moment, how does your computer know to deliver your email to Aunt Mary, who lives in Massachusetts?

There are probably hundreds, if not thousands of computers called "Mary's Computer" online at any given point in time. So how do things get routed and tracked on the Internet? Think about the last time you sent or received a package from UPS. Do you remember the driver using a scanning gun to scan the package's barcode? Barcodes are symbols that represent information such as the street number and name where the package is to be delivered. This barcode system allows UPS to track millions of packages around the world each day in real time via a quick scan, rather than having to manually reenter the destination address or the originating location each time.

Along those same lines, computers also use a numbering system to ensure that messages get routed to the appropriate place. That number is called an *IP address* (or *Internet Protocol address*).

Every time your computer connects to the Internet, it takes on an IP address. An IP address is temporarily assigned to a computer as it connects to the Internet by your Internet service provider (ISP). You usually don't see this address and probably don't know it's there, but it is. The entire Internet uses this same numbering scheme, so when you type in www.nasa.gov to visit the NASA website, the computer thinks 72.246.51.15, which is the actual IP address of the NASA site. Obviously, www.nasa.gov is much easier to remember. All of this translation of IP addresses happens in the background and is transparent to the user.

When you send an email to Aunt Mary, it gets routed correctly because it knows Aunt Mary is actually bestauntie@yahoo.com, and Yahoo! has a preset list of IP addresses, which are like ZIP Codes in a sense. Yahoo! also knows which account holder is "best auntie" and makes the delivery accordingly. All of this routing and IP address information is contained in a part of the email called the "headers," which most people usually don't see. In order to see them, you must enable "full headers" on your incoming email.

Here's how a cyber stalker might use the information gained in the email headers to further his or her efforts:

> *I now have the internet addresses of your computer and your Internet Service Provider (ISP). This minimally gives me something else to key a web search on, where no matter what email aliases you were using, I can find emails or other postings originating from your home system. And of course more information for more next steps. I would also take all the IP addresses and decode them at a website like http://www.dnsstuff.com/ or http://remote.12dt.com/rns/ to see what it tells me about the service provider you're using.*

It's frightening to think that someone with a little savvy can gain so much information about you just by reviewing the headers of your email. However, the reality is that it *is* possible, and this is something you need to be aware of prior to clicking the Send button.

Anonymizers and Anonymous Remailers

Anonymizers are programs, often available on the Internet for free, that claim to protect the privacy of someone surfing online or sending email (see Figure 3.2). They can also be used for more nefarious deeds, such as sending offensive emails and avoiding being traced.

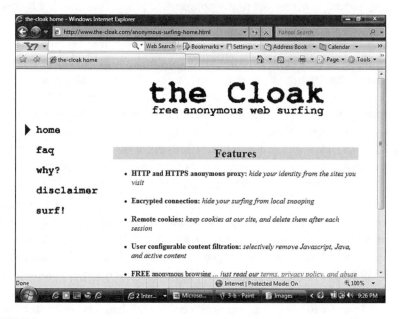

FIGURE 3.2

The front page of an anonymizer site called "The Cloak." Many variants of this site are available on the Internet.

Whereas the main function of anonymizers is to cloak Internet usage, anonymous remailers are programs that are specifically meant to strip the header information away from email and replace it with information that is untraceable.

Closely related to anonymizers and anonymous remailers are online websites that provide temporary email addresses that virtually disappear in as little as 15 minutes, leaving little trace of their existence behind (see Figure 3.3).

FIGURE 3.3

A site that will expire an email address after just 15 minutes!

An important point to understand here is that nothing is really ever truly "anonymous" when you are on the Internet. At some point, there is a trail that, to some degree, can be traced back to you. Let's say, for example, someone uses one of these anonymizer programs to visit a site containing sexually explicit images of children, which they then proceed to download.

First of all, a connection to the Internet must be established. If that person is sitting in the comfort of his home, he has an account with some company to connect to the Internet. Even if he is on a public Wi-Fi account, connection information is still being recorded somewhere. We will talk a lot more about the horrors of child sexual exploitation later on, but bear in mind that whenever you download something to your computer—an image, a file, or a program—it is very likely to be retrievable even if you delete it.

Second, even though many anonymizer sites claim not to keep records, there are logs that, if the site is based in a country subject to warrant searches, may be produced.

Finally, if any site raises suspicions as a target for potential illegal activity, it's an anonymizer site. Don't think for one second that local law enforcement hasn't already figured that out and that it wouldn't raise suspicions to see that someone went to an anonymizer site (because a trail of the actual site visit would still be there).

Fake Name Generators

The site shown in Figure 3.4 not only provides fake names, but fake addresses, social security numbers, credit card accounts, and so forth. Although this information is false, someone could use the site to very quickly come up with a false ID if they knew that the information wouldn't be checked immediately. The site has been touted by writers who are looking to make up character names and identities, but law enforcement deals with too many people giving false identification. This site makes it a lot easier.

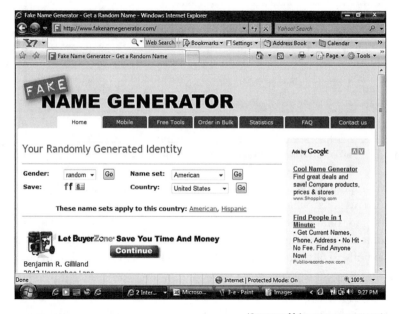

(Courtesy of fakenamegenerator.com)

FIGURE 3.4

Screenshot from www.fakenamegenerator.com. According to the website, up to 100 fake names are generated a minute.

Fake Caller ID

Another type of software allows Caller ID to be faked or "spoofed." Most people think if their Caller ID reads "XYZ Bank" that, in fact, the call is legitimate. This is not necessarily true. Caller ID spoofing is purported to be a "fun way to fake out your friends," but clearly the opportunity it presents for criminal activities is rampant. In fact, it's become key to attempts at defrauding people via their cell phones. This type of fraud is known as "vishing." (See Chapter 11, "Phishing, Pharming, Spam, and Scams.")

Felicia had an unusual, and not so pleasant experience, as a result of this type of program.

FELICIA GETS CAUGHT UP IN A HOMICIDE INVESTIGATION

The irony of this story is that on the particular day of this event, Felicia was working on her own department's unsolved homicides. She frequently assists a retired FBI Special Agent who lends his expertise to the department trying to find some small detail that may have been overlooked or a single name among thousands that could yield a clue and finally bring closure for the families of the victims of these cases.

Felicia was drilling down through a lot of data when her department-issued cell phone rang. The man on the other end identified himself as a New Hampshire State Trooper and indicated that the number in question had been involved in a homicide. He therefore wanted to know to whom he was speaking.

Felicia's first response was that one of her coworkers was playing a joke. She recognized the trooper's name, though they had never met in person. She began to run a list through her mind of who she might have joked around with recently and which of the many jokesters she works with could have pulled this off. Playing along with the trooper, she asked for a callback number to verify his identity. Everyone is entitled to do that and, given this story, should. It is her department's policy to always verify the number with a callback. She recognized the number not only as being legitimate, but as the Major Crimes Unit.

When she called back, she identified herself. "You're kidding," Trooper Jones (not his real name) said. Felicia assured him she was not and that the number in question was actually leased by the department. The trooper went on to tell Felicia that the number appeared several times in the days preceding a local homicide of a man. The man was a self-employed tradesman.

"Could you have called him about having some work done?"

"No."

"You must have called him at some point. This number appears on the sheet."

Fortunately for Felicia, because it was her department-issued cell phone, she knew they would have all the incoming and outgoing phone records. She advised the trooper she was going to do two things: Get her captain to call him back to assure him she was not inclined toward homicidal tendencies; and pull all the business office records and fax them over to him immediately.

The call records clearly showed she could not have made the calls and had not received any calls from the victim. (Thank heavens for accurate records!)

It wasn't until later on that Felicia realized what had happened. Her cell phone number (which is a bit unusual) must have been spoofed, or faked, hence why she doesn't particularly care for the availability of these programs. Not only do these "spoofing" sites allow the user to mask Caller ID, they can change the displayed Caller ID to anything they want (see Figure 3.5).

(Courtesy TelTech Systems, Inc. www.spoofcard.com)

FIGURE 3.5

A 60-minute card can be purchased for $10 online. The service even allows the caller to disguise his voice.

The ability to change Caller ID has led to an extremely dangerous new prank called "swatting." The term is derived from police SWAT (Special Weapons and Tactics) teams. The goal of swatters is to falsely report an emergency to a police department to cause a SWAT team response to a physical address. Caller ID spoofing just makes it that much easier for someone to claim she is someone else and

This dangerous prank not only puts innocent people, the people at the actual address, in extreme danger, it puts law enforcement in danger as well because they have no idea what they are facing.

that a dangerous person is inside her house with a weapon. This dangerous prank not only puts innocent people, the people at the actual address, in extreme danger, it puts law enforcement in danger as well because they have no idea what they are facing.

Think swatting sounds like fun? Just ask Jason R. Trowbridge of Houston, Texas, and Chad A. Ward of Syracuse, New York, who each just recently entered guilty pleas to "conspiracy to commit access device fraud" and "computer intrusions in furtherance of harassing and swatting telephone calls." They each face a maximum statutory sentence of 5 years in prison, a $250,000 fine, and restitution.

4

Upskirting, Downblousing, and Your Right to Privacy in the Cell Phone and Digital Age

Cell phones are really miniature computers and, as such, have become the new playing ground for cyber criminals. They are just now beginning to be exploited in ways you would never expect.

Upskirting and Downblousing

These two relatively new terms are still unfamiliar to many. Basically, upskirting and downblousing involve taking pictures of someone's "intimate parts" without their knowledge or approval in a location where there is a reasonable expectation of privacy.

SMILE FOR THE HIDDEN CAMERA

Jeanine went out with her girlfriends after work one night to a local lounge. The four young, attractive women traded stories as they sat around a cocktail table munching on snacks. One of Jeanine's friends noticed that a man a little older than them kept circling their group. He had his cell phone in his hand and paused for just a moment as he stood over each woman. Jeanine confronted the man and asked him what he was doing. He insisted he was just waiting for a phone call, but Jeanine had recently read an article about the dangers of "downblousing"—taking pictures of women's cleavage and posting it on the Internet—and suspected that was what he was doing.

What are Jeanine's legal rights at this point? Can she demand to see his cell phone? Should she call the police? Can she press charges if she thinks this man has been taking pictures of her and her friends?

The answer to Jeanine's dilemma depends on what state she lives in. Upskirting and downblousing fall under the realm of "video voyeurism" laws—the equivalent of a high-tech "Peeping Tom." Many states that used to have this crime categorized as a misdemeanor (meaning usually less than a year in jail time) are beginning to realize the seriousness of it. As of this writing, a total of 34 states now make video voyeurism a felony. Under certain circumstances, additional prison time can be added if the perpetrator is a repeat offender, if the victim is a child, or if the images are distributed.

THE SUSAN WILSON STORY

The story of Susan Wilson and her family, from Monroe, Louisiana, is shocking. Wilson could not understand how a long-time family friend and church member, Steve Glover, seemed to know so many things about her, including what she had just done. Wilson eventually got suspicious enough to look around in Glover's house one day when she was visiting. She found a videotape and was shocked to see her own bedroom appear on the screen after she pressed Play. As it turns out, Glover had planted hidden video cameras in Glover's bedroom and master bathroom. Wilson's story was brought to national attention and became the subject of a TV movie after she discovered that there were no laws in Louisiana prohibiting what Glover had done. Glover eventually pleaded to "unauthorized entry" and was ordered to pay $2,000 in restitution for the damage he caused in placing his equipment inside Wilson's home.

LOCATION, LOCATION, LOCATION

James Boudreaux, also from Monroe, Louisiana, bought a wireless color camera from Radio Shack for $20 and hid it inside his stepdaughter's entertainment center in her bedroom. For 4 months, Boudreaux video-taped his stepdaughter in various stages of dress and undress, including when she was completely nude. The discovery was made when the step-daughter went to Boudreaux's bedroom and found him standing naked in front of his TV with the video streaming. In December of 2007, Boudreaux became the first person convicted under Louisiana's newly adopted state video voyeurism law. He was originally sentenced to 56 years in prison, but appealed and was resentenced to 15 years in prison.

Coincidentally, in that same month, a retired Connecticut firefighter, Richard Stevenson, was sentenced for secretly videotaping his 17-year-old stepdaughter. After searching their home, Stevenson's ex-wife found 72 tapes taken of her daughter. The videos were taken in her daughter's bed-room, and the girl was often naked.

Stevenson had a shed behind their home, which he used as his own pri-vate retreat. He referred to the shed as "Paradise Ranch." In it was a mon-itor that played back video from no less than five cameras Stevenson had planted in the home, two of which were in his stepdaughter's bedroom. His sentence? Six months in jail.

These cases exemplify how drastically different laws and sentencing can be from one state to another. Unfortunately, this same scenario plays out for many cyber crimes, including cyber stalking and child predator cases. Because all of this is so new, states are scrambling to create laws to deal with "new" crimes. They remain largely inconsistent.

OHIO 2008 VOYEURISM CASE—30 DAYS IN JAIL

To illustrate this point further, take the recent case of a 25-year-old fitness center manager from Ohio who, in June of 2008, was found guilty of voyeurism when he hid a camera in the ceiling of a tanning booth. The man was found guilty of a second degree misdemeanor, a charge that netted him 90 days in the county jail with 60 days suspended. However, he will have to register as a sex offender upon his release.

We Fight for Changes in the Law

We are currently working with our state's legislators to change laws of this nature. Although it would appear to be a simple process to do what is "the right thing," it can be a battle to make changes that are in the best interest of victims. Unfortunately, politics play a huge role in determining what laws are passed or scrapped.

THE FLORENTINO AVILA CASE: OUR FIRSTHAND EXPERIENCE

Those in law enforcement will tell you that they see so much bizarre behavior it takes a lot to surprise them. We have a very commonly used saying for those times when we are surprised: "You just can't make this stuff up."

We handled a case not too long ago that was most interesting from a technical standpoint, and challenging from a legal one.

Florentino Avila had taken and archived *hundreds* of photos over the course of a couple of years. All these photos were taken up the skirts of women in various department stores. Avila hid in clothing racks and dressing rooms, and even blatantly knelt down in aisles while strategically **People are creatures of habit, and for those who cross the line into sexual deviance, our experience is that recidivism is generally guaranteed.** angling his cell phone camera to forever memorialize what dozens of unsuspecting women were wearing under their skirts.

Despite hundreds of disturbing images and hundreds of victims whose privacy had been violated, Avila could only be charged for a handful of images because in a crime of this nature, law enforcement must have an identified victim.

Coincidentally, Avila was caught for this same deviance in the state of Colorado. People are creatures of habit, and for those who cross the line into sexual deviance, our experience is that recidivism is generally guaranteed.

Avila could not be charged with the majority of the photos because most of the women had no idea they had been victimized. In other words, no victim, no crime. Picture an entire detective division reviewing hundreds of images in the hopes of identifying the department store where a photo might have been taken. After potential "crime scenes" had been identified, the public was notified of the upskirting incidences at various stores in the community. We reached out to the local media to request public assistance in trying to identify victims, but most people were not willing to come forward. Think about having to come to the local police station and say, "Yes, those are my white cotton panties under that flowered broom skirt." Even for those who might come forward, it would be necessary for each victim to make a written or verbal statement and then testify in open court in the event the case was taken to trial. Due process, as guaranteed by our Constitution, translates into a number of hurdles for victims and law enforcement that make sensitive cases extremely difficult to prosecute.

What's more, even when we have a viable victim, sometimes issues arise that throw a wrench into our ability to prosecute bizarre and deviant behavior.

Stickam: Voyeurism or Exhibitionism?

Launched in February of 2005, Stickam (www.stickam.com) is one of several websites whose main function is to provide social networking, but with a twist—it supports live webcams and live chat. As of this writing, Stickam had a membership of approximately 400,000 users (mostly 14- to 25-year-olds) with thousands more signing up each day. That's a drop in the bucket compared to MySpace, which has banned users from adding the Stickam code to their MySpace page.

Parents need to be aware of these sites and the fact that many new computers come preinstalled with webcams. Several parents have been shocked to walk into their children's rooms only to discover them chatting live, face to face, with a "virtual" stranger.

Sites such as Stickam are a cross between online voyeurism (anyone with web access can view hundreds of people doing just about anything) and online exhibitionism. Stickam has strict rules prohibiting obscene or indecent behavior, but this is difficult to enforce.

New Challenges to Voyeurism Law

A recent Florida case may have significant ramifications in challenging the laws states have established against voyeurism.

THE BRIAN PRESKEN CASE

A police report taken on July 8, 2007, tells the story of what can happen
at a seemingly innocent place—a bookstore. According to the report, the
26-year-old victim was slightly bent forward browsing bookshelves when
she noticed a flash of light. She said she thought a man had taken a picture of her. The Pensacola woman said she noticed another flash of light,
and when she turned around, the man's hand was beneath the opening
of her skirt, and there was something in his hand. The woman screamed,
and the man retreated. The woman caught up to Brian Presken, 32, a former Catholic high school teacher of Pensacola, Florida. She confronted
Presken and called the police. Someone in the store found a mirror on a
shelf and gave it to police.

Presken, who passed out while being questioned by police, told police he
kept a mirror with him to check his appearance. (Voyeurs often keep a
mirror handy, because if they can't capture an image up a woman's skirt,
they will resort to just viewing it with a mirror.) Presken filed a motion to
get his misdemeanor voyeurism conviction overturned because of the
legal argument that people do not have a reasonable expectation of
privacy in public places.

REASONABLE EXPECTATION OF PRIVACY

Presken was charged under the Florida Statute 810.14: Voyeurism. This
statute states, in part

> *"...a person commits the offense of voyeurism when he or she, with lewd,
> lascivious, or indecent intent, secretly observes another person when the
> other person is located in a dwelling, structure, or conveyance and such
> location provides a reasonable expectation of privacy."*

In the motion, Presken's attorney, Katheryne Snowden, claimed that the
Florida statute didn't define the phrase "reasonable expectation of privacy."

Interestingly, there is another Florida state statute that is meant specifically to deal with video voyeurism, meaning using video cameras or cell
phone cameras to commit the act. This statute defines *reasonable expectation of privacy* as "anyplace where a person can disrobe," but Presken was
alleged to have used a mirror, not a camera of any kind.

Voyeurism laws have been overturned in other states because the phrase
"reasonable expectation of privacy" has not been clearly defined.

CONVICTION OVERTURNED

On May 16, 2008, Judge George J. Roark III agreed and granted Presken's motion to dismiss the voyeurism charge. The Assistant State Attorney, Greg Marcille, said the ruling will not be appealed, but he did say, "We intend to ask the legislature in next year's session to consider amending the statute to cover situations such as what occurred in this case."

Presken was also charged with disorderly conduct, which is still being pursued.

RAMIFICATIONS

Presken's case has significant ramifications because too many states have adopted the language "reasonable expectation of privacy" without any clear definition of what that means. Too often, it is only after convictions get overturned that states close up these legal gray areas.

In Washington State, two men were convicted in separate voyeurism cases and used a similar privacy argument to appeal their cases to their state's supreme court. One of the men was accused of taking pictures under the skirts of two female employees at a mall. The other was suspected of videotaping under the skirts and dresses of women and girls at an event in Seattle.

The court acknowledged that the behavior of the men was "reprehensible," but the law they were charged under could not be applied to "public places." State lawmakers ended up amending the statute after both cases were overturned.

How Prevalent Is Voyeurism?

If you don't believe us when we say video voyeurism is huge, go to YouTube and do a search for "hidden camera." Then do a search for "upskirting." You will be shocked at how many videos are available for view.

People who have pictures unknowingly taken of them for the purposes of someone else's sexual gratification *are* victims. That means there are thousands of unsuspecting victims out there who probably don't even know they've ever been victimized.

> If you don't believe us when we say video voyeurism is huge, go to YouTube and do a search for "hidden camera."

How to Prevent Becoming a Victim of Voyeurism

The following are not only tips to prevent becoming a victim of a voyeur but important personal safety tips as well:

- Be aware of your surroundings. To commit the act of upskirting or downblousing, the perpetrator has to get in fairly close proximity to the victim. Be aware of that.

- When you enter a dressing room, look around. Pinhole cameras are sometimes very hard to detect and can be concealed in ordinary objects such as smoke detectors. Some stores allow same-sex monitoring of dressing rooms by policy, but usually must state that clearly in the dress-ing area. Look for small lights, red lights, or ceiling tiles that are slightly misplaced. If you see something that you may suspect is a camera, notify someone and ask to have it explained. In this era of "customer service," no reasonable store manager should object to you questioning these things, but be aware that store security systems may already be making recordings of you from the minute you enter the store.

- In public places, be aware of being jostled, especially if you are wearing a skirt or a dress. It is easy to be distracted and not realize you've been a victim of upskirting. Again, someone has to get within fairly close prox-imity of you to do this, so be aware of your "personal space."

- Cell phones are being used more and more for voyeurism because everyone carries one these days so it does not raise suspicions. However, if someone jostles you or bends down near you, you need to be aware of that.

- If you suspect someone has upskirted you, try and get a good cloth-ing description of the person and notify the police immediately.

- Finally, and most importantly, women have a sixth sense about someone being "creepy." Listen to that inner voice.

Is a Stranger Watching Your Nanny Cam?

Many parents, in an effort to ensure their children's safety, have installed "nanny cams." These webcams allow Mom or Dad to watch the activities of their child's caretaker, either overtly or covertly. The system is usually set up with a small webcam that can stream wireless video across the Internet. Many daycare centers are now using nanny cams, so parents can watch their children while they are at work. But what if you weren't the only one watching?

A VideoTek Finder (from VideoTek) can be purchased on the Internet for under $500 at www.PIMall.com. It's a handheld device that, within proximity, can detect wireless webcams and allow the person with the device to watch exactly what the webcam is broadcasting. It works by automatically scanning all commonly used video frequencies, like a police scanner does. In less than 5 seconds, the VideoTek Finder can lock in on any video transmitter. It has a small 2.5" display for watching what is being streamed on the video frequency. The antenna sensitivity can be set for distances of up to 500 feet away, depending on the power level of the source transmitter. Think about someone sitting in a car 500 feet away from your house. This person could easily be down the road or even around the corner and still be able to watch your nanny cam, or any other wireless video transmitter, without you even knowing about it.

The Voyeur's Backpack

And as if that wasn't enough to make you wonder, here's yet another device—a slim backpack specifically designed to capture streaming video. The Porta 2030 backpack with built-in video cameras can be worn slung over the shoulder or in traditional backpack style. It streams video across Wi-Fi networks. The user has controls that allow him to prioritize what is being streamed. Even if someone was found to be using the device for voyeuristic purposes, the video, which can be set to upload automatically to the Internet, would already be out there for millions to view.

For the James Bond 007 fanatic, many interesting gadgets can be purchased online for the purposes of "spying," including lipstick case cameras, pinhole cameras that can be hidden in any coat or bag, glasses cams, and pen cams.

Although it is fun for the civilian enthusiast to make a purchase for a spy game, for the sexual deviant, these toys just make it so much easier to find and exploit unwitting victims. (See Appendix A, "Toys They Don't Want You to Know About.")

Unfortunately, our judicial system, which tends to lag behind technologically due to budgetary constraints, has not been able to keep up with the new legal challenges digital video has created. As cameras get smaller and more capable, the opportunities for violating an individual's privacy expand exponentially. We cannot ignore the illicit activities this technological progression has brought about.

RESOURCES

- National Center for Victims of Crime (www.ncvc.org)

5

Identity Theft

There is yet another dark side to the online world: cyber criminals who seek to scam you, spam you, load nasty things onto your computer, steal your identity, and then steal you blind. They can wreak havoc with your bank account, your credit cards, your computer, your credit rating, your sanity—and never even touch you physically, although the financial and emotional damage is *very* real. We want to emphasize this point. Just because identity theft is not a physical crime against someone, do not underestimate the amount of fear and stress it puts victims under. It is *not* a victimless crime by any means.

Identity Theft: The Number-One Type of Fraud

In February of 2008, the U.S. Federal Trade Commission released a report of the top consumer fraud complaints. For the seventh year in a row, identity theft was the number-one consumer complaint category. Of 813,899 total complaints received in 2007, 32% were related to identity theft.

The most common form of identity theft was credit card fraud, a trend we're seeing in the police department where we work.

A bulk of these fraud cases (64%) happened as a result of an exchange on the Internet. Forty-nine percent of fraudsters used email to contact their eventual prey, and 15% used the web.

For the seventh year in a row, identity theft was the number-one consumer complaint category.

What do all these numbers mean to American consumers? Estimates are that losses range from $55.7 billion in 2006 to $49.3 billion in 2007 (Javelin Strategy and Research, January 2007).

23,000 Victims Per Day: One Every 3.5 Seconds

Let's crunch some more numbers. In that same report by Javelin Strategy and Research, it is estimated that there were 8.4 million victims of identity fraud in 2006. That's equivalent to 23,000 victims each day. Identity theft and fraud continue to be the most prolific and most profitable crimes committed.

When the Federal Trade Commission issued its "2006 Identity Theft Survey Report," it estimated that over 8 million Americans reported being victims of identity theft in 2005. That would equate to someone's identity being stolen every 3.5 seconds!

The fact that these numbers are so close, yet from completely different sources, suggests that they are fairly accurate. That means in the time it took you to read this section, someone's identity was stolen.

Cheap Credit Cards

Here are some of the realities of financial cyber crime: A credit card number with security code (the validation digits on the back) and expiration date can be purchased online for $7 to $25. Birth certificates can be purchased online for around $150, and a credit card number with its associated PIN can be bought for about $300.

What many people don't realize is that an entire "underworld" of the Internet exists solely for the purpose of propagating many different types of crimes, from trading sexually explicit images and video of children to trading credit card numbers. Access to such sites is very restricted, often requiring "sponsorship" by an existing member. Members use secret chat rooms where credit card numbers fly back and forth faster than a Ferrari.

A credit card number with security code and expiration date can be purchased online for $7 to $25. Birth certificates can be purchased online for around $150, and a credit card number with its associated PIN can be bought for about $300.

Identity Theft Versus Identity Fraud

Identity fraud usually involves the unauthorized use of credit and debit cards, where there's no or only limited liability, so long as the unauthorized use is reported.

Identity theft occurs when a person's information—date of birth, social security number, driver's license—is stolen and used specifically for the purpose of establishing a new identity and new credit using the victim's name.

To complicate matters, the FBI collects statistics on crime using "umbrella" categories. Therefore, when police agencies report crime statistics to the FBI's repository for crime data, the offense of identity theft is reported as "Impersonation," whereas identity fraud can be reported as either "Fraud" or "Credit Card Offense." You can see why it's so difficult to get a real number on these types of crimes.

What we do know is that when it happens, it can set off a chain of events that leave you exhausted and feeling just as violated and vulnerable as if someone had entered your premises.

ILLEGAL USE OF LEGAL NAME CHANGE

Identity thieves are incredibly clever. Take the case of Trina Caldwell, 31, of Washington State. In February of 2008, she was sentenced to 60 months in prison and 5 years of supervised release on the charges of Bank Fraud and Aggravated Identity Theft.

Caldwell, along with a ring of other women, including her own mother, went to the King County District Court under false pretenses and repeatedly obtained name change orders. They then used those name change orders to apply for driver's licenses and social security cards. With these two key items, they opened up bank accounts and made deposits from one account to the other and then withdrew the cash before the checks bounced. They did this to the tune of over $140,000. As soon as one account was closed, they would go back to the courthouse saying they were getting married, or wanted to take their father's name and, once again, would obtain yet another false identity.

Although certainly not the biggest identity theft case, this illustrates just how clever thieves are at being able to obtain new identities with relative ease.

The Long Road to Recovery

Until you've worked with or become a victim of identity theft, you cannot appreciate the amount of time it takes to recover from this type of crime. Victims must notify just about everyone they interact with—credit card companies, banks, doctor's offices, schools, and employers—and advise them their identity has been stolen. The paperwork trail is enormous, and every entity has its own version of forms that must be filled out. Police reports must be filed. Credit reporting agencies must be notified, the Social Security Administration must be notified, and so on.

What's more, new credit cards and social security numbers must be applied for. Copies of reports must be sent. All this takes an arduous effort and a large amount of time. Often victims have to take time off from work, resulting in a loss of wages. Any future attempts at obtaining credit means the whole story has to be dredged up again, and all the paperwork has to be dug back up and re-sent. Many victims still deal with the ramifications of identity theft years after the crime was committed.

Besides the physical labor of having to stay organized and on top of all your accounts, there is often a fear that someone is out there with all your information. He or she knows your name and where you live. The feeling of being violated is very real.

On a plus side, we can say based on our personal experience and research that identity theft rarely leads to actual physical harm. If there's any comfort to being a victim of a crime, let that be it. Still, this does not remove the sting of emotions—shame, fear, anger—that identity theft victims often feel.

The NCIC Identity Theft File

The NCIC (National Crime Information Center) Identity Theft File protects victims of identity theft by confirming that they are, in fact, the victims and not someone who has assumed their identity. Think about it: If someone has stolen your identity, what's to prevent him from using it if he gets pulled over for speeding or is arrested? Hence the creation of the NCIC Identity Theft File.

Information needed for the file includes a victim's name, date of birth, social security number, and type of identity theft. A password that is easily remembered is chosen by the victim and entered into the file. If the victim has any interaction with the police in the future, the police have access to the NCIC ID Theft File to confirm the password. This also serves as a red flag that someone might be using an assumed name so that identity can be confirmed.

Guilty Until Proven Innocent

One of the most frustrating aspects of identity theft is that it can be extremely hard for victims to prove they are innocent. Numerous cases, some of which we will highlight, demonstrate how difficult it is to untangle yourself from identity theft once you become a victim.

Identity theft victims face the added burden of having to prove that they really did not order that new laptop online or run up thousands of dollars in cell phone fees. That's what makes this crime so frustrating for both victim and law enforcement—it's like trying to follow two very clear sets of footprints going off from the scene of a crime in totally different directions. Add to that the fact that credit card companies receive so many reports of identity theft a year that they don't necessarily believe you were, in fact, a victim. Even if you can prove that you are a victim, they still want to get paid, but trying to sort through authorized and unauthorized purchases isn't always as easy as it seems, and you are still obligated to pay for any authorized purchases even if you dispute 90% of the balance on the account.

It takes a great deal of time to try and point out that right path. It's as if the victims become revictimized in the process of trying to clear their name. So why let it happen in the first place if you can prevent it?

> Credit card companies receive so many reports of identity theft a year that they don't necessarily believe you were, in fact, a victim.

Types of Identity Theft

The most common form of identity theft is credit card fraud. According to the nonprofit Identity Theft Resource Center, identity theft is subdivided into four categories:

- **Financial identity theft**—Using another's identity to obtain goods and services
- **Criminal identity theft**—Posing as another person when apprehended for a crime
- **Identity cloning**—Using another's information to assume his or her identity in daily life
- **Business/commercial identity theft**—Using another's business name to obtain credit

Delays in Notification

Another point of frustration for victims is that they often don't know their information has even been compromised for weeks, sometimes months, due to the significant financial and customer-confidence stigmas for companies to come forward and admit their data has been compromised. However, it is the right thing to do.

In May of 2008, the Staten Island University Hospital in New York became one of the latest organizations to admit that tens of thousands of patients had their data compromised when a hospital desktop computer was stolen from one of its billing offices.

What makes this situation troublesome is that the hospital waited 4 months to notify patients of the breach. The reasoning? Here's what one hospital spokesperson told the media:

> In taking a look at this, could it have been done sooner? I believe perhaps it could have been done sooner.

The spokesperson, Anthony Ferreri, SIUH president and CEO, went on to say that the hospital went through an 8-to-9-week process to identify a credit-monitoring program for all 88,000 patients with the national credit-reporting agency Equifax before it made notification to patients.

"We wanted to make certain we had the best possible vendor with the experience in the particular area who could protect the credit and the information of those who were affected," Ferreri said.

These kinds of delays substantially increase the chances that victims will have their identities stolen and compromised. We understand the public relations debacle this kind of breach incurs, but the victims deserve to be notified in a timely manner above the rights of the companies to save face.

Incidentally, this is not the only time data has been stolen from an organization. Laptop thefts are on the rise. Thumb drives can contain volumes of data. iPods and MP3 devices can store thousands of documents. Data is very portable these days, and we understand that despite best efforts, things can get lost. However, companies need to consider the ramifications of losing data and they must establish policies accordingly.

Why is this so difficult to do? That's easy—we are a mobile society that wants to be able to work anywhere, anytime.

Preventing Identity Theft

The two most important things you can do to prevent identity theft and the loss of your credit are fairly easy and simple: Monitor your bank and credit card accounts and monitor your credit reports.

Monitor Your Accounts

In this day and age, almost every bank and credit card company allows you to monitor your account information online. Do it! You should be checking your accounts on a monthly, if not weekly, basis to make sure there are no transactions you do not recognize. If there are, contact the bank immediately. Compare your monthly statements to your receipts and make sure they match. Visiting your bank online is safe as long as you know exactly where you're going, which is why we recommend that instead of clicking a hyperlink, type in the bank's URL (Internet address) in the Location tab. Do *not* ever go to your bank or credit card website from a link in an email because you may be going to a fake site. Start another Internet session and type in www.*nameofbank*.com yourself to make absolutely sure you are really at the bank's site. (See more on this in Chapter 11, "Phishing, Pharming, Spam, and Scams.") Check your accounts often so you see any discrepancies immediately.

> Check your accounts on a monthly, if not weekly, basis to make sure there are no transactions you do not recognize.

Get Your Free Annual Credit Report (annualcreditreport.com)

Memorize this web address: www.annualcreditreport.com. Better yet, bookmark it. Most states participate with this site to allow consumers free access to the three major credit-reporting agencies: Equifax, Experian, and TransUnion.

Prior to joining law enforcement, Felicia spent many years in the consumer credit industry. She remembers the days when credit reports were run on punch cards, then ticker tape. Many times when viewing credit reports of consumers, she was the first one to inform them of a delinquency or discrepancy. The reports were not as readily available to consumers as they are now. They are an important weapon in your online safety arsenal. Make use of them.

If you qualify (based on which state you live in), you are entitled to a free copy of your credit report each year. By staggering your requests and getting only one report from a single credit bureau at a time, you can actually see your credit report once every 4 months (once from each credit bureau per year). This is an extremely important technique in preventing identity theft.

Note that a variety of "free" credit report websites are out there. However, this is the only "official" site set up by the three major credit-reporting companies. Many others will claim to be free but dupe you into purchasing other services. Stick with www.annualcreditreport.com, but make sure you download the report and read it!

Credit Report Tips

Read your credit report thoroughly. Familiarize yourself with all the accounts listed so you can easily recognize any future discrepancies.

Notify the credit-reporting agencies immediately if you see any discrepancies in your credit report. These companies are a central repository for all the financial institutions that report to them, and their reputations rely on their information being accurate. Notify them immediately if you see an account (open or closed) on your credit report that you do not recognize. Someone may be attempting to commit identity theft in your name. The credit agencies are obligated to investigate any discrepancies you report to them.

Verify that your address information is correct. Identity thieves will often take out different addresses or use a P.O. box to have credit cards sent to them.

If you suspect identity theft, you have the right to ask that a "fraud alert" be placed in your file to let potential creditors and others know that you may be a victim. A fraud alert can make it more difficult for someone to get credit in your name because it tells creditors to follow certain procedures to protect you. It also may delay your ability to obtain credit, but this is a fair tradeoff to make sure someone else does not seek credit in your name.

You only need to request a fraud alert from one credit reporting agency. That company is then obligated to notify the others. (The contact information for these credit agencies is listed under "Resources" at the end of this chapter.)

There are different kinds of fraud alerts. An initial fraud alert stays in your file for at least 90 days. You must call to extend it if you need it beyond the 90-day period. An *extended* alert stays in your file for 7 years and requires a police report for documentation.

Be aware that although some identity thieves will sell stolen information immediately, many will warehouse it because they are well aware of this 90-day window. Newly stolen data is considered risky in the underworld of identity thieves, but thieves are still willing to chance getting caught by attempting to sell it.

Felicia Finds "Rogue" Account

We want our readers to understand that we come at this topic from all angles—as professionals, as law enforcement, as women, and, unfortunately, even as "victims."

When we make recommendations, it's because of all the cases we've seen that either could have prevented or could have been worse, or the recommendations come from our own personal experiences. In this case, Felicia became the victim of identity theft and there was little she could have done to prevent it.

Felicia was rather surprised to arrive home to find a collection call on her answering machine. Knowing that she had no outstanding bills, she immediately went online and pulled up her credit report. By staggering the reports, as recommended earlier in this chapter, she was able to see one right away. It was during this review of her credit report that she noticed an account for a cell phone taken out just a few months prior.

Felicia knew the account was bogus and immediately contacted the credit-reporting agency and assured them this was not her account. She followed this up with a letter in writing.

By stating in writing that an account is not yours, the credit reporting agency is obligated to investigate your claim. In this case, someone had taken out a cell phone account in New York under Felicia's name. The cell phone company was contacted, the account was immediately closed, and the negative information was removed from Felicia's credit report.

Felicia continues to carefully monitor her credit report knowing that she was, in this instance, very lucky. Millions of people have been through the nightmare of identity theft, with thousands of dollars being sucked out of their personal bank accounts and their credit being ruined—not to mention the exhaustive and lengthy effort it takes to correct everything.

Monitor Your Child's Credit Report

The Federal Trade Commission estimated that in 2006, 5% of identity theft complaints came from people younger than 18. That's over 500,000 child victims a year. Identity thieves are notorious for grabbing the social security numbers of children and opening up accounts because they are often overlooked and easy to hijack. If you have children, also request a copy of their credit records through www.annualcreditreport.com, and check your children's history using their social security numbers. Identity thieves love to open accounts under children's names because the crime can go undetected for years.

One interesting note on this topic is that it is estimated that more than half the cases of identity theft of a minor are perpetrated by a relative (see Identity Theft Resource Center at www.idtheftcenter.org).

THE ALICIA M. CASE

In a widely publicized case, Alicia M., a then 16-year-old from Illinois, went to apply for a job at a local department store only to find out that someone else had been using her social security number since she was 11 years old.

A man from Chicago was later charged with identity theft, a felony in Illinois. Police say that the man bought the social security number for $200 and had been using it to secure among other things, a $149,000 mortgage on his home, cell phones, and vehicle registrations.

Alicia was denied employment and cell phone service, and she nearly missed out on loans from the college she was enrolled in because of this nightmare.

Tips to Prevent Your Child's Identity from Being Stolen

Most schools require your child's social security number (SSN). It would be hard to not provide this information, particularly because many programs, such as Special Education, require a child's SSN in order to receive service. However, this does not mean the school's football team has to have it. The point here is to always challenge why an SSN is being required and to ask where that information is being shared. We are not aware of any students who were refused a public education, which is required by law, for not providing an SSN.

> Always challenge why an SSN is being required and ask where that information is being shared.

Even if schools have strict privacy policies, which most do, your child's information is being entered into some sort of database, which can be further compromised. Databases containing any personal information are a treasure trove to identity thieves, who can often acquire millions of pieces of data at a time.

Have a conversation with your children about the importance of not giving out personal information, including their social security number. Explain to your teenagers that they are likely to be required to provide their SSN on an employment application because of standard pre-employment credit screenings and the need to report their income to the IRS, if hired, but that they should safeguard their personal information, including their driver's license and debit cards, always.

More Identity-Theft Prevention Tips

The following tips don't take a lot of time, but they can save a tremendous amount of time in the long run by reducing your risk of becoming an Identity Theft victim:

- Make at least two copies of all your credit cards, your driver's license, your social security card, your insurance card, and any other cards you carry in your wallet. Make copies of both the front and back of each card. Store one copy at home and one copy somewhere safe outside the home. This will give you quick access to all your account numbers as well as the 800-numbers you may have to call should your purse be lost or stolen. This 5-minute task can save you hours of agony in trying to recall everything you had in your wallet.

- Don't forget other "minor" forms of ID, such as library cards and supermarket discount cards. Make front and back copies of everything and notify everyone because something as innocuous as a library card could be presented as a form of ID to request another form of ID.

- Going on vacation? Take the copies you made of the fronts and backs of your credit cards and other IDs and stick them somewhere in your luggage away from your wallet. Better yet, record all the info and put it in a file on a USB stick and hide it in your luggage. Remember that you are more vulnerable when traveling, so have the info, including the 800-numbers, readily available so you can get your cards quickly replaced. On that note, if you're traveling internationally, there's often a separate 800-number. Keep all this information in a safe place, but *not* in your wallet.

- Even if you think you may have just misplaced a card, notify the card holder immediately. Thieves will use stolen cards within minutes. Credit card companies have the ability to freeze your account to prevent fraudulent transactions almost immediately. We cannot tell you how many times police departments are notified of fraudulent activity by stores at the same time the victim is still looking around for their misplaced card. Don't take a chance. It is a lot easier to get a new credit card mailed out than it is to try and correct your credit because of credit card theft or identity theft. Notify the credit card company first, immediately, and then the police if the credit card company advises you of recent activity.

- Tear up or, better yet, shred those preapproved credit card offers that come in the mail. Someone could easily take them and apply for credit in your name. Some towns are even sponsoring "Shred Days," where citizens can bring sensitive documents to locations with certified commercial shredding trucks.

- Don't put mail in your mailbox to be picked up if you can avoid it. Those raised flags indicating that there's outgoing mail are a treasure trove for identity thieves who want to grab bills with account information and copies of your personal checks. Better to drop off the mail in the blue U.S. Mail collection boxes or take it to a post office.

- Make sure if you are moving that you stop your mail several days prior to the move. Do not chance mail being sent to a vacant house.

- One more reason to not put up that mailbox flag—mail theft is rampant these days. Identity thieves have a technique for "washing" checks you wrote out to pay your utility bills using acetone (nail polish remover) to remove the ink. They then use the blank check for wherever they want! Thieves know that a gel-based pen such as a Uni-ball is not washable, so they will first trace over your signature first with a gel-based pen, then wash the check in acetone. This keeps the signature intact, but blanks out the amount of the check. It is highly recommended that you fill out the entire check, including who it is to and the amount, using a gel-based pen rather than a ball-point pen.

- Opt out of the preapproved credit card solicitations. Call 888-5-OPTOUT or go to www.optoutprescreen.com.

- Be alert to bills you normally expect that are *not* coming. A frequent trick of identity thieves is to issue a change of address on an account.

- Have you ever been checking out at the register when the clerk asks for your phone number? Politely decline! All legitimate businesses expect customers to opt out of this request and have a means of bypassing it. All you're doing by providing your home phone number is allowing a marketing company to aggregate that much more information about your personal buying habits—thereby making it easier for you to become a target of unwanted solicitations and even scams.

- No matter what the circumstance, if you are asked for your SSN, challenge it! Ask why the information is needed and what the ramifications will be if you don't provide it.

Shred, Shred, Shred

Although identity theft is a cyber crime, it often begins the old-fashioned way—with someone picking through your trash or stealing from your mailbox. To that end, you should always try to shred any documents that contain any personal account information, receipts that have your credit card number, offers for new credit cards, and so on. Remember that thieves are clever and will use any "shred" (pardon the pun) of your identity to build a new one. That includes your address, your phone number, your date of birth—all of which can be gleaned from many ordinary documents you might not even think need to be shredded, such as a medical bill or a drug receipt. Think like a thief and don't give them any ammunition! Shred everything.

And remember, if you're an avid gardener, you can always use that shredded paper as mulch for your plants.

Many different models of shredders are available on the market, but the two most commonly purchased and widely available are the "strip-cut" shredder, which cuts the paper one way into strips, and the "cross-cut" or "confetti" shredder, which uses two contra-rotating drums to cut rectangular, parallelogram, or diamond-shaped shreds. The cross-cut shredder is usually more expensive, but worth the extra investment. The items shred-ded in a strip-cut shredder are much too easy to stitch back together.

We have seen the output of a strip-cut shredder that basically cuts right in between the space between the text, meaning the text was still completely readable. Make sure that if you opt for a strip-cut shredder that it cuts close enough to render the text unreadable. For added safety, make sure your shredder can shred plastic, including credit cards and CDs that may contain personal information. In other words, the purchase of a shredder is not the place to "cut corners."

Also, commercial shredding services are available for high-volume opera-tions. Many municipalities and medical facilities use commercial shred-ding services due to the confidential nature of the paperwork.

Fraudulent Donations

When a thief gets hold of a credit card number, the stakes are pretty high that the card could have already been reported stolen. How can the thief test whether or not the account number is good without risking getting arrested? By using the credit card number to make a donation to an online nonprofit agency. Think about it—they don't get any merchandise deliv-ered, so there's no trail of delivery; they don't have to appear anywhere in person and risk arrest, and they can test how much they can charge with-out sending up a red flag. Unfortunately, it's the nonprofit organization that gets whacked, not only with a fraudulent donation but then any asso-ciated costs with having to try to sort out the dummy donation.

If You Are a Victim of Identity Theft

Given how prolific identity theft is, chances are that you or someone you know may become a victim. When that happens, there are steps you can take immediately that will limit your liability. Here are some suggestions you may not have considered:

- Notify your credit card companies immediately. They can issue a stop on an account within minutes to prevent any further fraudulent charges.

- Gather all the documentation you have showing the charges and print everything out.

- Save the screens showing the fraudulent charges if you can. You can save a web page in Internet Explorer by using the File, Save As menu command and giving the page a filename just like you would a docu-ment. You can then call that file back up if you need it later on.

- Notify the police. Identity theft is a crime, and although the police may or may not be able to solve the crime, you may need the documentation to prove you were a victim if someone commits more crimes with your identity. File the report for your own future safety.

- Don't forget to notify the Social Security Administration (www.ssa.gov) and your local Department of Motor Vehicles. You might also want to notify your local postal service because often identity theft involves mail—either bills are sent for accounts you didn't open or your outgoing bills are stolen to obtain your account information.

- Report the incident to the Internet Crime Complaint Center (www.ic3.gov). This helps in identifying trends and gives law enforcement much needed information. This site has a wealth of resources to help you recover from the crime (see Figure 5.1).

One of the most interesting features of IC3 is somewhat buried on the site, but well worth the look. IC3 collects statistics for each state, including how it ranks compared to other states. To access this, at the top of the screen, select Press Room and then select Annual Reports along the right side of the resulting page. Alternatively, you could Google "IC3" and "annual reports." There are no major surprises in the top three complainant states: California, followed by Florida and New York.

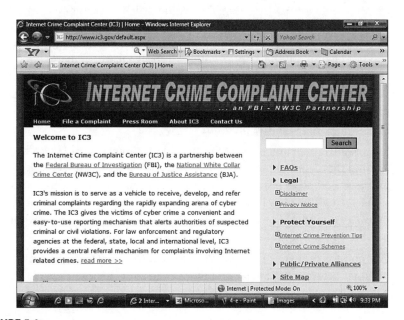

FIGURE 5.1

The Internet Crime Complaint Center (IC3) is a partnership between the FBI and the National White Collar Crime Center (NW3C). Online reports of cyber crime are accepted at www.ic3.gov.

Identity Theft Services

Every day more and more companies offer commercial identity theft protection for consumers—often for a price around $10 to $15 a month. The following list of companies is for research purposes only. We are not endorsing any product.

Do your own research before handing over your money. Some "identity theft protection programs" have recently come under scrutiny as a possible source of identity theft, so be careful and Google any company and research it prior to signing up.

- Identity Guard (www.identityguard.com)
- Trusted ID (www.trustedid.com)
- LoudSiren (www.loudsiren.com)
- NameSafe (www.namesafe.com)

More information about these different services can be found at Next Advisor (www.nextadvisor.com).

LifeLock Gets Sued

One such company, LifeLock, out of Tempe, Arizona, made its claim to fame when its CEO, Todd Davis, advertised his own social security number on the company's website, claiming that his firm could "protect my good name and personal information—just like it will yours." Unfortunately, it didn't. Davis's social security number was used successfully to apply for a loan, and over a hundred LifeLock members (of the supposed one million subscribers) have had their identities stolen while they were enrolled in the program.

Just recently, Experian, the credit-reporting company, sued LifeLock contending that LifeLock's advertising is misleading and that LifeLock's primary method of prevention—placing continuous fraud alerts on consumers' credit files—is illegal. To be fair, and we always try to be fair, there are a million of satisfied LifeLock customers who are quite willing to pay the $10-a-month fee for the protection it affords.

Our point is that your best bet is to be educated in ways to prevent identity theft before it happens—and that's free!

Attorney General Becomes ID Theft Victim

In May of 2008, Kentucky Attorney General Jack Conway announced the formation of a specialized cyber crime unit to combat, among many things, identity theft.

In June of 2008, Attorney General Conway revealed that when he went to buy music on iTunes, the company refused his credit card and informed him it did not match the ZIP Code on record.

Not only had thieves stolen his credit card information, they charged thousands of dollars on it for computers, phone services, and postage. The thieves changed the Attorney General's mailing address. That hurts. Felicia won't ever complain about being duped for a phony cell phone account again.

RESOURCES

The following is a list of identity-theft resources:

- IC3, the Internet Crime Complaint Center (www.ic3.gov)
- Identity Theft Resource Center (www.idtheftcenter.org)
- Free Annual Credit Report (www.annualcreditreport.com)
- Identity Theft Labs (www.identitytheftlabs.com)
- Privacy Rights Clearinghouse (www.privacyrights.org)
- Center for Identity Management & Protection of Utica College (www.utica.edu/academic/institutes/cimip/)

And here's a list of credit-reporting agencies:

- Equifax (1-877-576-5734; www.equifax.com)
- Experian (1-888-397-3742; www.experian.com/fraud)
- TransUnion (1-800-680-7289; www.transunion.com)
- Federal Trade Commission (www.consumer.gov/idtheft)
- U.S. Department of Justice (http://www.usdoj.gov/criminal/fraud/websites/idtheft.html)
- Card Cops (www.cardcops.com)

6

Online Dating—Are You Safe?

Online dating sites have proliferated over the last few years. Current research suggests that 200 million people visit online dating services a month (source: *Online Dating Magazine*). This new social venue offers people an opportunity to meet who might not ordinarily have a chance to meet because of their busy schedules. Online dating services offer many pluses—they allow someone to pick and choose his or her selection based on physical descriptions, interests, and goals. Unfortunately, online dating services also provide opportunities for those who have less-than-honest intentions. These services are no different from any other online venue. They provide a cloak to those who wish to portray themselves any way they want with very little validation.

THE JEFFREY MARSALIS CASE

None of the cases we've dealt with in our professional careers rise to the level of the case of Jeffrey Marsalis, a 34-year-old Philadelphia man who was accused, but later acquitted, of raping nine women, six of whom he met through Match.com (see Figure 6.1).

Marsalis claimed to be a doctor, a CIA agent, an FBI agent, and even an astronaut. During his trial, his fiancée testified that he often took her with him to a local hospital, dressed in a lab coat and scrubs, and went into cadaver labs and medical supply rooms—unchallenged by security guards.

(Courtesy Philadelphia Police Department)

FIGURE 6.1

Jeffrey Marsalis

Marsalis's victims were intelligent, professional women, including one attorney. Marsalis often produced official-looking badges that are easily purchased online and through police supply catalogs.

During the course of Marsalis's trial, all the victims gave almost identical testimony as to Marsalis's methods, including the fact that although they drank little alcohol, they all blacked out and lost their memory. By the time they regained consciousness, they realized they had either already had a sexual encounter or were in the midst of one with Marsalis. FBI chemists testified that they believed the women's drinks had been laced with the active ingredient found in Benadryl, which would explain the syringe found in Marsalis's apartment containing 50 mg of the drug in liquid form.

None of the victims reported the alleged rape to authorities until much later; therefore, there was no way to test their blood for the presence of drugs.

Marsalis's attorney claimed the sex was consensual in all cases and that the women were angry for being duped. The jury acquitted Marsalis on 24 total counts of rape, but did find him guilty of two counts of sexual assault—for which he could serve 10 to 20 years in prison.

Can Online Dating Be Made Safer?

Recently, online dating services have been in the press's spotlight when New Jersey became the very first state in the nation to require online dating services to disclose whether or not they perform any kind of background checks on members. True.com, an online service, lobbied for such a law. True.com's founder, Herb Vest, was quoted as saying, "The online dating industry tends to get a real bad rap, because of criminal activity. If we were to clean up, there's hordes of offline singles who'd come online to find their soul mate."

However, industry critics have been quick to point out that True.com's screening method—running names through state databases of criminal records—is incomplete and easily thwarted. This could lead to a false sense of security. Although some type of background check is better than nothing, unless the database utilized is a true criminal history check, the information cannot be validated. The most reliable source is the Interstate Intelligence Index (III), which is utilized by law enforcement through NCIC (National Crime Information Center). This database is controlled by the FBI and is not accessible to online dating sites. It cannot be emphasized enough that just because someone has no criminal history, it does not mean that person has no deviant or criminal tendencies.

Criminal History Checks—What Can You Really Find Out?

We'd like to elaborate a bit on just what running a criminal history check involves and what an organization other than law enforcement might get or not get.

The "official" repository of criminal history information is NCIC—the National Crime Information Center database—which is hosted by the FBI. Many different types of records are maintained in this database, including criminal history.

If someone is arrested and convicted as an adult, that information becomes part of that person's criminal history record, which is usually a public record. Note that we emphasize "if someone is arrested and convicted," because the reality is that someone could be investigated by a law-enforcement agency numerous times for rape or assault and it is never reported. Unless there is an actual arrest and conviction, no notification is made to any criminal database because, technically, there is no criminal record. And in order to have a criminal history, you have to have a willing victim report it, follow through with an investigation, have an arrest, get an indictment, and then get a conviction. If no conviction occurs, the subject can have the arrest record expunged. It is not at all unusual, or difficult, for criminals to have their convictions expunged. Another requirement for an arrest or conviction to be included in NCIC is that the fingerprints taken at the time of the arrest be accepted and classified. If fingerprints are rejected because they were of poor quality to be classified, that particular arrest and conviction will not find its way to a permanent criminal record.

Many law-enforcement agencies subscribe to commercial database services, such as LexusNexis and Accurint, that aggregate data from a wide variety of sources such as public records, death records, tax records, and credit reporting agencies. Law enforcement has greater access than commercial companies that might use the Accurint database in the course of job applicant screening.

We can tell you from our own experience that we run some services, which shall remain unnamed, for investigative purposes, and there is no guarantee they will have accurate criminal information. We have seen situations where registered sex offenders did not even show up.

An individual would have to agree, in writing, to a criminal history check by an online service. But again, depending on where that information is being accessed, it is very possible that criminal activity is likely to *not* be disclosed. Even in this day and age of information sharing, many law-enforcement agencies maintain their own, separate records on every person they have contact with. This information is only shared with other law-enforcement agencies during the course of an investigation, or if someone signs a release to allow their local and NCIC records to go to a potential employer or the military upon application.

Local police contact records are just that—local to the police department providing them. What one town or city provides will not include what the next town over has; therefore, it is easy for someone's real criminal profile to be completely missed. Only law enforcement can provide these records. Online dating services cannot. If someone's NCIC record is checked, this has to be documented with a report number by the local police agency requesting it—along with the reason why it was run—because this information is regularly audited by the FBI. Only trained personnel from a law-enforcement agency who have been granted access to NCIC by the state agency who runs it (generally the state police) can run a "Triple I" (Interstate Identification Index). This information is not accessible by the private sector or the public. Each time a record is run, the requesting agency must account for the request, referencing a case number. The agency then must keep a current log of all checks run. The state agency heading NCIC in a particular state is the only authorized agency allowed to run a criminal record check for employment screening. The potential employee must have signed a release authorizing the prospective employer to request the criminal check.

For any commercial online dating service to do a thorough criminal history check is simply impossible. Even State Boards of Education that screen potential teaching applicants do so through the state police, who, with the appropriate release forms, then run the applicant through the NCIC database.

Our biggest concern with this new law and with any online dating service that claims to run background checks, including criminal history checks, is that it creates a false sense of security for those who might use the service.

Another key point to keep in mind is that just because someone has not been arrested or convicted does not mean that person does not have some dark behavioral secret. Look at Ted Bundy—this charismatic charmer killed for years before he was caught. A criminal record check as criteria on a dating website would not have been helpful to potential dates if he had decided to become a member of eHarmony, Match.com, or True.com! The crime is committed *before* a person is caught, arrested, and convicted; therefore, never assume that "no criminal history" means no deviant behavior. Remember the movie *Stripes*, with Bill Murray and his classic line when he was being interviewed to enlist in the Army? Murray's character was asked whether he had ever been convicted of a crime. Murray replies with a mischievous grin, "Convicted? No, never convicted...."

Online Dating Dilemmas

We're barraged with commercials and ads for popular dating websites such as Match.com and eHarmony. Around the world, busy adults with demanding professional lives and little spare time are filling out profiles to find their perfect match. One no longer needs to sit at a bar with friends and hope that Mr. or Ms. Wonderful will appear in between Cosmopolitans and Appletinis.

We all know people who have met the love of their life through dating websites. Yet despite many success stories, there are also stories of not-so-happy endings.

We're not discouraging anyone from trying to find love online, but when you give out personal information in the hopes of finding love, real caution needs to be exercised.

We all know people who have met the love of their life through dating websites. Yet despite many success stories, there are also stories of not-so-happy endings.

Dating on the Internet is no more safe than meeting someone at a bar or through a friend. The package may be impressive, the first interaction may be positive, and the profile may make the potential date sound promising. However, you are not always getting what you see at first glance.

Every time we hear Brad Paisley's song "Online"—the one where the actor who played George Costanza on *Seinfeld* is the protagonist in the music video—we laugh. It is funny, but it is also disturbingly accurate, describing an overweight, middle-aged man with asthma who has never done well with women, but who can become a completely different person on his MySpace account.

Paisley talks about how the character in this song is really nothing to write home about, but when he goes down into his parents' basement and logs into his MySpace page, he becomes a good-looking, talented, successful, and wealthy ladies' man. This may be an exaggeration of sorts, but truth be told, people lie online because they can be something they are not, appear cooler or more successful than they are, and find someone who will believe it all. Often the "lies" are not so blatant; however, even those subtle pieces of "misinformation" could be significant in the big scheme of things. Remember that the person with whom you are interacting is a *stranger*. That stranger may wind up being the best thing that ever happened to you, or not. Either way, you must be perceptive, smart, and savvy about the people you meet online and allow into your life.

We have worked several cases involving dating sites where women became victims of their date. Two cases specifically come to mind involving educated, professional, intelligent women who took what they thought were the right precautions before going on what became the "date from hell." There is a misconception that those friendly, benign conversations online make someone less of a stranger and more of a friend than the person who slips you his or her phone number at a party or bar.

Two cases specifically come to mind involving educated, professional, intelligent women who took what they thought were the right precautions before going on what became the "date from hell."

JEANETTE'S STORY

Jeanette is a partner in an architectural firm. She is a single mother who puts in many hours per week at a job where she has an incredible amount of responsibility and where people rely on her experience and judgment. Jeanette spends several hours per week in a local gym where she maintains an excellent fitness level and has even taken self-defense classes. With no time for traditional dating, a friend encouraged her to set up a profile on a popular dating site that uses its own methods to match potential mates.

Jeanette's profile is matched with a local business man, Peter, who appears to have the same interests as she does. The two converse online and then on the phone. Jeanette agrees to meet Peter at a local bar and grill for a drink and some appetizers one weekday evening. Jeanette gives her itinerary to her best friend, Deb, and the two even have a "safety plan": If Jeanette has not called Deb by 9 p.m., Deb will give her a call and check in. The two have used this plan in the past, and it includes them calling each other when they have arrived home safely at the end of the date.

Jeanette meets Peter at the grill. He is dressed conservatively and appears to be well spoken and educated. The two talk and discover that they have a mutual interest in photography. After two drinks each and several appetizers, the two decide to go for a walk in the quaint downtown area. Peter points out that his apartment overlooks the river and is gorgeous at sunset. Jeanette is initially hesitant; however, Peter then tells her that he has some wonderful artwork in his collection and he would love to get her opinion.

Jeanette goes with Peter to his apartment, which is walking distance from the restaurant where they met. It is only 7:30 p.m. and still light out. Peter behaves as a gentleman at first and the two have a glass of wine while watching the water. Peter and Jeanette become affectionate and he suggests moving their make-out session to the sofa. When Jeanette stops and tells Peter that it is really too soon, Peter's attitude does a 180-degree turn. He grabs her and pushes her into the couch and tries to unbutton her pants. Jeanette tries pushing him off of her and actively resists his advances, but Peter ignores her pleas. He flips her over on the couch and continues to try to undress her. Jeanette is ultimately able to shove Peter off of her. Peter insists that he does not know what her problem is, and is rather nonchalant about the encounter. Jeanette reports crying and shaking but is still able to get her coat on. Jeanette states that as she turns around to head out of the apartment, Peter is standing in front of her with his hand on his penis, masturbating in front of her. Jeanette reports that he kept saying to her, "I know you like it, let me see you...."

Jeanette runs from the apartment to her car where she breaks down. She does not call the police, but does call Deb crying and hysterical. Jeanette drives to Deb's house where she relays the incident to her. The incident is not reported to the police for several weeks, primarily because the victim was embarrassed at having gotten into the situation.

Victim Reluctance to Report

Time, with any case investigation, is of the essence; however, it is extremely common for victims to delay reporting a crime, if they even report it at all. One of the common reasons for this delay is that they are embarrassed and feel as though they let themselves become victimized. Women report feeling stupid about letting someone take advantage of them, and they lay the blame on themselves. We continually tell them that the only one to blame is the criminal.

GENEVIEVE'S STORY

Genevieve, a European immigrant who speaks five languages and is in medical school, reported that she had been raped by a date she met on a popular dating website. Genny, as she's called, is educated, intelligent, and had several safety steps in place for when she decided to date someone she met online. Genny met Anthony and emailed him several times before exchanging phone numbers with him. He told her he was a salesman who traveled all over New England and was quite the world traveler. His profile was impressive, from his credentials, to his insistence that his family was a priority, to his photo. He liked expensive wines, traveling, being successful, and claimed always to get what he wanted.

Genny agreed to meet Anthony on two occasions for coffee in a local hotspot so they could meet and get to know each other in a public place. Genny said that Anthony was a gentleman who was articulate and confident. They made arrangements to meet for a date one evening when Anthony was back in the area.

Anthony called Genny the evening of the date telling her that he was running late, giving her what appeared to be a plausible excuse. He told her that he would drive north and meet her for drinks as soon as he could. Anthony's last-minute change of plans was not a red flag at the time, although she had told him that the evening could not be too late because she needed to be at work in the morning.

Genny met Anthony at his hotel parking lot. They took a cab to a popular bar and had a couple of drinks. Genny stated that they went to another bar known for special martinis, and even though the bar was quiet, it took Anthony quite some time—about 20 minutes—to get her drink. Anthony only sipped at his drink and wanted her to finish hers. Genny stated that the room seemed to get blurry and started to spin. She was unable to stand on her own and remembered Anthony having to help her down the stairs. She remembers going back to the first bar where Anthony bought her more drinks. She remembers dancing, remembers getting into a cab, and then remembers being in a pool. The next thing she remembers is lying under Anthony while he was raping her. Genny remembers trying to scream; however, she could not make her mouth move. She could not even move her limbs. She described the situation as being an almost out-of-body experience in that she could think, but could not speak or move.

The next morning Genny woke up in a strange motel room and remembers having been thrown into a shower after she passed out. She remembers waking up in an all-night breakfast restaurant and watching Anthony scarf down eggs and bacon. Genny said that she stumbled to a restroom, where she was sick, and then saw herself in the mirror. She recalled looking like a nightmare. Friends provided statements that Genny was always well groomed, no matter what the situation. Anthony would not let her make any calls, and told her that she had really been "into" him. Genny finally got out of the motel room and looked at her phone. She realized that Anthony had made a number of calls to pizza places, taxi services, and the all-night breakfast restaurant that she remembered being in. Genny thought this strange because he had a company car, expense account, and cell phone. Later it was apparent that the calls had been made on Genny's phone so as not to appear on any business expense that might link him to the crime.

Genny was so shocked that she initially did not report anything. It took her a day or so to try to make sense out of the events that had occurred. She realized that she was missing a special piece of jewelry, so she called the motel and discovered that it had been found in the pool area after hours.

By the time Genny realized that she had probably been drugged, it was too late for any blood test. Most date rape drugs pass through the system within 12 to 18 hours; therefore, there was no medical evidence. Also, no SAE (sexual assault evidence) kit was used because she reported the incident almost a week after it occurred.

Genny reported confusion, embarrassment, and shame. She had taken her time in meeting Anthony, had met him at a public place during the day, had spoken with him on the phone, and then chose a relatively neutral place for their date. She notified her friends and had made arrangements for a friend to call her if she had not returned home by midnight. When her friend called, she told her friend she was having a good time and would be home soon. The friend remembers the call. Genny does not.

Anthony was arrested. Although Genny was articulate and adamant about testifying against him, the District Attorney's office made the decision not to pursue the case because a "he said, she said" case is very difficult to prosecute because it does "not play well to a jury."

Those involved with the case believed her story then and still believe that she was raped by a predator who fully intended to take advantage of her. Anthony walks free. Our hope is that he does not do this again; however, we know better. On the day that arrangements were made for Anthony's arrest, he took down his dating website, which had his picture on it. After he was booked and released on bail, his dating website went up again, this time without his picture. We call that cocky and blatantly flipping off the system. Anthony obviously has not taken the situation seriously, and given the failure of the justice system to prosecute this crime, we wonder if he ever will.

DATE RAPE DRUGS

Just recently, a Ruby Tuesday waiter from Colorado Springs was lauded for saving a woman from a date rape. The woman had met her date online, and the two had gone out for dinner at a Ruby Tuesday restaurant. As the woman got up to use the restroom, the waiter observed the date put a pill in the woman's drink. He then watched as the man used the straw to crush and stir the pill in the drink. The quick-thinking waiter brought a fresh margarita to the table and took the spiked drink. He saved the drink, and the authorities were called. The Internet date was arrested on felony charges as a result of trying to spike a tranquilizer in the unsuspecting woman's cocktail.

Lack of Evidence and Empathy

One of the biggest problems in these cases is that there is usually no DNA evidence (particularly in a consensual encounter) and no witness in the room at the time that the crime happens. These cases need to be built based on "he said, she said" statements and circumstantial evidence. Combine that with the issue of a victim being too embarrassed to report the incident—along with society's view that a woman should not put herself in a position of being victimized by someone she has met online—and it's no wonder few

> One of the biggest problems in these cases is that there is usually no DNA evidence (particularly in a consensual encounter) and no witness in the room at the time that the crime happens.

of these cases are prosecuted. To add insult to injury (because there is always injury whenever someone is victimized, even if it's just the psychological trauma), when alcohol gets thrown into the mix, the common reaction is, "What did she think was going to happen when she went out with the guy, consumed alcohol, and then went back to his place?"

What many people fail to realize is that alcohol is often deliberately used as the "weapon" by predators. In many states, intoxication of a victim makes a woman incapable of giving consent, thus allowing charges to be filed. The problem is that an intoxicated victim often means very sketchy details for the investigation.

An investigator can interview friends, witnesses, bartenders, taxi drivers, and other passers-by; however, only the two involved actually know what happened during the sexual activity. These cases depend on putting enough pieces together to convince a jury that a woman **What many people fail to realize is that alcohol is often deliberately used as the "weapon" by predators.** was sexually violated against her will—often without physical evidence. Most often the perpetrator will admit that sexual activity happened, but will insist it was consensual. The victim will insist she was forced.

Even with an articulate, emotionally stable victim who is willing to testify, the weight of proof falls more on the victim. The suspect never has to take the stand, whereas the victim does. The victim's life is an open book and a cut-throat defense attorney will attack her to lessen her credibility with a jury. The victim is often revictimized by the very system set up to hold the bad guy accountable. The victim is put in a position where she questions herself and blames herself for what happened.

THE NURSE'S REVENGE

Women are not always victims in online dating cases. In all fairness, we will tell the story of an emergency room nurse in a well-publicized case that involved Match.com.

"Belinda," as we will call her, was an emergency department nurse supervisor, and she met her boyfriend, Harry, on Match.com. From her perspective, the relationship was going well as long as Harry gave her his complete, undivided attention. Belinda became jealous and obsessed, and Harry felt he needed to take a step back from the relationship. All of a sudden, Harry began getting text messages on his cell phone that he had "better watch his back."

Shortly after, Harry was visited by local police at his place of employment. He was taken into custody, handcuffed, and led out for a psychiatric evaluation at a local hospital. The officers had the legal right to do so as a result of a signed form known as a "prayer and complaint," which had been completed as part of a process known as an *involuntary emergency admission*, or *IEA*. Guess who had completed and sworn to the affidavit that Harry was unstable, dangerous to himself and others? In her capacity as a supervising nurse, Belinda had convinced a Justice of the

Peace at the hospital where she worked that Harry was a patient in need of an IEA. She omitted the fact that he was her boyfriend.

Although it was quickly determined that Harry was not a threat to himself and did not need admission into a psychiatric ward, the damage had already been done. Belinda was arrested for stalking, but Harry had been embarrassed in front of his coworkers and boss, and when the story made headlines, Harry had a difficult time putting the pieces of his life back together again.

During the course of the investigation, it was discovered that Belinda had attempted to do the same thing to an estranged boyfriend following a domestic incident where she had been the aggressor. Belinda sought revenge after the police were called to remove her from the ex-boyfriend's home. She completed the IEA paperwork; however, when the Justice of the Peace was made aware that she had sought to have her ex taken into custody for an involuntary emergency admission immediately after a domestic incident, he nullified the paperwork. Belinda was arrested for this incident as well. Her nursing license was suspended. Belinda entered guilty pleas on two stalking charges, both misdemeanors. In exchange for her guilty pleas, the prosecution dropped charges of false swearing and tampering with public records. Belinda was given two sentences of 6 months each, both suspended for 1 year. Belinda was also fined $1,000 on each count, with $500 suspended for each.

The phrase "Hell hath no fury like a woman scorned" epitomizes this case. It had many male coworkers on edge at the creativity of Belinda's quest to avenge her broken heart. Many joked about what had happened to the old-fashioned "get-even" behaviors such as keying the guy's car or replacing his hair conditioner with hair remover....

Neither one of these unsuspecting men had any idea that their online "match" had a jealous and spiteful streak. Her online profile certainly did not allude to her issues. A dating profile stating that someone is "looking for long-term commitment" can apparently be interpreted in several ways!

Online Dating Safety Tips

We recommend that all potential online daters heed the following list of precautions when using an online dating service:

- Trust your instincts. After the fact, so many women say, "I had a feeling about him." We believe that women need to listen to that inner voice or gut feeling first and foremost. They don't call it "women's intuition" for nothing! (Men, this point is directed at you as well, so don't dismiss it.)

- Never reveal personal information prior to meeting someone in person. Don't disclose where you work or what gym you belong to.

- Protect your personal email address. Most online dating services provide email services within their community that afford protection from tracing. Stick with these services for as long as possible. If need be, create a separate account with vague information to use specifically for online dating.

- If you need to provide a phone number to a potential date, use your cell phone number. Cell phone numbers are less easily traced and can be changed with relative ease. Do *not* use your home phone number, especially if it is publicly listed. Better to take the other person's phone number and advise that you will call him or her. If you do not have a private number, dial *67 (check with your local phone service) before dialing the number. This generally blocks your outbound Caller ID information for just that call.

- Always advise a trusted friend or family member where you are going and when you expect to be back. Provide this person with the profile information of the person you are meeting.

- Meet in a public place!

- If you have a drink with a date, never leave that drink unattended. Readily available drugs can easily be slipped into a drink unbeknownst to the victim that can render you powerless to fight off an attacker. If you have to run to the ladies room, finish your drink first or bring it with you.

- Use your head and do not assume anything you see on the Internet is true!

7

We Catch Sexual Predators—What You Don't See on TV

The Internet has helped transform what used to be a nearly hidden crime—child exploitation and pornography (referred to by law enforcement as KP or "kiddie porn") into what was estimated in 2006 to be a $20-billion-a-year criminal enterprise. According to the National Center for Missing & Exploited Children, there are more than 10,000 child porn sites involving more than 300,000 children.

The Dateline Debacle: *To Catch a Predator*

Millions of people have tuned in to watch Dateline NBC's *To Catch a Predator* series with investigative reporter Chris Hansen. This series chronicles undercover investigations in which alleged pedophiles are lured to a house after conversing online and expressing the desire to have sex with someone they believe to be a minor, but who is in actuality an adult member of a group called Perverted Justice. The first episode aired in 2004. Since then, 11 *Predator* segments have aired. Although the television viewing public can't get enough of the series, the show has turned out to be a nightmare for law enforcement.

Although the television viewing public can't get enough of the series, the show has turned out to be a nightmare for law enforcement.

Perverted Justice and *To Catch a Predator* in Action

Perverted Justice has been called an "anti-pedophile activist organization," a "civilian watchdog" group, and a "civilian vigilante" group. The
site began in 2002 and started out by publicly posting chat logs to shame
men who engage in sexual chats with purported children. Some members
of the site allegedly went further by harassing in real life the sex chat
perpetrators, as well as their friends, neighbors, employers, and family.
The group now focuses on working with law enforcement to have the perpetrators arrested.

According to an article in Wikipedia, "...in 2006, Perverted Justice
received $802,000 from NBC for its work on *To Catch a Predator*. In 2007,
the site expects to receive another $450,000, and in 2008 another
$600,000."

According to that same article, "In May 2007, Perverted Justice was criti-
cized in a now-dismissed employment lawsuit brought by former Dateline
producer Marsha Bartel." In the filing, Bartel alleges that NBC provides
financial incentives to the group to use trickery and to humiliate targets
to "enhance the comedic effect of the[ir] public exposure." According to
Bartel, some of the men caught in the *Predator* sting operations have
reported that the decoys begged them to come to the sting houses, even
after they had decided to walk away. Perverted Justice responded to the
criticism by labeling Bartel a disgruntled former employee motivated by
financial gain. The lawsuit was eventually dismissed after the New York
Supreme Court ruled that "an employer is free to terminate an employee
at any time for any reason or no reason."

During the first two *Predator* "sting" operations, law enforcement was not
involved. Since then, law enforcement in the local jurisdiction has been
involved. The setup leads to some pretty dramatic footage. The predator
arrives at the house, which is set up with covert cameras, and is lured
inside by a legal-aged adult actress pretending to be a minor. Chris
Hansen appears out of nowhere and grills the suspect about why he's
there and describes in sexually explicit terms what the suspect had offered
to do with the minor via the chat logs. Hansen then lets him walk out of
the house, where he is met at gunpoint by law enforcement and is
arrested.

Although this makes for great television, experts have questioned the
partnership between Dateline, Perverted Justice, and police agencies—in
some cases calling it an "unholy alliance."

Problems with *To Catch a Predator*

There are some stumbling points in the Dateline NBC series. First of all, law enforcement must be very careful to steer clear of any possible charges of entrapment. They don't want to provide a defense attorney with ammunition from an investigation that might be tainted by questionable tactics. Someone doing this type of investigation should not be lurking in chat rooms that have any ties to sexual content or sexual deviance, because this immediately casts a negative light on the case. Furthermore, a good investigator adhering to accepted ethical standards will not harass or prod a target to make a case.

Does *To Catch a Predator* Hinder Law Enforcement?

From an investigative standpoint, *To Catch a Predator* has made it more difficult for law enforcement to pursue predators who exploit children. The purpose of the show is not to aid law enforcement or prevent victimization, but rather to win ratings. Investigative techniques have been disclosed by the series that have helped educate the perpetrators on how to circumvent the law. This has made our job so much harder while making things more convenient for the bad guy. The evidence collected in the *To Catch a Predator* series has been questioned. Questionable evidence can result in a case being thrown out entirely. When law enforcement conducts its own undercover pedophile operations, all online chats are carefully logged and documented. The investigator must be willing to swear in court that the evidence has not been compromised in anyway. This kind of integrity cannot be sworn to when the evidence—Internet chat logs—come from an outside source.

As the predators are confronted by reporter Chris Hansen, they often make "on-the-air" confessions. This has raised the question of whether Hansen is acting as law enforcement's "legal agent." If so, the suspects should be advised of their legal rights before being spoken to.

NBC Settles Suicide Lawsuit

In 2007, the family of Louis W. Conradt, Jr., filed a $105 million lawsuit against NBC. Conradt was a Dallas, Texas prosecutor who committed suicide after investigators brought an NBC camera crew to his house as part of an online sting.

Patricia Conradt's lawsuit claimed her brother fatally shot himself in the head after he was accused of engaging in a sexually explicit online chat with an adult posing as a 13-year-old boy. Dateline was working with the Perverted Justice group on the episode.

Key to the lawsuit were allegations that NBC "steamrolled" authorities into arresting Conradt after telling police he failed to show up at a sting operation 35 miles away.

In February, a federal judge issued a scathing ruling in the case, saying a jury might conclude the network "crossed the line from responsible journalism to irresponsible and reckless intrusion into law enforcement."

In June 2008, NBC reached an out-of-court settlement with the family. NBC has not disclosed the amount paid to the family.

The Good and the Bad

We understand what the intent of the show is and that many who were caught in the trap have plead guilty to charges.

As women and mothers, we're all for bringing this heinous crime to the forefront, especially if it encourages parents to keep a closer watch on what their children are doing online. As members of law enforcement, however, we're frustrated that while *To Catch a Predator* had good intentions, the show has made it a *lot* harder for us to conduct these types of undercover operations.

In our opinion, *To Catch a Predator* has not reduced the number of predators soliciting minors online for sex. These individuals, commonly referred to by investigators as "travelers" because they actually travel to a destination to meet with their target victim, are not rare. A captain of ours has likened finding "traveler" suspects to "shooting fish in a barrel."

At any point in time, Kristyn can go online posing as an adolescent and receive numerous solicitations within minutes. The only thing *To Catch a Predator* has done is to spook the pedophiles so much that they are now far more cautious. This leads to many difficulties in trying to run these operations.

For example, when Kristyn began doing this kind of work, the predator would take her word during the chat that she was a legitimate underage child. This is no longer the case. Predators demand phone calls, pictures, and even live video. Many will offer to provide a live webcam at their own expense to ensure that the undercover detective or real victim can give them live video. This presents a major problem to law enforcement who cannot use a real juvenile in these types of operations. Dateline hires actresses to portray minors. Law enforcement cannot and will not because of protocols, ethics, and safety standards.

OUR VERSION OF *TO CATCH A PREDATOR*

WARNING
The following contains graphic and sexually explicit material.

The following "chat session" has been modified to protect sensitive information, but it is very typical of the chat sessions Kristyn would engage in posing as a 13- or 14-year-old girl. What we ask you to pay attention to is the timeframe as things unfold, which has not been altered. We have changed screen names and locations. Kristyn might choose to log in to a chat room such as a teen music chat room or a Miley Cyrus fan club— sites that might appear to be safe and appropriate for the average teen.

    LITTLEONE (1:51:23 p.m.): 14 f nh

    COOLMAN32 (1:51:27 p.m.): ok

    COOLMAN32 (1:51:31 p.m.): where u from

    LITTLEONE (1:52:01 p.m.): Podunk

    COOLMAN32 (1:52:04 p.m.): cool

    COOLMAN32 (1:52:06 p.m.): newville here

    COOLMAN32 (1:52:10 p.m.): what do u look like

    LITTLEONE (1:52:20 p.m.): blond blue long hair

    COOLMAN32 (1:52:26 p.m.): nice

    COOLMAN32 (1:52:29 p.m.): how tall ar eu

    LITTLEONE (1:52:44 p.m.): like 5 5

    COOLMAN32 (1:53:00 p.m.): nice

COOLMAN32 (1:53:03 p.m.): im 6'2
COOLMAN32 (1:53:09 p.m.): u really 14
LITTLEONE (1:53:16 p.m.): yea
COOLMAN32 (1:53:24 p.m.): ok
COOLMAN32 (1:53:30 p.m.): no school today
LITTLEONE (1:53:47 p.m.): home "sick"
COOLMAN32 (1:53:52 p.m.): oh
COOLMAN32 (1:53:56 p.m.): ar eu really sick
COOLMAN32 (1:54:23 p.m.): do u have a pic
LITTLEONE (1:54:48 p.m.): no mom caught me putting a pic in my profile and she freaked
COOLMAN32 (1:54:57 p.m.): oh ok
COOLMAN32 (1:55:00 p.m.): u alone
LITTLEONE (1:55:06 p.m.): yup
COOLMAN32 (1:55:34 p.m.): oh ok
COOLMAN32 (1:55:40 p.m.): where u in your room
LITTLEONE (1:55:43 p.m.): yup
COOLMAN32 (1:55:46 p.m.): me to
COOLMAN32 (1:55:54 p.m.): how much u weigh
LITTLEONE (1:56:06 p.m.): like 120
COOLMAN32 (1:56:10 p.m.): nice
LITTLEONE (1:56:22 p.m.): thanks
COOLMAN32 (1:56:28 p.m.): u really 14 and not someone pretending to be
LITTLEONE (1:57:23 p.m.): 14 i wish i was older it sux to be 14
COOLMAN32 (1:57:49 p.m.): im 32
LITTLEONE (1:58:01 p.m.): thats awesome
COOLMAN32 (1:58:01 p.m.): do u play any sports
LITTLEONE (1:58:32 p.m.): i like soccer, ride horses
COOLMAN32 (1:58:57 p.m.): cool
COOLMAN32 (1:59:01 p.m.): wha tu wearing
LITTLEONE (1:59:38 p.m.): t shirt and shorts
COOLMAN32 (1:59:44 p.m.): nice
COOLMAN32 (1:59:47 p.m.): no panties
LITTLEONE (2:00:17 p.m.): yes panties
COOLMAN32 (2:00:24 p.m.): nice what color
LITTLEONE (2:00:53 p.m.): purple my favorite color
COOLMAN32 (2:01:00 p.m.): nice
COOLMAN32 (2:01:04 p.m.): are u shaved
LITTLEONE (2:01:17 p.m.): yup - everyones doin it now
COOLMAN32 (2:01:24 p.m.): nice

COOLMAN32 (2:02:02 p.m.): u rub it a lot
COOLMAN32 (2:02:11 p.m.): ill stop this is bad
COOLMAN32 (2:02:15 p.m.): your to young
LITTLEONE (2:02:29 p.m.): not really
COOLMAN32 (2:02:42 p.m.): oh
COOLMAN32 (2:02:50 p.m.): have u had sex
LITTLEONE (2:03:01 p.m.): not yet but almost
COOLMAN32 (2:03:05 p.m.): nice
COOLMAN32 (2:03:13 p.m.): are u flexible
LITTLEONE (2:03:19 p.m.): yeah
COOLMAN32 (2:03:22 p.m.): nice
COOLMAN32 (2:03:28 p.m.): would ulet me push it in
LITTLEONE (2:04:18 p.m.): i guess
COOLMAN32 (2:04:56 p.m.): your just to young
COOLMAN32 (2:05:06 p.m.): and im no perv
LITTLEONE (2:05:06 p.m.): k
COOLMAN32 (2:06:01 p.m.): where in podunk ar eu
LITTLEONE (2:06:25 p.m.): near newtown
COOLMAN32 (2:06:46 p.m.): ok
LITTLEONE (2:06:56 p.m.): u know where that is
COOLMAN32 (2:07:03 p.m.): not really
COOLMAN32 (2:07:16 p.m.): ive probably been by it severl atimes
LITTLEONE (2:07:23 p.m.): oh its kinda near hampfield
COOLMAN32 (2:07:28 p.m.): ok
COOLMAN32 (2:07:37 p.m.): down by the beach
LITTLEONE (2:07:43 p.m.): yeah near the water
COOLMAN32 (2:08:03 p.m.): id get in trouble if i did that
LITTLEONE (2:08:44 p.m.): nuh uh not if u dont get caught
COOLMAN32 (2:09:02 p.m.): thought your parents ar ehome
LITTLEONE (2:09:10 p.m.): no
COOLMAN32 (2:09:17 p.m.): when the ygetting home
LITTLEONE (2:09:44 p.m.): later
COOLMAN32 (2:19:58 p.m.): ok
COOLMAN32 (2:29:11 p.m.): u horny
LITTLEONE (2:29:17 p.m.): maybe
COOLMAN32 (2:29:23 p.m.): really
LITTLEONE (2:29:32 p.m.): yup
COOLMAN32 (2:29:38 p.m.): i have a weird feeling about this
LITTLEONE (2:30:03 p.m.): whatever
COOLMAN32 (2:30:21 p.m.): how long will u be alone until

LITTLEONE (2:30:48 p.m.): til like 4 or 5

COOLMAN32 (2:30:51 p.m.): ok

COOLMAN32 (2:30:59 p.m.): what would u wear

COOLMAN32 (2:31:02 p.m.): u have a skirt

LITTLEONE (2:31:10 p.m.): yeah

COOLMAN32 (2:31:20 p.m.): thats hot

LITTLEONE (2:31:25 p.m.): really

COOLMAN32 (2:31:36 p.m.): yes

COOLMAN32 (2:31:41 p.m.): is it real short

LITTLEONE (2:31:47 p.m.): i have some short ones

COOLMAN32 (2:32:02 p.m.): nice

COOLMAN32 (2:32:07 p.m.): do u have a cam

LITTLEONE (2:32:46 p.m.): not yet mom wont let me

COOLMAN32 (2:32:54 p.m.): i see

COOLMAN32 (2:32:58 p.m.): that sucks

COOLMAN32 (2:33:14 p.m.): would ulet me push it all the wa yin

LITTLEONE (2:33:26 p.m.): I dunno

COOLMAN32 (2:33:41 p.m.): i bet your very tight

COOLMAN32 (2:34:06 p.m.): nice

COOLMAN32 (2:34:17 p.m.): i want to do this but im so nervous to

LITTLEONE (2:35:02 p.m.): what r u nervous abou

LITTLEONE (2:35:04 p.m.): about

COOLMAN32 (2:35:13 p.m.): im nervouse u might be a cop

LITTLEONE (2:35:36 p.m.): i am so not!

COOLMAN32 (2:36:09 p.m.): ok

COOLMAN32 (2:38:41 p.m.): i have a big dick id hurt u

LITTLEONE (2:38:45 p.m.): omg

LITTLEONE (2:38:46 p.m.): really

COOLMAN32 (2:38:52 p.m.): 7 inches

LITTLEONE (2:39:01 p.m.): no way

COOLMAN32 (2:39:07 p.m.): yes way

COOLMAN32 (2:39:10 p.m.): 2 thick

LITTLEONE (2:39:16 p.m.): u measure it

COOLMAN32 (2:39:20 p.m.): i have

COOLMAN32 (2:39:38 p.m.): ud scream

COOLMAN32 (2:40:39 p.m.): id go hard if u wanted

LITTLEONE (2:40:45 p.m.): i dont know

COOLMAN32 (2:40:57 p.m.): pump in and out fast

LITTLEONE (2:41:28 p.m.): omg

COOLMAN32 (2:42:46 p.m.): id slide it in an dout

COOLMAN32 (2:43:49 p.m.): is there anywhere we could meet

LITTLEONE (2:43:59 p.m.): theres a ton of places around here

COOLMAN32 (2:44:18 p.m.): but i cant come see u like at astore

COOLMAN32 (2:44:35 p.m.): are uat a friends

LITTLEONE (2:44:40 p.m.): im home

COOLMAN32 (2:44:57 p.m.): are u by hiway

LITTLEONE (2:45:07 p.m.): yeah like above that

COOLMAN32 (2:45:17 p.m.): are u by a park

LITTLEONE (2:45:22 p.m.): my parents wor late tomorrow

COOLMAN32 (2:45:50 p.m.): wan to plan for tomorrow nite

COOLMAN32 (2:46:05 p.m.): when u get home from school

LITTLEONE (2:46:06 p.m.): not really a park near a golf course

LITTLEONE (2:46:34 p.m.): school is out at 230 but i can leave at luch cuz they dont check

COOLMAN32 (2:46:47 p.m.): oh ok i get out of work around 3

LITTLEONE (2:47:07 p.m.): oh thats cool

COOLMAN32 (2:47:12 p.m.): im just trying to figure where u are

COOLMAN32 (2:47:24 p.m.): so uwill be all alone

COOLMAN32 (2:48:50 p.m.): were would we go

COOLMAN32 (2:48:53 p.m.): back to my house

LITTLEONE (2:49:13 p.m.): i guess so

LITTLEONE (2:49:22 p.m.): could u pick me up somewhere

COOLMAN32 (2:49:30 p.m.): yeah i could

COOLMAN32 (2:49:35 p.m.): depends where

COOLMAN32 (2:49:43 p.m.): do uhave a phone

LITTLEONE (2:49:49 p.m.): do you know podunk good

LITTLEONE (2:49:54 p.m.): i have a cell

COOLMAN32 (2:49:55 p.m.): sorta

LITTLEONE (2:50:02 p.m.): what places do u know

LITTLEONE (2:50:13 p.m.): u could call me when u got here tomorrow

COOLMAN32 (2:50:29 p.m.): I can pick u up downtown

LITTLEONE (2:50:40 p.m.): yeah i could even walk there from school

COOLMAN32 (2:50:49 p.m.): i was wondering if u would call

LITTLEONE (2:51:18 p.m.): u ahve a number

COOLMAN32 (2:51:22 p.m.): i do yes

COOLMAN32 (2:51:27 p.m.): cell

COOLMAN32 (2:51:39 p.m.): u have 2 way

LITTLEONE (2:51:43 p.m.): yup

COOLMAN32 (2:51:50 p.m.): beep me

COOLMAN32 (2:52:19 p.m.): my direct connect is 555*555*5555

LITTLEONE (2:53:26 p.m.): i dont know my push to talk by heart cuz my friends just call my number but ill find it

COOLMAN32 (2:53:42 p.m.): its in your myinfo

LITTLEONE (2:53:51 p.m.): ill find it

COOLMAN32 (2:53:56 p.m.): yes

LITTLEONE (2:54:08 p.m.): so u want me to walk somewhere after school

COOLMAN32 (2:54:24 p.m.): yeah we could

LITTLEONE (2:57:47 p.m.): cuz i cant be out too late in case my mom checks on me

COOLMAN32 (2:57:57 p.m.): i thought u were going to be alone tomorrow

LITTLEONE (2:58:12 p.m.): i am but she'll call around 5 to check on me

COOLMAN32 (2:59:05 p.m.): can we meet now

LITTLEONE (2:59:32 p.m.): i promised my mom id stay around

COOLMAN32 (2:59:37 p.m.): she could just call your cell

LITTLEONE (2:59:39 p.m.): im supposed to be sick!

COOLMAN32 (2:59:45 p.m.): we could go back to your house

COOLMAN32 (3:00:55 p.m.): would we stay there we could use ur parents bed!!

LITTLEONE (3:01:10 p.m.): sure she womt be home till like 7 probly

COOLMAN32 (3:01:29 p.m.): yes that gives us time

COOLMAN32 (3:01:47 p.m.): take me half hour 45 minutes to get to u

LITTLEONE (3:01:52 p.m.): k

COOLMAN32 (3:02:07 p.m.): have u sucked before

LITTLEONE (3:02:10 p.m.): maybe

COOLMAN32 (3:02:21 p.m.): did u swallow it

LITTLEONE (3:02:25 p.m.): ???

COOLMAN32 (3:02:39 p.m.): he cum on your face

COOLMAN32 (3:02:56 p.m.): were u on your knees

LITTLEONE (3:03:03 p.m.): one time

COOLMAN32 (3:03:12 p.m.): just one guy

COOLMAN32 (3:03:42 p.m.): he put it in u

LITTLEONE (3:03:47 p.m.): no

COOLMAN32 (3:04:08 p.m.): just half way

LITTLEONE (3:04:25 p.m.): he didnt have condoms

COOLMAN32 (3:04:35 p.m.): i would wear one

COOLMAN32 (3:05:27 p.m.): u didnt try anal

LITTLEONE (3:05:31 p.m.): no way

COOLMAN32 (3:06:18 p.m.): did he cum on your face or titties

COOLMAN32 (3:07:19 p.m.): are u far from that bowling alley

LITTLEONE (3:07:37 p.m.): school isnt but i dont live near there.

COOLMAN32 (3:08:09 p.m.): what's your address?

LITTLEONE (3:08:10 p.m.): i live liek a mile from school on Smith Street

COOLMAN32 (3:08:26 p.m.): ok

COOLMAN32 (3:10:23 p.m.): i thought theres a movie theatrer there

LITTLEONE (3:10:54 p.m.): the movie theater is next to the plazas -

COOLMAN32 (3:11:19 p.m.): ok got ya

LITTLEONE (3:12:25 p.m.): theres an alley behind it near the woods by the projects there

COOLMAN32 (3:13:07 p.m.): oh those houses

LITTLEONE (3:13:43 p.m.): well its called angel terrace and its apartments on the other side of the woods

COOLMAN32 (3:14:10 p.m.): will u be on later tonite

LITTLEONE (3:14:24 p.m.): ill try

COOLMAN32 (3:14:27 p.m.): we could meet there

COOLMAN32 (3:14:48 p.m.): but i dont get ouft of work until 3 or so – ill beep u

LITTLEONE (3:15:03 p.m.): ill be on tonite or before school

COOLMAN32 (3:15:08 p.m.): me to

COOLMAN32 (3:15:17 p.m.): please dont say anything

LITTLEONE (3:15:22 p.m.): no way

LITTLEONE (3:15:33 p.m.): how will i know its u

COOLMAN32 (3:15:45 p.m.): ill call u

COOLMAN32 (3:15:53 p.m.): i have a truck-its got lots of room!! I can't wait!

Note that within minutes of entering the chat room, our 14-year-old female from New Hampshire was approached at 1:51 p.m. by a 32-year-old male. He asked her age and where she lives. He immediately asked her for a physical description and to confirm that she is really 14 years old. After verifying her age, he asks if she has a photo. This request occurs within the first 3 minutes of the conversation.

At 4 minutes into the conversation, the 32-year-old male has asked her if she is alone. Within 8 minutes, he wants to know if she is wearing panties and what **Within 8 minutes, he wants to know if she is wearing panties and what color they are. He seeks information regarding whether she shaves her private area, whether she masturbates, and whether she has had sex.**

color they are. He seeks information regarding whether she shaves her private area, whether she masturbates, and whether she has had sex. At 13 minutes, our 32-year-old pervert knows intimate details about this child. By 2:03:28 p.m., he has already asked if she would let him "push it in"—meaning have sex with her.

FOURTEEN MINUTES

In less than 14 minutes, someone located this child in a chat room and then propositioned her for sex. Based on our experience, this is not unusual. Although some predators take their time grooming or seducing a child, our experience is that in the majority of cases, child exploitation occurs within minutes.

Reading further on, the sex offender elicits information about where the child goes to school, where she lives, when her parents are home, and what her sexual experiences have been. He prods her about various sexual activities, including anal and oral sex, and talks about using her parents' bed when they meet. He even obtains a cell number from her—all while he thinks her parents are away.

Many kids come home after school to an empty household while their parents are at work. Parents call to check in and know their children are safely in their room at home, hopefully completing their homework. The Internet access on a child's computer is seen as safe and a means to help with homework assignments, network with their friends, and essentially keep them out of trouble. Better to be on the computer at home than hanging out at the food court in the mall buying drugs, right?

Adults are often shocked that their kids will even chat with a stranger, let alone reveal intimate details. It starts off as innocent and even fun. For some, however, that adult in the chat room can quickly become a friend. For a child going through the turbulence of puberty and the ups and downs of high school, having an adult show interest in them is a huge high.

There are no set characteristics for a child predator—this is a far cry from the age-old stereotypical child molester who lives with his mother, is out of work, shuffles around in orthopedic shoes, and wears thick Coke-bottle glasses.

It is flattering and makes the child feel special, especially a child who might be experiencing self-esteem issues. And let's face it, what teenager does not go through a period of low self-esteem? It might even be a way to become the envy of your friends by having an "older guy" show interest in you.

The bottom line is, adults are out there seeking children to exploit. They do it from home and at work, during the day and late at night. They come from all walks of life, all socioeconomic backgrounds, and various professions. Many of them are married with children of their own. There are no set characteristics for a child predator—this is a far cry from the age-old stereotypical child molester who lives with his mother, is out of work, shuffles around in orthopedic shoes, and wears thick Coke-bottle glasses. They sit in their homes, anonymous, lurking, and actively searching for a child who will engage in their seduction. They fully intend to molest a child if they can get away with it, and while they take precautions to elude law enforcement, they seek the perfect online victim who will agree to meet them and keep it a secret. Whereas some offenders travel far for their liaison, others offend very close to home.

Every one of the offenders Kristyn has arrested has made the admission that had a young girl been at the meet, he would have engaged in sexual activity with the child. Some had made arrangements for a hotel room, some expected to consummate the relationship in their car, and others intended to go back to the child's home. Many bring condoms, alcohol, or drugs. They don't care that they are going to hurt a child. Their only concern is fulfilling their need to sexually assault a child without getting caught.

THE ARREST

In this particular case, a "meet" was scheduled for the next day, and when the male arrived at the prearranged location, he was promptly arrested and charged with "Certain Uses Computer Prohibited," a felony. In some states, this charge might be called "Online Solicitation of Minors" or "Dissemination of Harmful Matter." The case resulted in a conviction, and following a jail sentence, the defendant was placed on probation and is now required to register as a public sex offender for the rest of his life.

Misdemeanor Versus Felony

Any crime is generally classified as a violation, misdemeanor, or felony. A violation is akin to a speeding ticket, where a conviction results in a fine but no jail time. A misdemeanor-level crime can result in a monetary fine up to a couple of thousand dollars and a potential jail sentence of up to 1 year.

A felony, the most serious level of crime, can result in many thousands of dollars in fines and many years in prison. States vary on their sentence structure, and courts have the discretion to be creative on whether the standard minimum is even ordered. We routinely see multiple felony-level offenses, which would theoretically result in a sentence of 3 1/2 to 7 years for each charge, get pled out to less than a year in jail, with most of that time suspended. It is frustrating, to say the least. The federal system has mandatory minimum sentences for crimes that meet its criteria; however, meeting those criteria is often difficult, and therefore, cases will customarily proceed in state courts. We are seeing more and more Internet crimes in which children are exploited being accepted by the United States district courts. These cases result in a considerable amount of time behind bars in federal prisons.

Laws Vary from State to State

Ironically, in several states, certain crimes where children are exploited are not felonies, but rather misdemeanors. For example, in Maryland, possession of child pornography is a misdemeanor, not a felony. Even in our home state of New Hampshire, child pornography possession was a misdemeanor up until approximately 10 years ago. There are still certain online behaviors that occur during Internet chat sessions that are misdemeanor-level crimes and are not necessarily even covered under statutes in some states—but things are changing. These laws are finally being scrutinized across the United States by lawmakers in an effort to appropriately criminalize any behaviors that sexually exploit minors. Laws across the country are becoming more consistent from state to state.

Although laws vary from state to state, with the passage of the Adam Walsh Act and federal initiatives such as Project Safe Child, states are working toward more consistency in cases involving the possession, manufacture, and distribution of child sexual assault images, as well as online enticement, in regard to legislation and penalties.

Lessons Learned

Whenever we do Internet safety presentations, we emphasize that had this been a real 14-year-old girl chatting with the predator in the chat room, and had the man met and had sex with the child, the resulting crime would have been rape. The 32-year-old male subject was coming to New Hampshire to rape a 14-year-old child in her parent's bed. Regardless of a conviction and resulting prison time, if a real child had been victimized, no jail sentence could make up for that. It often takes this harsh and graphic description of the incident to put things into perspective. This is reality—a scary and common occurrence on the Internet.

THE TEACHER AND HIS "STUDENT"

As an example of the great inconsistency in computer crime law from state to state, we can look at the arrest of Scott Simoncini in Worcester, Massachusetts in January of 2008. This case began in New Hampshire in December of 2006. Simoncini approached who he thought was a 14-year-old female in a chat room. The 14-year-old child was really Kristyn working on an undercover Internet child exploitation case. The immediate disclosure that the girl was a minor did not dissuade Simoncini from chatting with her. On the contrary, Simoncini became involved in a lengthy conversation with the child, and he very quickly pursued sexually explicit chat and introduced the idea of getting together with the child for the purposes of sexual activity. Going one step further, Simoncini sent the "child" images of himself naked and in sexually suggestive poses. During one of the chats, Simoncini used his webcam to stream real-time footage of his genitals and masturbated over the Internet to the purported 14-year-old.

Kristyn and Felicia were able to positively identify Scott Simoncini as a history teacher and coach from Massachusetts. Simoncini had no prior criminal history. Despite us having definitive corroborating information on Simoncini and evidence of the online chatting, Simoncini could not be arrested on a felony warrant because he had not suggested a specific date, time, and location to meet the "child" for sex, as our state law required at the time. Sending sexual images to a child over the Internet was not covered in state statutes, and although Simoncini suggested meeting for sexual activity and had a very graphic chat with the "child," that also was not sufficiently addressed in the state statutes.

Fast-forward to January of 2008, when Massachusetts State Police began an investigation into the online activities of a suspect using the same screen name as Simoncini. This involved another case where he was engaged in explicit chats with what he thought to be an underage child. Investigators had not identified Simoncini; however, their investigation led them to Kristyn because she had entered the contact into a specialized database utilized by investigators. When Massachusetts State Police called, she was able to provide them with Simoncini's identity and other biographical information. Because the computer Simoncini used was in Massachusetts, and the statute of limitations had not yet expired, Kristyn forwarded her case file to the Massachusetts State Police. The criminal code in the Commonwealth of Massachusetts addressed sexually explicit chatting with minors, as well as sending naked or sexually graphic images to children. The Massachusetts law made "Dissemination of Harmful Matter" a felony.

Simoncini was arrested on several felony-level charges as a result of Kristyn's case and the Massachusetts State Police's case. Initially, Simoncini and his attorney claimed that he was innocent and only online as a "fantasy," except Mr. Simoncini was not in a fantasy or role-playing chat room. The idea of a teacher claiming to be playing out an online fantasy involving sex and a child is outrageous and pathetic at best. Needless to say, the evidence was solid, and in March of 2008, Simoncini took a guilty plea to several of the charges. He was sentenced to 1 year, given a suspended sentence of 2 years, with 2 years of probation, including GPS monitoring, surrendered his teaching license, forfeited his computer, and instead of having his picture in a yearbook, is now in the gallery of the Commonwealth of Massachusetts' Sex Offender Registry as a registered sex offender.

This case was a wakeup call that our laws were inadequate. It was used in testimony to a legislative committee as an example of how important it was to tighten our child exploitation laws and close the loopholes that allow people like Simoncini to webcam themselves masturbating and having sexually explicit and graphic conversations with children during an online chat.

Free Babysitting

Of course, the question arises as to why children are in chat rooms to begin with. Many parents are naive to the dangers of the Internet and even their own children's activities online. Parents assume that if Suzy is in her room "doing her homework" on the computer, she is safe under their roof. They know where their child is, and because the child is not technically outside of parental supervision, she is certainly not in any danger. If the choice were to have your child at home in her room on the computer or hanging out at the food court in the mall, out of sight, which would you choose? Some parents have allowed the computer to take on the role of babysitter in the same way that television once did, but there's little chance your child will be inappropriately approached or solicited from a television set.

The Internet is a double-edged sword—it is an amazing tool that opens an infinite number of doors to new ideas, education, cultures, art, and different people and places. It can also be a very dark place for a child if not monitored carefully. Felicia likens the Internet to a car. Would you hand over the car keys to your child who has never driven before without any training or warnings about the dangers of driving? Of course not. Yet every day, millions of children are speeding across the Information Superhighway, with no supervision and no driving rules. The Internet should be thought of as a privilege. If the "rules of the road" are not adhered to, you need to take away the keys.

> Every day, millions of children are speeding across the Information Superhighway, with no supervision and no driving rules. The Internet should be thought of as a privilege. If the "rules of the road" are not adhered to, you need to take away the keys.

The Internet—A Pedophile's New Playground

Just recently, the Spanish periodical *El Pais* in Madrid printed an article quoting child pedophile expert Guillermo Canovas, who stated that there is "no doubt that the use of the Internet by pedophiles has led to the increase of this type of crime [child exploitation]." Canovas said that, "the web has broken the isolation and guilt of pedophiles, allowing them to get in touch, to justify and encourage each other, to give each other tips on where to find pornography or children." Canovas further stated that while pedophiles often find themselves attracted to children at an early age, "the majority of them develop the tendency later on," but the Internet can precipitate the tendency.

The daily *El Pais* further reported that "far from being a marginal loner, the typical pedophile is a socially integrated and successful person." The Internet simply opens the door to a target-rich environment that is not limited to the perpetrator's community. No longer does the child molester have to place himself in a social setting where children are located, volunteer for child-related projects, or hang out in playgrounds or school yards—he simply has to jump on the Web and log into his Instant Messenger account.

12 Million Hits in 72 Hours

To put this ease-of-access in better perspective, consider that in June of 2008, 70 men were arrested in Australia as part of a global crackdown on online child pornography after they visited a site created by a hacker who posted child porn images on a legitimate European website. That number of 70 arrests, in and of itself, is significant, but what is even more disturbing is the fact that the website attracted over 12 million hits in only 76 hours.

Soon after this story broke, Australian Federal Police quickly stated that not all hits were deliberate. Some of the hits were inadvertent when users were redirected from a legitimate website to the kiddie porn site, but we still find this disturbing because we know it was not 12 million "accidental" hits. We know from other cases that, unfortunately, kiddie porn sites attract hundreds of thousands of hits in very little time. Among the men arrested by Australian police was a federal police officer. A million images of child pornography were seized.

THE JERRY JONES CASE—A TRIPLE THREAT

In the world of theater, a *triple threat* is an artist who is an accomplished singer, dancer, and actor. In sports, the *hat trick* refers to three hockey goals scored by a player in a single game, whereas the *trifecta* is a bet the horse race gambler places hoping to accurately predict which horses will cross the finish line in first, second, and third place. In the world of child predators, we have our own diabolical "triple threat."

In October of 2005, Jerry Jones was arrested for showing up at a shopping plaza after making arrangements with what he thought was a minor child for the purposes of sexual activity. At the time, the arresting agency had not seized his computer.

When his picture appeared in a local newspaper, a 7-year-old disclosed that Jones had molested her. During a forensic interview, the young child spoke of the multiple times that Jones had sexually molested her over the course of several months. Jones had manipulated himself into a caretaking role with the child and, thus, had almost unlimited access to the little girl over this period of time. The child spent nights at Jones' home, and Jones took her on daytrips and a couple overnight trips. She stated that he had videotaped her, had taken photos of his exploitation of her, and had introduced her to inappropriate websites.

Although search warrants did not locate any evidence that the child sexual assaults had been photographed or recorded, computers were seized and analyzed. Jones was in possession of many files containing erotica and child sexual assault images.

Jones was charged with multiple counts of Aggravated Child Sexual Assault and Possession of Child Pornography in addition to the Certain Uses of Computer Prohibited charge from an Internet chat case. The cases were separated, most likely in the defense's hope that he would not be convicted on all charges if the cases were tried at different times with different juries. Jones was ultimately found guilty on charges in all three cases, and he is doing no less than 30 years in jail.

As if the sexual victimization of a very sweet young child wasn't egregious enough, she was revictimized by being required to testify at trial. She was brave and pulled it off without a hitch, thus sending Jones to what all hope will be the rest of his life in state prison. One cannot help but be heartbroken at the thought of how this child was hurt, physically and emotionally, by Jones. She was robbed of her childhood and her innocence—things that can never be given back to her.

Male Versus Female Offenders

Although the offender in the preceding scenario is a male—and the majority of sex offenders are males—make no mistake that there are female perpetrators out there. It is more common for a child to be victimized by a male adult; however, there are many documented cases where a female is the abuser. We generally hear about these cases in the news when a female teacher takes advantage of a male student. New Hampshire holds the dubious distinction of being host to one of the most notorious predators, teacher Pamela Smart, who seduced some of her male high school students and then orchestrated a plan for them to execute her husband. She took child exploitation to the extreme.

Unfortunately, society still has not accepted that a male can be victimized by an older female. Even male teenagers might not see themselves as victims of the "older woman." Not too long ago, Kristyn was involved in the investigation of a 31-year-old woman who provided alcohol to several underage boys and sexually assaulted some of them. During the course of the case investigation, interviews, and arrest, Kristyn heard numerous jokes about how lucky the boys were and how they must have been the envy of their friends. When the arrest hit the media, even Jay Leno on *The Tonight Show* chimed in with a few zingy comments about the woman's activities with the young males. Sexual assaults involving males as victims are still underreported, possibly because of a combination of societal expectations and the embarrassment of being a male who has been taken advantage of by a female.

Although this stereotypical notion of the strong invincible male who cannot be victimized is changing, we are still not there yet. It is still difficult for a male to come forward, and when these cases are reported, we believe that juries still have a hard time seeing a 14-year-old male as a victim, particularly when the victim is often near adulthood by the time the case goes to trial.

> Unfortunately, society still has not accepted that a male can be victimized by an older female. Even male teenagers might not see themselves as victims of the "older woman."

Much to our dismay, the female suspect in this case was acquitted at trial despite her victims testifying about what she had done. Part of the problem in obtaining a conviction may have been the fact that the young teenage victims were not seen as victims by the time the trial occurred. The boys' appearance had dramatically changed and they more closely resembled men than the children they truly were at the time of their victimization.

Recently, a female public sex offender came in to register—a requirement since she had just moved into the community. At the age of 18, she lured and seduced three 13-year old boys in the area in which she lived. All three boys gave statements confirming the sexual assaults; however, only one jurisdiction sought an indictment. Although the woman was convicted on one count of Aggravated Felonious Sexual Assault against a 13-year-old child, the investigating officer relayed that other law enforcement officials gave him a hard time for pursuing the case. Had the roles been reversed and the victim been a 13-year-old female, our guess is that all three communities would not have hesitated to seek indictments against an 18-year-old male perpetrator.

The Cyber Playground

We want everyone to understand that although many parents feel their children would never be exposed to the horrors of sexual predators online, it happens with a great deal of frequency. We understand that parenting is hard enough without the added complication of having to police your child's Internet activities, but we both feel strongly that this has become the "virtual playground" for our children. Just as you wouldn't send a young child off by himself to a playground with no adult supervision, you must think of the Internet as the child's "cyber" playground, which requires the same parental oversight and monitoring as any other activity your child might be involved in.

Awareness is the key. Parents who are aware of the dangers of the Internet are already armed to prevent intrusions on their children's innocence.

8

Child Sexual Assault Images—The New View on Child Pornography

Chat rooms have been a hot topic in terms of child exploitation because they are frequently the vehicle law enforcement has found by which predators find, groom, and exploit young teenagers.

A less familiar manner to exploit children was recently seen in an investigation of a New England–based soccer coach who was finding victims from his high school and elite soccer camp in order to manufacture and collect teenage pornography.

THE JACOB SILVA CASE

Jacob Silva, shown in Figure 8.1, is a 27-year-old man from Manchester, New Hampshire, who set up an elaborate scheme to take advantage of unwitting high school males by posing as a young female on the popular social networking site MySpace. The misconduct, which may have spanned all over New England for over 4 years, involved Silva pretending to be a female who would send explicit pictures and videos of herself in exchange for the young males sending sexually explicit images and videos of themselves engaging in various sexual activities.

Silva has been charged with 26 offenses, including using a computer to entice a child to commit indecent exposure, soliciting children to engage in child pornography, endangering the welfare of a minor, and prostitution. (He allegedly offered to pay someone under the age of 18 to engage in sexual activity.)

(Courtesy Concord Police Department, New Hampshire)

FIGURE 8.1

Jacob Silva

Silva introduced the pretend female persona to members of his soccer teams and then actively solicited the males to engage in sexual activity on their webcams. The boys unwittingly were responding to Silva, who was pretending to be the female while capturing the images and collecting them.

The number of victims Silva may have had over the past 4 years is undetermined, but could reach into the hundreds. It is also undetermined as to where else these child pornographic images and videos could have reached because child porn collectors commonly trade and distribute their collections in exchange for other's collections. Once the videos are on the Internet, there is no way of determining the extent of the distribution, nor is it possible to contain the videos and pull them back. Law enforcement may never know the magnitude of the victimization Silva has perpetrated.

Teenagers need to understand that the decision to webcam themselves in a compromising position or even cell phone-cam themselves is a permanent one. Once these images have been sent, they can *never* be retrieved. An immature decision made in the folly of youth can come back to haunt an individual for years to come. Every time the video or image is sent or viewed, the victim is revictimized. Yet another repercussion is that many colleges and prospective employers have realized the significance of the Internet in doing background research on an applicant and will specifically research social networking sites and Google applicants. The damage is immeasurable and can haunt an individual for years to come.

Teenagers need to understand that the decision to webcam themselves in a compromising position or even cell phone-cam themselves is a permanent one.

Fritz Does Federal—Enticement Across State Lines

We currently have a federal parolee on our city's sex offender list who exemplifies the term *online child exploitation across state lines*. On October 24, 2000, Fritz, a 36-year-old man, was convicted in a United States District Court after he met up with a young girl who was under the age of 13 while he was living in Alabama. The child resided in Georgia. The child was enticed online and then brought across state lines from Georgia to Alabama for the purpose of sexual activity. The perpetrator further victimized the young girl by forever memorializing his sexual deviance with her on video. He was arrested for enticement and manufacturing child pornography. Upon his release from a federal penitentiary in New Jersey, Fritz chose to make New England his home. Because he is currently on a short leash in regard to our sex offender registry and his federal probation, we will forego mentioning Fritz's last name.

The important point is that many people out there get convicted of crimes of this nature and often serve relatively minor sentences. Although our perpetrator spent more than 6 years in a federal prison, which is often much more than a state sentence

How many are out there who have committed similar egregious crimes but have not yet been caught?

will bring, he was released into society while still in his 40s. You can either look at this as young enough to start over and learn from the error of his deviance, or young enough to victimize again. Another point to remember is that we can only be certain of the victimization for which he was convicted. How many other victims might there have been before he was caught? How many are out there who have committed similar egregious crimes but have not yet been caught?

Child Pornography Collectors

They say that reality is stranger than fiction, but we have a habit of saying, "You just can't make this stuff up." We've dealt with several cases in which the child porn suspect has such deviant behavior that it results in a jaw-dropping reaction from the investigating officers.

As an example of how disturbing an individual's penchant for collecting child pornography can be, how about the suspect who had such a *huge* collection, the computer server storing the images was too big for transport in the back of a police cruiser. In order to get the server to the location where the evidence was We've dealt with several cases in which the child porn suspect has such deviant behavior that it results in a jaw-dropping reaction from the investigating officers.

to be stored and examined, a local ambulance was called for transport. Probably one of the oddest "medical" calls that ambulance crew had ever responded to.

THE PUMPKIN MAN

No, not like, "Do you know the Muffin Man...who lives on Drury Lane?" The Pumpkin Man—a nickname coined for now-72-year-old David Cobb, a former English teacher at Phillips Academy in Andover, Massachusetts— is a far cry from the Muffin Man (see Figure 8.2). He is more akin to "Run, run as fast as you can, you can't catch me, I'm the Gingerbread Man." The difference being that his deviance was sexual in nature.

(© AP Photo/Jim Cole)

FIGURE 8.2

David Cobb (a.k.a. "The Pumpkin Man")

Cobb was convicted in New Hampshire for attempted sexual assault of a 12-year-old boy. He was arrested in August of 1995 in Farmington, New Hampshire, where he had a summer home. Cobb was walking with the victim and had a backpack full of what was referred to as child pornography, a pumpkin mask, and a price list for sexual acts. The list was titled "Pay Scale for Helping Pumpkin," and the nickname stuck because he wore the pumpkin mask when soliciting children for these sexual acts.

Cobb had also taken a guilty plea in Maine for unlawful sexual contact with a 9-year-old girl and a 12-year-old boy in 1985. He was sentenced to an 18-month concurrent sentence.

At the time that Cobb was arrested in New Hampshire, possession of child pornography was a misdemeanor-level offense. The attempted sexual assault was a felony-level charge. He served 11 years in the New Hampshire State Prison for the felony-level charge. The sentence called for Cobb to have a year after his prison sentence to complete a sex offender program. Then a court would decide whether to send Cobb to the county jail for the remaining year.

COBB REFUSES TREATMENT: SAYS "NOT CHILD PORN"

Cobb asked the court to forgo the 1-year period and leave him in prison because he refused to complete the sex offender treatment, saying he believed the images he possessed were not pornographic. The images were collages of children's faces cut out of clothing catalogues and pasted on photos cut from adult magazines. Cobb had been given a 12-month deferred sentence on the misdemeanor child pornography charges, and would then be expected to complete sex offender treatment within that time frame. A deferred sentence is different from a suspended sentence in that when an offender receives a deferred sentence, the individual must come back to the court and show that he or she was of good behavior and fulfilled all court-imposed conditions. A *suspended sentence* means that the sentence is suspended as long as the individual does not get into any trouble with the police for a certain period of time. Once that time has passed, the sentence essentially goes away without the individual coming back to court.

In order for a suspended sentence to be imposed, the prosecutors must motion the court with information that would warrant a judge bringing forward the jail time. In a deferred sentence, the individual must go in front of the court after a specific amount of time in order to show the court's order has been successfully fulfilled. Cobb was released in June of 2007 and registered as a sex offender living in the Commonwealth of Massachusetts.

THE PREDATOR'S FAMILY HEIRLOOM

After we thought we'd heard it all, we learned of an interesting case involving Alan Wirth Atwood, of Stillwater, Minnesota, who claimed that the only reason he had acquired and saved child sexual assault images was because he insisted they would someday become "collector's items." A cyber tip had been reported to the National Center for Missing and Exploited Children that a pornographic photo of a child had been uploaded through a Yahoo! email address. The Minnesota Internet Crimes Against Children Task Force provided a report to the Stillwater Police when the email address and account were traced back to Atwood.

According to the police complaint, the 64-year-old Atwood had saved in excess of 70 images of child pornography because he believed they would become collectors' items as "the time would come when they would no longer be available." Atwood admitted to knowing that collecting and distributing child pornography was wrong when police raided his home. In that raid, three computers were seized, and police found that Atwood had saved images from more than a hundred different people, and that images had been exchanged in emails and instant messages. It is probably a safe bet that these images will never be featured on an upcoming episode of *Antiques Roadshow* or be placed on the auction block at Sotheby's.

THE NEW HYGIENE

Some child porn collectors are so obsessed with obtaining images that their entire lives revolve around downloading and viewing their child sexual assault acquisitions. One case involved investigators finding that the suspect had been wearing a diaper so he would not have to be interrupted if he needed to use the toilet. Here's the visual: Picture an overweight, middle-aged man wearing nothing but an extra-large Depend adult diaper as the search warrant team makes entry. In another case, investigators observed a cat litter box in the basement room where the suspect had been downloading and viewing his child sexual assault images. Not a big deal when they learned that the suspect's mother changed the cat litter box daily. The disturbing discovery was that the cat litter box was *not* for a cat. Apparently,

Nope, you just can't make this stuff up.

this deviant urinated and defecated in a cat litter box because he could not break away from his 24/7 child pornography hobby. Sounds sick, but consider the fact that his mother emptied the waste for him and gave him fresh litter every day.

Nope, you just can't make this stuff up.

THE LINGERIE CONNECTION

Imagine the looks on the faces of investigators who discovered in excess of 500 pairs of women's panties in the bedroom of a suspect. This large-scale collector admitted that he had been cross-dressing since he was a teenager and did not own any men's undergarments. He stated that he was embarrassed to "come out" and subsequently dressed up as a woman privately every day. He had videos and pictures of himself in wigs, dresses, and pink tights. Having been unemployed after getting fired from a large department store, he spent his day downloading pornography for hours at a time. He admitted to downloading any type of pornography he could find, including so many child sexual assault images that investigators still only have an estimation of his illegal files. He even downloaded very disturbing cartoons that took actual Sunday news child cartoon characters and portrayed them in situations where the parent cartoon characters were having intercourse with the cartoon children. The "cartoons," although not actual children, were still very graphic and disturbing. Also among the evidence, investigators found a child-size sexual blow-up doll.

The preceding actual case anecdotes are truly a part of what law enforcement categorizes as the jaw dropping, "you can't make this stuff up" behavior we see everyday on these investigations. Reality some times is stranger than fiction.

Sex Offender Websites: Facts Versus Fiction

In July of 2006, on the 25th anniversary of the abduction of Adam Walsh from a Florida mall, the Adam Walsh Act was passed in the United States. Adam Walsh was the young son of John Walsh, the host of *America's Most Wanted*. Adam was murdered, and the perpetrator was never definitively identified. The Adam Walsh Act has restructured the responsibilities of the 50 states in how they handle sex offender registration.

Sex offender registration still varies from state to state, although states are becoming more consistent with one another and working more closely together to ensure sex offender compliance. At the beginning of 2007, it was estimated that 128,000 of the 565,000 registered sex offenders were noncompliant in the United States. This translates into over a 20% non-compliance rate. For the public, this means that many offenders are unaccounted for and could be living anywhere.

Sex offender registries have become a hot topic for many communities, and as usual there are those who are trying to make money from them, including websites such as the National Alert Registry (http://www.nationalalertregistry.com/), which charges a "one-time setup fee" of $10 for a report and child safety kit and $5 a month for updates. A plethora of sites allow you to enter your address or ZIP Code and will give you the registered sex offenders residing in your neighborhood. Some are free; some (such as the National Alert Registry) charge

> At the beginning of 2007, an estimated 128,000 of the 565,000 registered sex offenders were noncompliant in the United States—over a 20% noncompliance rate.

for their services. Such sites allow a visitor to pinpoint every sex offender within an entire community.

We have to wonder why a site would charge a monthly fee if its true intent is to safeguard communities, especially for information that is already in the public domain (see the section "The National Sex Offender Public Registry" later in this chapter).

Some sites are free and can be located simply by typing "sex offender registry" in Google. Free or not, these sites are not necessarily accurate. They are not regularly updated, particularly if an offender moves out of a community. These sites are also missing the many offenders that are classified as nonpublic or public by request only—often classified as Level/Tier I and II. Only law enforcement can obtain nonpublic information, and only law enforcement has access to the most current sex offender lists. So much for those websites.

For law enforcement, these sites are a double-edged sword. Although the public has become better informed of the predators who might be living in their neighborhoods, the intent of the sex offender registry was for law enforcement to keep track of sex offenders who had served their sentences and had been released back into society. Part of the premise was that a registry might be a safeguard in helping to prevent recidivism if the offenders know they are being tracked and watched.

The problem has been the overzealous community members who have taken the information from the websites and have plastered posters in neighborhoods, have accosted convicted sex offenders, and have raised all holy hell with city councils, school departments, and police departments about offenders living in their neighborhoods and near schools. Just recently we had to handle a situation where a number of parents felt the need to hand out fliers of a registered sex offender living near a local elementary school to parents as they dropped their children off at school one morning. The panic that ensued was irrational. Kristyn received a call from a grandmother who asked her to speak with her 10-year-old grandchild because the child had seen the flier and panicked. The little girl told Kristyn that she was "freaked out" that she and her friends might be raped by the sex offender near their playground. No 10-year-old should be put in a position where she is worried about becoming a rape victim. This is an example of how reason and good judgment must be used by parents in teaching their children about safety and awareness. The fact that these children were subjected to this information in this manner is, in our opinion, irresponsible. Safety is a topic that school departments and police departments address with students every day, with a set curriculum that teaches the fundamentals without causing stress and panic. A parent's fear that something bad may happen to a child is certainly real; however, it is important to address these fears with reason and information.

Knowledge is power. However, we have to put this in perspective. First of all, many states have registries where offenders are categorized as public or nonpublic. These classifications are often made dependent upon the nature of the criminal conviction or whether the victim is a child. Any conviction where a child is victimized or the crime involves child exploitation is generally a public view category. Nonpublic offenders are those with misdemeanor convictions or felony-level convictions where the victim is an adult. These classifications are still changing across the country. Some states even have offenders who are only required to be on the registry lists for a set number of years because the severity of their crime is of a lesser degree. Only the public offenders will find their way to a website, assuming that the website is even accurate. Of the sites we have visited, none of the private ones were even accurate, many listing more offenders than were actually living in a community. These sites must be maintained with accurate, up-to-date information, and it is often questionable where the sites obtained the information to begin with. We recommend that concerned citizens visit the sex offender registry sites that are sponsored by the state sex offender registration offices. In most states, the sex offender registry is often maintained by the State Police or Department of Safety of that state. Only there will you be able to access the most up-to-date information on offenders in your area.

We cannot emphasize enough how important it is to keep this information in perspective. First, only public offenders are listed on the sites. Lists of nonpublic offenders aren't accessible to the public.

Second, in order to be required to register as a sex offender, an individual has to have been *convicted* of a qualifying sexual offense. Only after the conviction and the completion of the court-ordered sentence will an individual appear on a registry. One must keep in mind that *many* offenders will never make it onto the sex offender registry for a number of reasons: First, the sex offense must be reported; then the case must be investigated and charges must be filed. Ultimately, a conviction must be handed down through a plea, a judge's ruling, or a jury finding the defendant guilty in order for a predator to become a registered sex offender.

Many cases of sexual abuse are never reported. Of those that are reported, many never make it to a court room due to lack of evidence or the inability of a victim to handle the emotional stress of a trial.

> Many cases of sexual abuse are never reported.

Oftentimes, an individual charged with a sex offense will plead out to a lesser offense that may not be a qualifying sex offense. Pleas are a way to ensure that the wheels of justice continue to turn. A plea bargain will ensure that an offender is punished and that the system does not get bogged down with too many trials.

The problem with a plea in a sex offense case is that a truly violent sexual predator might never have to register as a sex offender as a result of the plea. For example, we have a predator in our community who has been investigated for molesting at least two children. He was initially charged with aggravated felonious sexual assault in New Hampshire, which was for the rape of a minor. The case was pled down to second-degree assault, a charge that is usually associated with someone being severely beaten up and sustaining a serious injury that might require long-term recovery, such as a broken limb. A conviction of second-degree assault does not require the perpetrator to register as a sex offender, even if the underlying case was a sexually based crime. Although state legislatures are addressing this type of issue, it is still a problem. In many cases, the way to encourage an offender and his or her defense attorney to take a plea is to sweeten the deal by not requiring the offender to register.

Another recent example involved a case where the offender was charged with aggravated felonious sexual assault and felonious sexual assault, involving a 15-year-old. Convictions of these charges would place the offender on the public view list. However, the plea agreement allowed the offender to take a conviction for a misdemeanor sexual assault, which, in New Hampshire, only requires the offender to register as a nonpublic offender for 10 years.

Whereas kidnapping in many states would require an offender to register, homicide might not, even if there was a sexual component to the case, depending on how the crime was charged and the plea agreement. We hate to say it, but there are individuals in our communities who are not registered offenders but whose history make them more dangerous than some of the offenders listed in the registry. And because these predators have not been convicted, the public cannot be warned in any way of their perversions.

THE DOUGLAS SIMMONS CASE

Take Douglas Simmons, a convicted child murderer from Connecticut who also kidnapped and sexually assaulted the 6-year-old child he killed. Simmons spent 22 years in prison for the murder of Michelle Spencer in 1981. He relocated to southern New Hampshire following his release from prison. The community found out and was outraged. Despite committing a sexual assault, Simmons was not convicted for the sexual assault in the plea agreement; therefore, when he moved to New Hampshire, the murder charge was not a qualifying charge to mandate him to register as a sex offender against children. Ultimately, a conviction for kidnapping in relation to the case did place him on the public view list. However, had kidnapping not been part of the plea, he would not have been on the New Hampshire sex offender registry.

Obviously there are loopholes in many state laws and sometimes no forethought when prosecutors are making plea offers. Just because a predator commits a sexual assault does not mean that he or she will be convicted of a sexual assault and end up on a sex offender registry.

We see communities in an uproar when a sex offender moves in; however, what people forget is that it is often the unknown that is more of a threat to their children. Although the sex offender website might point out a local offender for public awareness, can you really be certain that you don't have a dangerous predator in your area who has just never been caught? How do you know that your neighbor might not be a sex offender or a drug dealer or a robber? You don't. That is why it is imperative to put these websites in perspective and realize that although the information is important for your family's safety, the offender you

As we often tell concerned parents, your child is more likely to be approached by a drug dealer in your neighborhood than a convicted sex offender, and there is no public view drug dealer list on any website.

don't know about is much more dangerous than the one you do know about. You should be no less careful and vigilant with your child's safety, even if you live in a neighborhood free of public sex offenders. As we often tell concerned parents, your child is more likely to be approached by a drug dealer in your neighborhood than a convicted sex offender, and there is no public view drug dealer list on any website.

In all of her years as a police officer, the majority of the sex offenses Kristyn has investigated involve individuals with *no prior criminal history*. This should make one stop and put the concept of sex offender registries into rational perspective.

The National Sex Offender Public Registry

Bookmark the website for the National Sex Offender Public Registry: www.nsopr.gov. Many local police departments have links to statewide versions of this registry. You need to visit it and get familiar with the names and pictures (many are posted) of those on the public registry in your area.

Again, remember that there are many sex offenders whose names are not required by law to be released publicly, and they pose a danger to your children, as well. Do not fall into complacency because there are no publicly registered sex offenders

Do not fall into complacency because there are no publicly registered sex offenders living in your neighborhood.

living in your neighborhood. We have seen a website that supposedly maps the locations of sex offenders, but its contents were not up to date. This concerns us because it can create a false sense of security. Our experience tells us that you need to be as worried about the person your child is talking to online (even if he or she claims to be another 13-year old) as you do the pedophile who is registered and living down the road.

COP GETS 14 YEARS FOR DISTRIBUTING KIDDIE PORN: THE JOHN SCHENBERGER CASE

Nothing seems more heinous than someone in authority abusing his position to perpetrate a crime against children. In a recent case that leaves us both utterly disgusted, John E. Schenberger, a 17-year police veteran from the Pennsauken (New Jersey) Police Department, was sentenced to 14 years in federal prison for shipping child pornography using his own department's computers.

The following is from the Attorney General's press release:

> While all of the files were sexually explicit in nature, about 373 of those files portrayed prepubescent children participating in sexually explicit poses and/or acts, Schenberger admitted. Furthermore, Schenberger admitted that about six of the eight digital movie files portrayed prepubescent children participating in sexually explicit poses and/or acts.

On July 5, 2008, Schenberger, by his own admission, again used a computer at the Pennsauken Police Department to log onto the instant messaging feature of the Hello.com website and transfer approximately 532 digital picture files and three digital movie files to the same individual. Schenberger also admitted that about 426 of the 532 picture files and all three of the movie files portrayed prepubescent children participating in sexually explicit poses and/or acts.

What makes this case so much more heinous is that Schenberger was depicted as the department's computer "czar" who got caught up in an undercover operation by the Memphis Crimes Against Children Taskforce. He was indicted by a grand jury in Tennessee, but the case was later transferred to a Camden, New Jersey federal court. His reasoning for using his own department's computers to transfer kiddie porn? He didn't want his own children to see the porn on his home computer.

PRIEST GETS 4 YEARS

As we stated earlier, we find it particularly offensive when someone in a position of authority abuses that position to perpetrate a crime against children. In June of 2008, 51-year-old Raymond Ethier, a now-defrocked Roman Catholic priest from Hudson, New York, was sentenced to 4 years in federal prison after pleading guilty to downloading child pornography. Ethier was found to be in possession of videos and still images of children engaged in sexual acts while he was the pastor of a local church. Upon completion of his sentence, he will be required to participate in a sex offender program.

Sexual offenders come from all walks of life and from all different backgrounds.

Our point is that sexual offenders come from all walks of life and from all different backgrounds. We regularly conduct research on sexual offenders and their backgrounds. There is no one "profile" of an offender. We know of doctors, priests, politicians, and, yes, even professional clowns, who have been arrested for possession of child pornography. All the more reason for parents to never let their guard down in monitoring their children's activities online.

U.S. Supreme Court Rules CG Kiddie Porn Is Perfectly Legal

Table 8.1 traces the development of child pornography laws in the United States. As you can see in this table, in 2002 the U.S. Supreme Court issued a historical and rather disturbing ruling when it announced that computer-generated images of child pornography are perfectly legal as long as no actual child is used in the production of the image.

Table 8.1 Development of Child Pornography Laws in the United States

Date	Legislation/Ruling	Comment
1978	Sexual Exploitation of Children Act	First federal law specifically dealing with child pornography. Prohibited the manufacture and commercial distribution of obscene material involving minors under 16.
1982	New York v. Ferber	Child pornography not protected by the First Amendment. Child pornography separated from obscenity laws, to be judged on a different standard.

Date	Legislation/Ruling	Comment
1984	Child Protection Act	Age of minor covered by child pornography legislation was raised to 18, and distinction between child pornography and obscenity codified.
1986	United States v. Dost	Expanded the definition of child pornography to include sexually suggestive depictions of a lascivious nature.
1988	Child Protection and Obscenity Enforcement Act	Illegal to use a computer to depict or advertise child pornography.
1990	Osborne v. Ohio	Private possession of child pornography ruled to be illegal.
1996	Child Pornography Protection Act	Definition of child pornography expanded to include virtual images of children and images that appear to be of a minor.
1998	Child Protector and Sexual Predator Punishment Act	Internet Service Providers (ISPs) required to report known incidents of child pornography to authorities, but not required to actively monitor customers or sites.
2002	Ashcroft v. Free Speech Coalition	Virtual images ruled not to be pornography; 'appear to be a minor' ruled to be too broad.

(Source: Wortley, Richard and Stephen Smallbone. May 2006. "Child Pornography on the Internet." Problem-Oriented Guides for Police Problem-Specific Guides Series, Guide No. 41. U.S. Department of Justice, Office of Community Oriented Policing Services.)

If you don't know anything about computer-generated images, look at Figure 8.3 to see if you can tell if it is real or computer-generated.

(Source: AutoDesk)

FIGURE 8.3

Image of a car

The answer? The photo is computer-generated.

Digital Images

Computer graphics technology has come a long way because of high-end graphic imaging and manipulation programs such as PhotoShop. Although these programs have led to amazing advances in many fields, including medical science, art, and business, they have also led to the creation of "virtual" child pornography, which is excluded under the law. Millions of dollars are spent every year by law enforcement in an attempt to determine what is real and what is computer-generated.

The 2002 Supreme Court ruling struck down an earlier ruling from 1996 that banned all material that "appeared to be" a child in a sexually explicit situation. The new ruling excluded child pornography that was computer-generated, although the process of "morphing" (pasting a real child's face onto a naked body) remains illegal.

Congress Reacts

In reaction, Congress passed a law in 2003 making it a crime to exchange online messages about "any material or purported material" that would cause "another to believe" it depicted a minor engaged in sex, whether "actual or simulated." Violations of this law call for at least 5 years and as many as 20 years in prison, but the law has been repeatedly challenged as being "too broad" and could ensnare a grandmother who sends an email with the subject "Good pics of kids in bed" depicting her sleeping grandchildren.

The original 2002 ruling has placed a huge burden on prosecutors, who now have to prove at a great expense, that an image is, in fact, real.

The National Center for Missing and Exploited Children

The cornerstone for those of us in law enforcement who work cases involving child exploitation is, without question, the National Center for Missing and Exploited Children (NCMEC). From 1984 through the present, NCMEC has been involved with more than 133,000 missing children cases. NCMEC has assisted in reuniting more than 115,700 children with their loved ones. Every day in the U.S., 2,200 children are reported missing, an annual total of 1.3 million runaways. Five thousand of these children die every year due to homicide, disease, and suicide, a number

NCMEC works tirelessly to reduce every day. NCMEC's reported recovery rate in 2007 was 96%, up from 62% in 1990, with an estimated one in six children having been recov-

Every day in the U.S., 2,200 children are reported missing, an annual total of 1.3 million runaways.

ered as a result of a photograph. Also, since 1984, the NCMEC hotline (1-800-THE-LOST) has received 2.2 million calls, an average of 283 calls each day.

NCMEC's cyber tipline has received more than 524,876 reports since 1998, with more than 29,729 reports of online enticement. Because of the SAFE Act, which established guidelines for the reporting and preservation of information, 325 electronic service providers are legally obligated to report exploitation of children online. NCMEC is currently averaging 2,000 cases per week, 1,500 of which are illegal activity. In 2007, NCMEC handled more than 105,000 cases.

Child Victim Identification Program (CVIP)

NCMEC's Child Victim Identification Program (CVIP) was formally estab-lished in 2002 following the Ashcroft v. Free Speech decision, in which law enforcement was held to the standard of positively identifying minor chil-dren in sexually graphic images and videos. Thirteen million images have been reviewed since 2002, with 5 million images being reviewed in 2007 alone. Currently, the FBI has 28,000 identified images catalogued for law enforcement.

Law-enforcement agencies submit images with unknown victims, and CVIP goes to work. CVIP has handled 13,000 requests for victim identifica-tion and have identified more than 1,300 child victims. They have identi-fied single videos or images, as well as "series" of images involving specific victims. As of April of 2008, five to six new victims were being reported to NCMEC each week.

Data from June 2006 gives the following picture of "child sexual abuse images":

Age of Victim

- Prepubescent child: 70%

- Pubescent: 24%

- Infant/toddler: 6%

Number of Victims per Series

- One child in 80% of images
- Two children in 11% of images
- More than three children in 9% of images

Relationship of Abuser to Child

- Neighbor/friend: 27%
- Other relative: 10%
- Parent/step parent: 35%
- Online enticement encouraging image on webcam or photo: 10%
- Babysitter/coach: 4%
- Guardian's partner (girlfriend/boyfriend): 4%
- Self-produced (that is, using one's own camera phone): 5%
- Relationship unknown to child: 5%

It is common for children not to disclose victimization regarding child pornography, and given that victims in child sexual abuse images are statistically more exploited by people they love and trust, it is no wonder.

NCMEC is also a leader in educating professionals working to stop child victimization. To date, NCMEC has trained more than 227,700 law enforcement, criminal justice, and healthcare professionals in the U.S. and Canada. They have distributed more than 15,000 law-enforcement guides.

CVIP costs about $1 million a year to run, with this program having reviewed millions of images to authenticate that they are indeed real as a result of Ashcroft v. Free Speech. Absent an assessment by the Center, pediatricians and other experts can be called in to testify to physical characteristics of children at different ages to try to authenticate a photo. Sometimes computer graphic experts are called in.

Some recent rulings allow jurors to decide whether an image is fake. Bear in mind that although this type of ruling places a burden on prosecutors, our experience is that pedophiles are likely to have much more than just one or two images on their computer. Even if a few proved to be computer-generated, there's more than likely many more that are not.

Despite that, our right to free speech forces law enforcement to jump through this victim identification hoop in order to prosecute child pornographers and child pornography collectors. NCMEC and CVIP have really placed the focus on the identification of the victim for the safety of children, not solely for the prosecution of perpetrators. Saving children from victimization, regardless of the court outcome, is what we truly work for—and NCMEC has set the standard.

Operation Avalanche

In 1999, 30 Internet Crimes Against Children (ICAC) task forces throughout the U.S. were partnered with U.S. postal inspectors in a proactive, 2-year undercover operation that took down what was then the largest child pornography enterprise ever known. Landslide Productions, Inc., was a multimillion-dollar child pornography business that was discovered to be selling child pornography websites to customers worldwide. Monthly fees allowed subscribers access to hundreds of websites containing very graphic child pornography.

During the course of the investigation, NCMEC received in excess of 270 complaints from all over the world in reference to this case.

Landslide Productions

Subscribers to Landslide paid $29.95 each to access the child porn websites. It had a list of 300,000 customers in 37 states and 60 countries. Landslide Productions, Inc., which was owned and operated by Thomas and Janice Reedy of Fort Worth, Texas, grossed over $1.4 million in 1 month. For 2 years, Landslide Productions took in almost $10 million.

The Reedys were convicted of 89 counts of conspiracy to distribute child pornography and possession of child pornography. Thomas Reedy was sentenced to life in federal prison, while Janice Reedy received a 14-year sentence.

In the course of this investigation, over 160 state and federal search warrants were executed, and more than 120 arrests were made for trafficking child pornography through the U.S. mail and the Internet. This operation identified predators and victims. One of the arrests stemming from this investigation was that of a 36-year-old computer consultant from North Carolina who had rigged a pinhole camera in a smoke detector to record the molestation of several children, one of whom was only 4 years old. That case resulted in a 17 1/2–year prison sentence.

Operation Avalanche crossed boundaries and borders, joining state, local, and federal law-enforcement agencies on a mission that impacted 60 countries and brought many pornographers and molesters to justice. This cooperative effort continues today through Project Safe Child, where local, state, and federal partners are working with ICAC task forces from state to state to combat the exploitation of our most innocent victims.

How Far Does "Private Fantasy" Go? The Zidel Case

In June of 2006, Marshall Zidel was sentenced to 1 to 7 years in prison following an April conviction on child pornography charges in Hillsboro Superior Court in New Hampshire. He had been convicted on eight other counts, which included a 1-year suspended sentence.

Zidel had been a photographer at a children's camp in Amherst, New Hampshire, and he digitally combined the faces of girl campers with obscene photos of adult women. There were nine "morphed" digital photos in which Zidel used the faces of 14- and 15-year-old girls who attended the camp. Zidel had been an employee of the camp for more than 20 years. Several of the pictures were labeled with lewd captions, which contained some of the names of the campers, similar to the aforementioned case of David Cobb (a.k.a. The Pumpkin Man).

Zidel's attorney argued that these were never intended for distribution but were rather for his client's own "private fantasy." The nine images were discovered when Zidel inadvertently left them on a CD of photos that were to be used for a camp yearbook.

Zidel and his attorney appealed the conviction, arguing that these images were not what legislators intended to be outlawed as child pornography. The argument was that digitally manipulated images that do not involve naked children, and would not appear to involve naked children to a reasonable person, are not child pornography. This was yet another complication in the definition of child pornography as a result of computer software that can manipulate an image to appear lewd or obscene without an actual child sexual assault photo of real victims having been taken.

The New Hampshire Supreme Court overturned the conviction in January of 2008, with Associate Justice James Duggan writing the following:

However distasteful, reprehensible, and valueless this conduct might seem, the First Amendment protects "the individual's right to…observe what he pleases…. This protection is central to our long and sacred tradition of prohibiting the government from intruding into the privacy of our thoughts and the contents of our homes.

Essentially, the case was overturned because Zidel never intended to distribute the morphed images. The First Amendment goes a long way toward protecting everyone's freedom, but it does not protect someone's right to create or distribute child pornography. How can one say that the children whose faces were placed on obscene pictures were not harmed? How can one say definitively that Zidel was not satisfying the deviant urge of a pedophile? Who is to say that this wasn't a precipitating behavior to live child exploitation? And does it matter that Zidel never intended for the morphed images to be made public, because they did become very public. This case emphasizes the notion that "the road to hell is paved with good intentions." We can't think of any reason why the manipulation of a child's photograph in this manner should not be illegal—we can only hope that legislators wake up and label this what it really is: deviant and wrong.

Recent Developments

In May of 2008, the U.S. Supreme Court upheld a federal law prohibiting the possession of child pornography as part of the PROTECT Act (Prosecutorial Remedies and Other Tools to End the Exploitation of Children Today Act). It sets a mandatory 5-year prison term for promoting or pandering, even if someone doesn't actually have child pornography in his possession. In a 7-2 decision, the Supreme Court ruled that "offers to provide or requests to obtain child pornography are categorically excluded from the First Amendment."

This means that someone still has to have the intent of committing the crime of promoting or pandering child pornography. The case reinstated the conviction of a Florida man, Michael Williams, who was convicted of "pandering" child pornography when he was caught up in an undercover operation in April of 2004. Williams had offered to trade nude photos of his toddler to an undercover agent, but when his computer was seized, he did not actually have any photos of his toddler, though he did have 22 other sexually explicit photos of other children on his computer. The case was centered around the charge of *pandering*, which is defined as "promoting or distributing real or purported material that would reflect the belief that there actually is child pornography."

Williams pleaded guilty to possessing the child pornography and was sentenced to 5 years in prison, but lawyers challenged the pandering charge, claiming that the wording was "overly broad" and violated the First Amendment right to free speech.

The case was heard in a federal appeals court and overturned. One of the arguments made, which the federal appeals court agreed with, was that offering a video of *Snow White* could be considered illegal if the person making the offer claimed that the video depicted minors engaged in sex.

Supreme Court Overturns Ruling

The U.S. Supreme Court ruled against the federal appeals court. The key to this decision is that prosecutors no longer have to prove the underlying material is illegal. The actual criminal offense is the language that offers to sell or trade in illegal material.

Because this ruling is so new, we're eager to see how it plays out in the cases where "virtual" child pornography is involved. It opens the legal basis to charge someone regardless of whether the kiddie porn is real or "virtual" if someone has the intent to sell or distribute it. In any case, here's what Justice Scalia said:

> *Child pornography harms and debases the most defenseless of our citizens.... We hold that offers to provide or requests to obtain child pornography are categorically excluded from the First Amendment.*

We couldn't agree more. Excluding the fact of whether or not an actual child is used, "virtual" child pornography is still dangerous because it feeds deviant compulsions. In addition, it places a huge burden on prosecutors to try and prove that the child porn is, in fact, real, not virtual. Digital imaging experts need to be called in along with a host of other "experts" to testify at a great expense. Children are still at risk, virtual or not.

CAN YOU KEEP YOUR PASSWORD PRIVATE? THE SEBASTIAN BOUCHER CASE

We've been closely following the case of Sebastian Boucher, a Derry, New Hampshire resident who was arrested with his father at the Canadian border in Vermont on December, 17, 2006, on charges of transporting child pornography on his computer.

According to court documents, Boucher was pulled over by a Customs and Border Protection Officer for a secondary inspection when he was crossing over from Canada into the U.S. The officer noticed a laptop in Boucher's vehicle and attempted to inspect it to see if it contained child pornography. Boucher is a Canadian resident who is a lawful permanent resident of the United States.

Boucher's laptop had 34,000 or so image files on it, several of which had names suggesting child pornography, including one that was called "Two-year-old being raped during diaper change." Boucher was read his Miranda rights, waived them, and told the customs agents that he sometimes visited newsgroups from which he downloaded pornographic images and that he may have, unknowingly, downloaded child pornography, but added that he deleted those images whenever he saw them.

Boucher voluntarily showed the border agents files on what was called drive "Z." These files appeared to be graphic child pornography, including many with preteens. What happened next thrust this incident into what may turn out to be a landmark court case—Boucher's laptop was shut down after he was arrested. Prosecutors obtained a subpoena for further inspection on December 19th, but it wasn't until the day after Christmas, December 26th, that a Vermont Department of Corrections Officer tried to access the laptop and discovered that drive "Z," which contained the suspect images, was encrypted and password protected with a program called PGP, or "Pretty Good Privacy." PGP is available for free and is one of the more popular data-encryption programs.

Prosecutors sent Boucher a subpoena requesting the password. Boucher refused to provide the password, citing his Fifth Amendment rights against self-incrimination. In a November 26, 2007 ruling, U.S. Magistrate Judge Jerome Niedermeier agreed and wrote in his decision that, "Compelling Boucher to enter the password forces him to produce evidence that could be used to incriminate him."

We will continue to follow this case, as it is likely to be appealed.

Laws and Loopholes

Child pornography laws are still being changed and loopholes being closed in many states. As we write this, the state of New Hampshire is in the midst of debating changes to current legislation regarding child pornography or "child sexual assault images" and what age can be considered a victim. One of the issues is that the Adam Walsh Act has made the possession of child pornography illegal if the child is under the age of 18. Many of us have lobbied and testified for our state to change the age from 16 to 18. Unfortunately, some legislators feel that a 16-year-old can make the decision to star in their own sexually explicit video. Others feel it would be too hard to tell if a child was 16, 17, or 19 in order to prosecute.

As a parent, how would you feel if someone videotaped your 16-year-old daughter having sex or simply in a state of undress? How would you feel if the videographer was a 43-year-old male? Should that be illegal?

What if a 16-year-old child is being sexually abused and videotaped by a perpetrator—maybe a family member? Shouldn't that be illegal because it occurred during a sexual assault?

What might seem like a fun idea on prom night could end up haunting that naive 16-year-old child. We are aware of a case involving a boyfriend who paid for the prom, limo, and hotel for his girlfriend. They willingly videotaped their sexual escapades that night. They both graduated and went off to separate colleges. The boy paid for a trip to see his girlfriend at her college, only to be dumped. He spent the night on the street. As payback, the creative, jilted lover made his own "Priceless" ad, similar to the well-recognized series of MasterCard advertisements, and posted it and the video of their sexual activity online. Now that the video is posted, it will haunt the woman forever, because it can never be removed from cyberspace. The evidence of an immature decision at 16 years old can legally be posted without that person's permission. In states where child sexual assault images are illegal under the age of 18, this case could be criminally pursued. In states where the laws have not caught up to the federal age of 18, this case cannot be pursued other than in civil court.

Internet Crimes Against Children (ICAC) investigators can charge a suspect for possession of child pornography only for videos or images where the victim has been positively identified or the age of the victim is readily apparent (infant, toddler, prepubescent child). Therefore, a suspect would only be charged for possession of a video or image of a 16- or 17-year-old if the child had been positively identified.

Laptops and Customs Searches

Customs Agents do not need any evidence of wrongdoing to search the contents of your laptop if you are at an international border. You may have heard the term *probable cause*, which refers to specific evidence or the standard of reasonable suspicion that a police officer must have in order to arrest someone or to conduct a personal or property search. However, the courts have ruled that at an airport, a laptop is no different from a suitcase, a car, or any other piece of property and can be searched without "probable cause."

This ruling came as a result of a case from July of 2005 when a 44-year-old math teacher from Orange County, California, returning from a flight from the Philippines, was subjected to a search that included his laptop. The man was asked by a Customs Agent to turn on his computer, and images of what appeared to child pornography were found. The defendant's attorney will appeal the ruling.

Laptop Search by Customs Is Challenged

Just recently, Democratic senators Russell Feingold (Wisconsin) and Patrick Leahy (Vermont) issued a challenge to the scope and authority of U.S. Customs and Border Agents. They have asked for a review of policy that allows U.S. Customs to assume they have the right to inspect a laptop. Senator Feingold was quoted as saying, "If you asked [U.S. residents] whether the government has a right to open their laptops, read their documents and e-mails, look at their photographs, and examine the websites they have visited, all without any suspicion of wrongdoing, I think those same Americans would say the government has no right to do that." ("Senators Question Border Laptop Searches," *PC World*, June 25, 2008.)

Sex Offender Caught at Border

Although we understand the concerns over the rights to privacy, were it not for the search of a Texan man's laptop, Canadian border officials might not have found the child pornography of a known sexual offender. When 45-year-old Kevin D. Moore of Texas was asked if he had any illegal documents on his laptop as he arrived at an Ottawa airport, he replied that he didn't; however, he reported that his brother also used his laptop, as a means to divert suspicion from his own activities. Moore had already been sentenced in 2003 for sexually assaulting a child. He will now spend 30 more years in prison and be on supervised release once he gets out.

A Balancing Act

The right to privacy is sometimes difficult to balance with the rights of the public to be safe and for the law to be enforced. In law enforcement, we hear that infamous term "Big Brother" all the time. Felicia recently commented on a blog regarding the difficulties law enforcement faces regarding sharing police information and was immediately flamed by privacy advocates (replying as "Anonymous," of course), who challenged law enforcement's right to share information and who drew all kinds of correlations to a communist state.

There is always a balance to be found here, but laws are made to protect people, and we do advocate for any law that will further protect our children. We'd be jumping for joy if law enforcement never had to draw up another search warrant, forensically examine another computer, or tap another phone; however, the reality is that our children are still at tremendous risk—more so now than ever before—due to the proliferation of technology.

People's perspectives change when they realize the lengths that law enforcement will go to protect a child from getting hurt. People's perspectives also change when they, themselves, become victims of crime. We'll respect and defend your rights, but let's put the rights of those that cannot protect themselves first.

The point we need to emphasize is that there is no magic "profile" for a sexual offender. Trust us, they come in all shapes and sizes, sexes, and orientations. If it were as simple as finding the sketchiest-looking guy and hauling him off, knowing our children are safe, we'd be thrilled. However, that's not reality. As such, law enforcement operates on information, and often that information is contained on computers that require searching.

SAFE Act

On December 5, 2007, the SAFE (Securing Adolescents From Exploitation Online) Act was introduced and passed by a House vote of 409 to 2. At the time of this writing, the bill has yet to be voted on by the Senate, but has already caused some controversy because of the changes it brings.

Laws already exist that require any Internet service provider (ISP), such as Comcast or AOL, to report the presence of child pornography to NCMEC (the National Center for Missing and Exploited Children) through a cyber tipline if they become aware of it.

The SAFE Act, in essence, creates stiffer penalties and broadens the definition of "Internet service provider" to include wireless (Wi-Fi) hot spots such as hotels, libraries, and municipalities. This does not mean that your local cyber café will be monitoring your activities or searching your hard drive for illicit images. It does, however, mean that the penalties against ISPs who do *not* report the presence of kiddie porn just tripled—from $50,000 per day per image for the first offense to $150,000, and up to $300,000 per day for repeat offenders.

Social Networks and Sex Offenders

It is well known that social networks have become the playground of predators. How better to fuel a predator's deviance than to offer hundreds of thousands of children ready to be solicited, groomed, and potentially molested?

> It is well known that social networks have become the playground of predators.

Facebook and MySpace Get Tougher on Sex Offenders?

On February 2, 2007, MySpace.com announced they had partnered with Sentinel Tech in donating a Sentinel Safe database to the National Center for Missing and Exploited Children (NCMEC). The database, jointly developed by MySpace and Sentinel, enables websites to identify convicted sex offenders and then remove and block them from online communities.

On January 15, 2008, MySpace announced several initiatives to lock out sexual predators, including "date of birth" validation. This came 3 months after Facebook took similar initiatives. Although we applaud any efforts to try and restrict pedophiles' access to children, the painful reality is that many of these policies are too easily thwarted.

We recently had a case in which a public sex offender against children had a MySpace page using his real name, date of birth, and biographical data. If notified about the offender, MySpace would shut down the page. However, just as kids make up data to set up a page, so can an offender. It is all too easy. We are able to maintain juvenile accounts on many venues for undercover and investigative work despite all the new policies. If we can maintain them, surely others can and will—including predators.

The bottom line is, and always will be, this: There is no substitute for parental oversight when kids go online. Be aware!

Our local high school was very public about blocking student access to sites such as MySpace; however, students were able to get around the firewall in a matter of minutes. When Kristyn was the high school resource officer, she had a student who utilized her Internet time during geography class purporting to be a 26-year-old exotic dancer using the online name "Raging Redhead."

This young woman chatted with several older men from other New England states and made plans to "hook up." The young woman's geography teacher conceded that she had assigned a project to her students, but had trusted them to handle the online assignment maturely. Luckily, "Raging Redhead" had a mother who had also been monitoring her daughter's online activity, and we were able to confront the young woman and keep an eye on her risky tendencies.

KIDS Bill

In December of 2007, the Senate unanimously passed the Keeping the Internet Devoid of Sexual Predators (KIDS) Act. It requires sex offenders to register and submit their email addresses and online screen names to the National Sex Offender Registry. The bill has received support from social networking venues such as MySpace and Facebook. Although we support any effort to try to legislate and curtail the activities of sexual offenders, our experience tells us that this will not stop someone who has a compulsive need to harm a child. He will simply assume a new persona. Without the legal authority to monitor whatever computers a sex offender uses, we would not assume that this is a valid deterrent.

Child Porn Sites Shut Down?

As we write this, several major Internet service providers (ISPs), including Verizon Communications, Sprint Nextel, and Time Warner Cable, have agreed to block Internet newsgroups and websites that contain and disseminate child pornography. The three also agreed to donate more than a million dollars to combat child pornography. Together, they represent millions of customers.

It is expected that tens of thousands of Usenet discussion groups will be shut down. These actions come as a result of an agreement with New York Attorney General Andrew Cuomo after many websites and Usenet groups (online groups with specific areas of interest) were found to contain child pornography. Reports indicate that the agreements follow an 8-month investigation in which undercover agents from Attorney General Cuomo's office, who posed as subscribers, complained to the ISPs about the child porn and little was done despite user agreements that prohibit the transmission or dissemination of sexually exploitive images of children. The Internet service providers were compelled to act or face charges of fraud and deceptive business practices. Cuomo was reported as saying, "The ISPs' point has been, 'We're not responsible, these are individuals communicating with individuals. We're not responsible.' Our point was that at some point, you do bear responsibility."

NCMEC, the National Center for Missing and Exploited Children, will maintain the "blacklist" of sites and newsgroups to be shut down. Authorities have the tools to identify 11,000 known images of child pornography because these same photos are often traded over and over again. Images can be identified by what is known as the "hash value" or a digital identifier. Once an image is identified and catalogued, its hash value can be scanned and searched for in other places.

The three companies agreed to take down child porn websites as NCMEC identifies them or after complaints and investigations. Shortly after this story broke, the Internet filled with comments on blogs and news sites— both for and against the action. As always happens whenever organizations move to block content on the Internet, an outcry is heard from those who feel this is an infringement on First Amendment rights and that "Big Brother" is wielding its mighty sword. Others are concerned about their own groups being shut down because they are mistakenly blacklisted.

We have both worked child pornography cases. We have seen the horrific images and what lengths pedophiles will go to satisfy their sexual deviance. As parents, we are far more concerned about the rights of the victimized children and their safety than the rights of those who may be crossing the line with sexually explicit photographs.

On a side note, at the same time the U.S. companies entered into this agreement, France's Interior Minister announced that beginning in September 2008, users would be given a way to flag sites that carry child pornography. This information would be used to develop similar "blacklists," which would be forwarded to French Internet service providers who have agreed to block the sites. The French minister also said that France would pass on information about any illegal sites to the host countries. Other states in the U.S., including California, are following suit with asking for voluntary compliance by ISPs. As of the time of this writing, AT&T

and Time Warner's America Online (AOL) unit have also agreed to shut down known sites trading child pornography. AT&T is the largest ISP in New York, with approximately 18.3 million subscribers. AOL is second with 9.3 million subscribers.

We are watching these stories closely as they unfold because 1) they represent a major shift in most Internet service providers' attitudes about not interfering with content, and 2) they can make a significant dent in the child porn trafficking industry because of the sheer number of subscribers affected.

ICAC: The Internet Crimes Against Children Task Force

The ICAC task force, composed of law-enforcement officers across the country, is funded by the Department of Justice through the Project Safe Childhood initiative. It recently (October of 2007) got a $3 million boost in funding to create an ICAC presence in all 50 states. ICAC has made over 10,000 arrests since its inception 9 years ago.

THE "TARA" SERIES: A HORRIFIC, YET BITTERSWEET SUCCESS STORY

Just recently, a young child was identified and saved through the efforts of the Maine Internet Crimes Against Children (ICAC) task force, other state ICAC agencies across the country, NCMEC, and the FBI. The now-9-year-old victim, in what has been dubbed the "Tara" series, had been abused for several years and had appeared online in images and videos between the ages of 5 and 9.

The series was first seen by law enforcement approximately 2 years ago when a suspect in an unrelated case told agents about the "Tara" series and gave police encryption keys that would allow access to the series online. The investigation actually began in Brisbane, Australia, where law-enforcement officials began probing a group of collectors with ties in the United States. The group made use of elaborate encryption and passwords to elude police.

The images of "Tara" became more and more violent, with one of the images showing the male perpetrator holding a large knife toward the small child victim. The images and photos were taken in various locations, including a bedroom, a hotel room, and in vehicles. The search for "Tara" went nationwide.

CLUES IN PHOTOS AND VIDEOS

A forensic examiner with the Maine State Police Computer Crimes Unit gets much of the credit for tracking down the accused abuser by looking for clues from the online images, including such tiny details as a bow made from a ribbon seen hanging on a wall.

An analysis was made on a unique painting titled "Inspired Hillsides" that was visible in one of the images. A spreadsheet with all sales of the painting was developed. Some of the paintings were sold to a specific hotel in Carrollton, Georgia.

In January 2008, pictures of "Tara" inside the interior of an automobile were shown to a representative from a Chevrolet-Buick-Pontiac-GMC car sales firm in Richmond, Virginia. The representative believed that the pictures were taken inside a vehicle consistent with a 2003–2005 Pontiac Aztek with exterior paint color Sunburst Orange Metallic. An offline search was conducted for all registered users of 2003–2005 Pontiac Azteks in Georgia.

An analysis of a bedspread viewed in some of the images indicated that it was a product of a specific online shopping company. The company confirmed that products were sent to the address listed for James and Sherri Ann Huskey of LaFayette, Georgia.

Investigators were able to connect specific paintings and fabrics in a room in one of the videos to one of two hotels in Georgia. At one hotel in Carrolton, Georgia, the manager was able to confirm that James Bartholomew Huskey had registered on July 21, 2007. Huskey drove a 2000 white van, but a check of his motor vehicle information indicated that a 2005 Pontiac Aztek was registered to Sherri Ann Huskey, James's wife.

Armed with a possible name, investigators turned to Huskey's wife and found a MySpace account in her name that had background images similar to those in the Tara series.

Huskey, the son of a preacher and local tennis coach, was arrested on June 16, 2008, and made admissions that he had been sexually molesting the young girl since she was approximately 6 years old. Huskey stated that he had been posting images of the molestation on the Internet, sharing it with an international, secretive group. Huskey admitted to having several thousand images of the molestation of the child and several hundred videos of sexual molestation on his computer. The camera he used to manufacture the images was recovered.

Huskey has been charged in United States District Court for manufacturing child pornography. The little girl Huskey victimized and exploited for years is now safe. However, the investigation into the "Tara" series is far from over, because there is no way to determine how far-reaching Huskey's Internet sharing actually is or how many other children have been victimized. Unfortunately, this innocent little girl will live the rest of her life with the horrors of her victimization and the knowledge that those images can never be eliminated from the World Wide Web. Every time a predator sends or receives one of these images, she will be victimized yet again.

ORGANIZED, SECRETIVE GROUP

One thing we want to emphasize about this case, beyond the incredible investigative work that was done, is that groups of child pornographers who trade photos and videos of children being raped often operate in a highly organized, very secretive manner. Here's an excerpt from the affidavit in this case:

> The group currently consists of approximately 48 members. There is a defined hierarchy or structure to the group and all members must abide by strictly enforced written security measures and standard operating procedures in order to retain their membership status. To become a member of the group, one must be invited in by an existing member, and must pass a timed written test to determine their knowledge of child pornography material (e.g., knowledge of the names of various child pornography series; must be able to describe a particular series in question, etc.). The test also serves as a measure to assess whether the interested party could be a law enforcement officer attempting to infiltrate the group. Members of the group are told to never provide their true identities to another member of the group. They are never to communicate with one another using traditional email, chat, Yahoo!, ICQ, or telephone. For the security of the group as a whole, their relationship with other members of the group is strictly cyber in nature. This way, if one of the members of the group is ever arrested by law enforcement, they cannot provide any identifying information to law enforcement on other members of the group. (Source: http://groups.google.com/group/alt.privacy/browse_thread/thread/3f24d5f70cbe392d)

The Child Advocacy Center: A Victim-Centered Approach

We think often about the young victims of predators such as Huskey and all the children who have crossed our paths as victims of sexual assault. To that end, we'd like to explain what does happen to these young victims.

When a child victim of sexual abuse or exploitation has been disclosed or has been identified, the investigation process is a far cry from that of a computer forensic investigation. The focus shifts from objective, stark data, to a more human approach into behavior. Law enforcement has come a long way in handling the youngest victims of crime—we are compassionate, empathic, patient, and determined to put the needs of the victim well before the need for a conviction or a statistic.

The Child Advocacy Center model was created from the vision of Robert E. "Bud" Cramer, then a District Attorney in Alabama and now a Congressman, who in 1985 organized an effort to better serve abused children. His notion was to minimize a child victim's emotional distress and lack of trust in adults, while maximizing interagency cooperation in the effort to investigate these egregious crimes as well as to provide prevention, education, and services. The team approach includes professionals from law enforcement, medical, mental health, and child protective services. This multidisciplinary approach focuses on the well being of the child and still affords investigators the best opportunity to prosecute predators.

In the best-case scenario, the child victim should only be subjected to one in-depth interview, which reduces the revictimization of the child and provides law enforcement with the most comprehensive, consistent information with which to proceed with the investigation. Whereas large agencies have specialized investigators and specialized units of trained personnel, most smaller agencies (which in reality are often the norm) usually do not. On top of this, we often deal with very young victims or victims with cognitive or emotional disabilities. The case still requires a solid forensic interview using a specially trained interviewer.

As law enforcement is focusing on criminal charges, child protection agencies often run parallel investigations focusing on child protection through a civil (nonpunitive) process. Multiple interviews with the same victim, conducted by different people from the various agencies involved, can lead to inconsistencies in the victim's statements, as well as forcing the victim to relive the trauma of abuse each time the story has to be told again.

The Child Advocacy (CAC) model involves a multidisciplinary approach in a neutral setting. A trained forensic interviewer, not associated with any investigative agency, meets with the child in an offsite setting away from any police department or child protection office. The room is pleasantly decorated and child friendly. The interviewer and the child sit at a table and get acquainted with basic conversation. The interview is audio and video recorded, being streamed in real time into a room where law-enforcement officers, social workers, and prosecutors can monitor the proceedings. Special headsets allow the "team" to direct questions that arise from the interview to the interviewer through an ear piece. The child only speaks with one person during this interview process. The child decides the direction of the "conversation," and the interviewer follows the child's lead in gathering pertinent information. The child is told that the interview is being monitored and recorded, and that he or she can decide to stop if the conversation becomes uncomfortable. No child is forced to speak with an interviewer. The resulting interview can be used for both law enforcement and child protection investigations.

The family is briefed as to the process prior to the interview and meets all team members, including the forensic interviewer, affording them the opportunity to ask questions or express concerns. An advocate from a sexual assault support agency is present to offer support and comfort for the family and victim during the process. The family does not witness the interview, but rather waits with an advocate in another room. Following the interview, parents are given resources and information as to the next steps in the case investigation.

The video recordings are entered into evidence, used only for the prosecution of the case. Video recordings allow investigators and prosecutors to review the interview in the victim's own words and minimizes the need to re-interview at a later time.

Child protective services, social services, child advocates, mental health intervention, and medical services can be brought into the process as deemed appropriate for the victim and family, regardless of whether the case ever sees a courtroom. Child Advocacy Centers are set up regionally across the country, accessible by any law-enforcement or child protective agency in that region. They are also especially convenient when a case crosses jurisdictions, with more than one law-enforcement agency investigating multiple incidences of abuse of a victim, in that one interview is used by all investigating agencies involved in the case.

This model has been successful, not only for prosecution, but for making the investigative process as "victim oriented" as possible, keeping the needs of the child first and foremost. The child is the center, and the process will focus on the individual needs of that specific child throughout the investigative process. Whether or not a case is prosecuted depends completely on what is in the best interest of the child and his or her needs.

For more information on the history of Child Advocacy Centers and the prevention, training, intervention, and therapy the National Child Advocacy Center offers, visit www.nationalcac.org.

Missouri: 30 Days, 7,000 Computers Trading Kiddie Porn

The Western Missouri Cyber Crimes Task Force conducted a survey in March of 2008 for which they had been preparing for well over a year. Investigators searched for computers that were trading known images of child pornography, as identified by NCMEC (National Center for Missing and Exploited Children). They took a 30-day snapshot of files being shared through computers in Missouri. The results were unsettling. More than 7,000 computers using peer-to-peer (P2P) software like that used to trade music were found to have traded child pornography. Seven thousand computers in 30 days. How much more can be said about how pervasive and prolific a problem this is? Investigators are preparing search warrants and subpoenas.

NCMEC Survey

The National Center for Missing and Exploited Children has conducted several surveys about online behaviors that have yielded some startling results. The surveys uncovered the following facts concerning what kids say about their online activities:

- Thirty-three percent of 13- to 17-year-olds said their parents know "very little" or "nothing" about what they do on the Internet.

- Four percent admitted to being exposed to sexual material online they did not want to see.

- Fifty-two percent who were exposed did not report the incident to anyone.

And here are some interesting facts about what parents have to say about their kids and their online activities:

- Fifty-one percent admitted they do not know whether they have software on their computer(s) that monitors where their teenager(s) go online and with whom they interact.

- Forty-two percent of parents do not review the content of what their teenager(s) read and/or type in chat rooms or via instant messaging.

- Ninety-five percent of parents couldn't identify common chat room lingo that teenagers use to warn people they're chatting with that their parents are watching. Those phrases are POS (Parent Over Shoulder) and P911 (Parent Alert).

- Ninety-two percent don't know what the net lingo "A/S/L" (Age/Sex/Location) stands for.

Internet Safety Guidelines

Here are some basic steps you should take, at the very least, to protect your kids online:

- Place the computer in a common area, not your child's bedroom.
- Talk with your kids about online dangers.
- Limit time online.
- Discuss the appropriate use of chat, instant messaging, email, and social networking sites.
- Do not let kids post pictures of themselves on the Internet.
- Use parental controls through Internet Explorer to block inappropriate sites.

RESOURCES

- Child Victim Identification Program (CVIP): http://www.missingkids.com
- The website www.nystopchildporn.com, developed by Gov. Cuomo's office, will maintain a running list of Internet service providers who have agreed to shut down child pornography trafficking sites.
- National Center for Missing and Exploited Children (www.missingkids.com; 1-800-THE-LOST or cybertipline.com)
- NetSmartz (www.netsmartz.org)
- Netlingo (www.netlingo.com)
- Wired Safety (www.wiredsafety.org)
- Get Net Wise (www.getnetwise.org)
- Polly Klaas Foundation (www.pollyklaas.org)
- Protect: National Association to Protect Children (www.protect.org)
- National Sex Offender Public Registry (www.nsopr.gov)

9

Social Networks/Social Nightmares

Years ago, the only form of social networking that existed on the Internet was bulletin boards that offered lines of green text against a black screen and were perpetually slow and difficult to navigate. Along came high-speed networks that could support photos as well as streaming video and audio, and the world of social networking emerged.

There are so many social networks available today, it is mind-boggling: MySpace, Technorati, Facebook, Xanga, Sconix, Gather—just to name a few. There are topic-specific social networking sites such as Shelfari and GoodReads for book lovers, BlackPlanet for African-Americans, Buzznet for music and culture fans, and Care2 for "green" living enthusiasts. There are literally thousands of different social networking sites that millions of people have joined. We're going to share with you some of the "darker" sides of social networking that this new frontier hosts.

Online Societies

According to a survey in June of 2007 by Compete.com (shown in Figure 9.1), MySpace had 72 million visitors that month, which made up 12% of the social networking market. Those are pretty staggering numbers—72 million visitors in a single month. But what is even more compelling is the fact that the supposedly "smaller" social networking sites still have millions of visitors each month.

Just because your children are posting on hi5.com or Friendster.com does not mean they are immune to any danger. Hi5.com reports almost 3 million visitors a month. Friendster has 1.3 million visitors a month. You wouldn't turn your children loose in a room filled with a hundred strangers, so there's no reason to not monitor them in a chat room with 3 million strangers.

Attention Rank	Site	Monthly Visitors	A
1	myspace.com	72,505,214	
2	facebook.com	22,609,677	
3	bebo.com	3,547,940	
4	tagged.com	3,304,563	
5	blackplanet.com	1,972,670	
6	myyearbook.com	2,894,318	
7	hi5.com	2,987,372	
8	classmates.com	11,043,070	
9	friendster.com	1,384,957	
10	xanga.com	3,713,235	
11	orkut.com	460,781	
12	asiantown.net	147,949	
13	flixster.com	3,090,311	
14	migente.com	1,280,000	
15	reunion.com	6,299,700	
16	quepasa.com	177,617	
17	tickle.com	2,121,767	
18	piczo.com	659,844	
19	multiply.com	656,808	
20	linkedin.com	1,421,393	

(Source: http://blog.compete.com/2007/07/24/top-social-networks-june-myspace-facebook/)

FIGURE 9.1

This chart from Compete.com measures how much time users spend on a site, compared to the number of total people who use the site, to give a better indicator of what users are viewing.

More and More Specialized Social Networks

As social networks proliferate, we're seeing more and more "specialized" sites, many of which are tailored to specific interests. Surely you've heard of MySpace and Facebook, but have you heard of Habbo.com (the "hangout for teens"), Bebo.com, MocoSpace.com, Fubar.com, Twitter.com, Gather.com, Sconex.com (teens), JuicyCampus.com, eCrush.com, CrushorFlush.com, GossipReport.com, eSpintheBottle.com, GaiaOnline.com (for anime fans), or VampireFreaks.com?

We're not quite sure what to make of the site Rotten Neighbor (www.rottenneighbor.com), which allows and encourages neighbors to leave anonymous posts about each other. The site was founded under the premise that realtors are not allowed to say whether a neighborhood is good, so neighbors do the reporting.

The site also purports to display the locations of known sex offenders. We put in the ZIP Code for the city we work in and the information was inaccurate. Remember that Kristyn's job is to track known sex offenders. The potential for people thinking someone will not harm their child because of the false security sites like these perpetuate is bothersome. The potential for someone to post something untrue about someone else is enormous.

What does all of this tell you? In addition to a lot of people using social networking sites such as MySpace and Facebook, there is a social networking site, a newsgroup, or a multiuser virtual website for any person with any interest or behavioral tendency. **There are infinite opportunities for deviant individuals to network and validate their odd behavior through chatting, blogging, and email.** Some of these sites may not be interactive but still provide a justification for the miscreants of society.

They Call It Love, We Call It Pedophilia

Take, for example, NAMBLA. NAMBLA stands for North American Man Boy Love Association. It is exactly what it sounds like—a group of men who want to justify having sex with underage male boys, even infants, calling it consensual and loving. They started in Boston in 1978 and had a newsletter. Thirty years later, they still exist and have an intricate website touting their pedophilic deviance. Years ago, investigators working on cases involving child sexual assaults had difficulty obtaining the NAMBLA newsletter because NAMBLA was almost a type of secret society. Today, anyone can jump on the computer and read about how NAMBLA insists upon the notion that it should be acceptable for men to be in a loving, physical relationship with boys, and that age of consent laws should be changed because the relationship is harmless since the child desires it as well. They hang their hat on the notion that a small child can consent to sex and often will make the first move on an older male. There is even a place on their website where you can join, donate, and become an active member. They are not the only one: www.boylinks.com, an Internet site promoting man-boy love, is similarly stomach turning. They are not difficult to access and are upfront with their messages. Of course, the phrase "child sexual assault" will not be found on their pages as a descriptor of what they are all about—but that is simply semantics. Child sexual assault is really what these groups are all about.

Suicide "Assistance" Sites—alt.suicide.holiday (ASH)

Just as disturbing is the number of sites where one can be guided by strangers on the best way to commit suicide. One site, called alt.suicide.holiday (ASH), has group discussions and guide files with instructions on the various methods one can use to take his or her life. ASH is a newsgroup that was set up in late 1989 allegedly to discuss why suicide rate increase around the holidays. The ASH FAQ spouts their philosophies and tries to justify the site's purpose; however, the FAQ clearly states, "The ash subculture does not encourage suicide, i.e., we do not persuade people to commit suicide. However we believe that people have a right to commit suicide and thus, in general, do not try to dissuade people from doing so." They claim that people have the right to choose. They purport to be a support group, but not in the conventional sense—more of a "support platform." The site states, "If you are seeking a forum aimed at supporting people not to commit suicide, or a forum with the purpose of eliminating suicidal feelings then ash is not for you." ASH claims to allow visitors to openly discuss feelings and ideas of suicide.

It is possible that the alt.suicide.holiday site may have been linked to numerous suicides. Julia Scheeres wrote a series for *Wired* in 2003 about cyber suicide, called "Suicide 101: Lessons Before Dying," an expose of sorts about ASH. She details how one of ASH's victims, a 24-year-old computer programmer from Ohio, posted a message asking for help on the best way to kill himself because he did not think he would be able to procure a gun. He was given a wide variety of suggestions, but ultimately purchased a shotgun at Wal-Mart and took his life. According to *Wired*, "No one [on the ASH site] asked him why he wanted to die or tried to change his mind."

ONLINE SUICIDE PACTS

In 2000, ASH was connected with a suicide pact involving a 20-year-old Norwegian man and a 17-year-old Austrian girl whose bodies were found off a 1,900-foot cliff in Norway. The male had posted an ad for a suicide partner on the site. A similar pact resulted in the deaths of a 42-year-old man who flew from Amsterdam in 2001 to meet with a 49-year-old woman in California who had posted on the site. The two shot themselves to death in a hotel room in Monterey. In 2002, a 17-year-old boy from Kansas posted his plans for his own suicide, and one ASH user actually spoke with the teen on the phone and "kept him company while he was taking his drug overdose." Other members wished him luck, while one offered a bet that the plan would not work. The question has been raised as to whether there is any culpability for members who goad and encourage someone to take their own life or act in a way that threatens someone else's life.

ONLINE SUICIDES

On January 12, 2003, Brandon Vedas broadcast his own death via the webcam in his bedroom in Phoenix, Arizona to an audience of "virtual" friends who urged him on, while his mother was in the next room doing a crossword puzzle with no idea her son was dying.

Vedas began his chat/webcam session in the #shroomery IRC channel by smoking marijuana and then consuming psilocybe mushrooms. He then reportedly consumed 8 mg. of Clonazepam and a bottle of Methadone. Vedas also consumed Propranolol, Vicodin, and Temazepam at some point during the session. While some of his audience expressed concerns about Vedas' behavior and others pleaded for him to stop or seek medical attention, they continued to watch Vedas go unconscious, with most not contacting the authorities for fear of an ensuing police investigation. According to chat logs, one user claimed to have called 911 and asked the group if he had done the right thing. Another user responded, "NO." Vedas had given his audience instructions if things were to go awry, including calling the police and giving them the license plate number of his car, which could easily be found in his driveway. Apparently that information was not passed on to authorities.

Vedas died as a result of a drug overdose, and his mother discovered his body later that afternoon. He was 21 years old. His family has set up a webpage in Brandon's memory at http://brandonvedas.com/.

MORE ONLINE SUICIDES

Kevin Whitrick, a 42-year-old British man, hung himself while visiting a chat room of 100 users, some of whom goaded him to complete the act. The chat room Whitrick logged into was an insult chat room where people trade insults back and forth at each other. This "cyber suicide" occurred in March of 2007. At that time, it was estimated that there had been 17 Internet-related suicides in the United Kingdom between 2001 and the time of Whitrick's death.

Where is the social conscience? What are the responsibilities of those in online communities when these types of incidences occur?

Never Say, "My Child Will Never..."

Many parents will say, "My child is not allowed to be on social networking sites or have a MySpace page," and they think that their children are actually obeying their rules. This naivetè is a huge issue. We have one word for the remedy—*awareness*. We also have the adage, "Never say, 'My child will never....'"

A lobbyist who works for a prominent social service agency in our state recently met a client for dinner. The conversation steered to MySpace, and the well-educated and in-the-know client made the comment that his 11-year-old son was not allowed to be on MySpace and that he did not have a MySpace page. The lobbyist whipped out her Blackberry and within minutes asked the client, "Is this your son?" Lo and behold, the client's 11-year-old had his own page under his own name.

> Parents are usually very surprised to see their children's social networking sites appear once they know how to access them.

Parents are usually very surprised to see their children's social networking sites appear once they know how to access them. We recommend you start by doing a school or location search and see who pops up.

For those who think this constitutes spying, we wish that they could hear the voices of parents whose children have disappeared, have been violated by online predators, or, as in the following story, have taken their own lives.

THE MEGAN MEIER STORY

The nation was recently stunned as the details of 13-year-old Megan Meier's death unfolded. Megan, a quiet child from Dardenne Prairie, Missouri, suffered from depression and Attention Deficit Disorder (see Figure 9.2). She thought she had made a new friend online via her

MySpace account when she began exchanging messages with a young man named "Josh," who claimed to have just moved from Florida into a nearby neighborhood. He told Megan he was homeschooled and didn't have a home phone number yet.

(© AP Photo/Tom Gannam)

FIGURE 9.2

Megan Meier

For a month, Megan and Josh corresponded and built their online friendship. On October 15, 2006, Megan received an email from Josh stating he didn't want to be friends anymore because he had learned that Megan wasn't nice to her friends. Megan's mother, who described Megan as "upbeat" prior to the incident, left the house to take another daughter to an orthodontist appointment. Megan called her mother saying messages were being posted about her online saying, "Megan Meier is a slut. Megan Meier is fat."

A few hours later, Megan hung herself in her bedroom. She died the next day.

It wasn't until several weeks later that more details about "Josh" emerged. The account was allegedly created by the mother of another child in the neighborhood, along with the assistance of an 18-year-old man. The mother claimed that she allowed the site to be created because she wanted to "monitor" what Megan was saying about her child.

Woman Charged

On May 15, 2008, the 49-year-old mother of the other child was indicted on federal charges for fraudulently using an account on MySpace. The exact charges were one count of conspiracy and three counts of accessing protected computers without authorization to obtain information to inflict emotional distress. The indictment alleges that the mother violated MySpace's terms of use prohibiting users from using fraudulent registration information and harassing other members. She faces up to 20 years in prison.

This is an extremely rare occurrence of applying an End User License Agreement, or EULA (that check box that pops up whenever you download software or take out an online account), but prosecutors felt the outcome warranted it. Typically, this is only applied to hackers who access accounts and infiltrate them. The case is being tried in California, home of MySpace, not Missouri, Megan Meier's home state, because there is no such law on the books in Missouri. This will be an interesting case to follow.

Make a Difference for Kids: The Rachel Neblett Story

In that same year, Rachel Neblett, a 17-year-old from Kentucky, committed suicide after being cyber bullied on the Internet. Her father, Mark Neblett, worked to push legislation through the Kentucky General Assembly for an anti-bullying bill. It did not pass. Why? According to one news report, "Many feel the reason the bill died in the Republican Senate is because some felt it would protect gay children." (Source: WAVE 3 TV, Louisville, Kentucky, February 5, 2008.)

The bill is being revisited this year. In the meantime, Mark Neblett, along with his sister, have founded a website at www.makeadifferenceforkids.org to promote awareness and prevention of cyber bullying and suicide.

Online Murder Plots

In September of 2006, a murder conspiracy was foiled by authorities when a 22-year-old Arizona woman attempted to hire a hit man to kill another woman. The jealous, homicide-seeking woman found photos of another woman on her boyfriend's MySpace page, and offered $1,000 to have the other woman killed. She provided a photo of the target, home and work addresses, as well as instructions for the woman to be shot in the head and for the hit man to provide a postmortem photo as proof of the done deed. Upon making a $400 down payment to an undercover officer in the parking lot of a grocery store, the jilted woman was arrested for conspiracy to commit murder.

THE ART OF MURDER: THE TAYLOR BEHL STORY

On September 5, 2005, 17-year-old college freshman Taylor Behl left her dorm room at the Commonwealth University in Virginia around 10 p.m. with her car keys, her cell phone, and about $40. Behl never returned, and on September 7, 2005, she was reported missing. Eleven days after her disappearance, an AMBER Alert was issued for her and the case became a criminal investigation.

On September 17, 2005, Taylor's car was located 2 miles from her dormitory. Taylor's Virginia license plates had been replaced with Ohio license plates that had been stolen 2 months prior.

LIVEJOURNAL BECOMES DEATHJOURNAL

During the investigation, it was discovered that Behl had a LiveJournal account. LiveJournal is a free online blog service. Behl's screen name, "tiabliaj," was *jailbait* spelled backwards. Behl had been involved in a relationship with a 38-year-old photographer she met online by the name of Ben Fawley. From Behl's journal entries, the relationship appeared to be romantic in nature. Fawley wrote under the screen name "skultz67." It appears that the two became involved in April of 2005.

Fawley was questioned by the police and told them he had last seen Behl earlier in the evening on September 5th when she had gone to his apartment and had borrowed a skateboard. In an odd twist, Fawley reported that on the morning of September 6th, he had been abducted and robbed and then dumped off on a dirt road. He alleged that an old girlfriend was behind the robbery.

Suspicions were immediately raised. Police began looking into Fawley and found that he maintained several websites where his photographs were posted. His photographs contained images of death and decay, skeletons, and young women in erotic poses.

On one of his sites, he had a model named "Taylor." He had several online journals, including one at www.deviantart.com. He referred to himself on one of the sites as an "ex-con." There were a number of entries on his sites from former girlfriends, some of whom described Fawley as having a "dark side."

On September 19, 2005, Fawley posted that he "must do the laundry...and the sheets!!!!!!!!!" on his www.deviantart.com site. Investigators executed a search warrant on his residence, and among the evidence taken was a sample from Fawley's box spring mattress that had a reddish-brown stain consistent with blood.

Eighteen days after her disappearance, at 11:23 a.m. on September 23, a comment was left on Taylor Behl's LiveJournal blog essentially stating that she had not been found because she did not want to be found. Investigators do not know who left the posting.

Unrelated to Behl's disappearance was Fawley's arrest on September 23 on 16 counts of child pornography.

A computer was also seized during the search warrant. Detectives spent some time reviewing sites with Fawley's photographs of "urban decay," deserted or rundown places, which Fawley seemed so fascinated by. Several locations were pinpointed as requiring closer examination. One of the locales was a dilapidated farm, which a former girlfriend of Fawley's identified for investigators. On October 5th, exactly 1 month to the day after Taylor Behl disappeared, her badly decomposed remains were discovered behind the barn.

In January 2006, Fawley was indicted for premeditated murder, abduction, and rape. In February, the indictment was amended to offer the alternative rationale that Fawley murdered Behl "while committing another felony, such as rape, sodomy, or abduction." As a result, the indictment was changed to second-degree murder. In August of 2006, Fawley accepted a plea for second-degree murder, which is not an admission of guilt, but rather a legal maneuver that concedes the state had enough evidence to convict him on the murder of Taylor Behl. Fawley maintained that he accidentally strangled Behl during rough, consensual sex. Although Behl's death was ruled a homicide, the body was so badly decomposed that the autopsy could not determine an exact cause of death.

Taylor Behl's LiveJournal is still accessible today. The URL is http://www.livejournal.com/users/tiabliaj/.

Blogging About Cannibalism

WARNING

The following section contains graphic material.

In April of 2008, a judge approved the death penalty as a sentence for the horrific 2006 murder of a 10-year-old girl that was planned and carried out by Kevin Ray Underwood of Oklahoma. The 26-year-old's blog, "Strange Things Are Afoot at the Circle K," included the question, "If you were a cannibal, what would you wear to dinner?" As time progressed, Underwood openly wrote, "My fantasies are getting weirder and weirder," and later, "...dangerously weird. If people knew the kinds of things I think about anymore, I'd probably be locked away." The victim, who lived near Underwood, was located in Underwood's apartment in a plastic container in his bedroom. The child had been asphyxiated by duct tape and beaten about the head. There were deep cuts in her neck where Underwood allegedly attempted to decapitate her.

In Underwood's apartment, investigators located meat tenderizer and barbeque skewers, items Underwood intended to use on the child's remains. During a press conference, the Police Chief went into very graphic detail about Underwood's plans with the body, including raping the body and cannibalism. Underwood's blogs can still be found online.

Common Interest Guaranteed

Any individual with a bizarre fetish or deviant behavioral tendency can find justification and validation on the Internet—one can remain virtually anonymous, never leave home, and still connect with a potential pool of hundreds of millions of people across the globe. This not only pertains to websites and newsgroups—even Yahoo! and AOL Instant Messenger allow one to go into chat rooms with a wide variety of interests and fetishes. With that many people connecting through cyberspace, success in finding someone who shares a deviant interest is guaranteed.

Any individual with a bizarre fetish or deviant behavioral tendency can find justification and validation on the Internet.

Words Can Never Hurt Me?

Many law-enforcement agencies realize the value in watching social networking sites. We've had juveniles who claim never to have tried illicit drugs post pictures of themselves smoking pot on their social networking account. These sites have become valuable tools in the course of investigations. Social networking pages are often printed out and reproduced in court. As the old saying goes, "A picture is worth a thousand words." Going one step further, our Juvenile Court judges are even ordering juveniles to stay off of social networking sites, regardless of what the original juvenile charge was that brought them into court.

Above and beyond law enforcement's use of social networking sites, it should be noted that many potential employers are now combing social networking sites to see if candidates have a presence. What they say today could come back to haunt them tomorrow, or 5 years from now.

Internet Safety Guidelines

The Federal Trade Commission has some important safety tips to follow when visiting social networking sites. (For more information, visit http://www.ftc.gov/bcp/edu/pubs/consumer/tech/tec14.shtm.)

- **Think about how different sites work before deciding to join a site.** Some sites will allow only a defined community of users to access posted content; others allow anyone and everyone to view postings.

- **Think about keeping some control over the information you post.** Consider restricting access to your page to a select group of people—for example, your friends from school, your club, your team, your community groups, or your family.

- **Keep your information to yourself.** Don't post your full name, social security number, address, phone number, or bank and credit card account numbers—and don't post other people's information, either.

- **Be cautious about posting information that could be used to identify you or locate you offline.** This could include the name of your school, sports team, clubs, and where you work or hang out.

- **Make sure your screen name doesn't say too much about you.** Don't use your name, your age, or your hometown. Even if you think your screen name makes you anonymous, it doesn't take a genius to combine clues to figure out who you are and where you can be found.

- **Post only information you are comfortable with others seeing— and knowing—about you.** Many people can see your page, including your parents, your teachers, the police, the college you might want to apply to next year, or the job you might want to apply for in 5 years.

- **Remember that once you post information online, you can't take it back.** Even if you delete the information from a site, older versions exist on other people's computers.

- **Consider not posting your photo.** It can be altered and broadcast in ways you may not be happy about. If you do post a picture, ask yourself whether it's one your mom would display in the living room.

- **Flirting with strangers online could have serious consequences.** Because some people lie about who they really are, you never really know who you're dealing with.

- **Be wary if a new online friend wants to meet you in person.** Before you decide to meet someone, do your research: Ask whether any of your friends know the person, and see what background you can dig up through online search engines. If you decide to meet this person, be smart about it: Meet in a public place, during the day, with friends you trust. Tell an adult or a responsible sibling where you're going, and when you expect to be back.

- **Trust your gut if you have suspicions.** If you feel threatened by someone or are uncomfortable because of something online, tell an adult you trust and report it to the police and the social networking site. You could end up preventing someone else from becoming a victim.

10

Sexual Deviance Online (Child Sex Rings, Prostitution, Sexual Victimization, and Other Bizarre Stories)

The Internet has opened up a whole new marketing opportunity for the "working girl," "lady of the evening," or "call girl." The trade actually uses the title "sex trade worker," a gender-neutral term that almost appears at first glance as benign as "construction worker" or "landscaper." Despite being illegal, the prostitution trade still flourishes, not only under the guise of a high-class escort service or on a drug-infested street corner, but hidden among the online personal ads of Craigslist and eBay, as well as more openly on sites such as SeekingArrangement.com, "The Premier Dating Website for Sugar Daddies, Mommies, & Babies." The description of what a Sugar Daddy or Mommy might want is rather obvious. Here's how the website describes it:

> Rich and successful. Single or married, you have no time for games. You are looking to mentor or spoil someone special—perhaps a "personal secretary"? Secret Lover? Student? Or a mistress for an extramarital affair?

Equally obvious is the Sugar Babe description:

> Attractive, ambitious, & young. Sugar Babes are college students, aspiring actresses, or someone just starting out. You seek a generous Benefactor to pamper, mentor, and take care of you—perhaps to help you financially?

We're not saying outright that this is a prostitution site, but any site that claims to promote "mutually beneficial relationships...perhaps to help you financially" doesn't leave much to the imagination. In its description of an "arrangement," the site explains, "Such a relationship is usually between an older and wealthy individual who gives a young person expensive gifts or financial assistance in return for friendship, or intimacy."

The Sugar Baby can look at profiles of potential benefactors and pick out a gentleman worth between $750,000 to $1,000,000 with a profile name such as "Daddy Big Bucks." The Sugar Baby posts profiles listing what he or she expects as a monthly income from a potential Sugar Mommy or Daddy, as well as what he or she can be expected to do for the benefactor of choice. By the way, if you can't find what you're looking for there, the site recommends you visit its "sister" sites: SeekingMillionaire.com and SeekingFantasy.com.

Interestingly enough, these types of "mutually beneficial relationships" can be found on Craigslist as well, with young men and women looking for someone to generously provide for them in exchange for a no-strings-attached relationship that includes sex. Whether it is a Sugar Daddy with a Sugar Baby, or male escort or call girl, the common denominator here is that the transaction includes money for sex.

The Darker Side of the Online Sex Trade

WARNING

The following section contains sexually explicit material.

The Internet connects people with common interests and allows the deviants and miscreants of society to anonymously find others of their perversion with whom to communicate and even form their own social groups. This is certainly no different for an individual with special sexual interests. Whether it is the W4M (woman seeking man), M4M (man seeking man), ww4mm (two women looking to party with a couple of guys), or the bi-m4wm (bisexual man looking for a bisexual couple), the Internet provides a wide array of possibilities. Perusing Craigslist in the personal section for casual or erotic relationships, one can easily locate ads that are actually soliciting sex in exchange for money, whether it be the "John" seeking a quick rendezvous while in town or the paid "sex worker" looking for a quick income.

For instance, you might come across something like this:

Waz up? My name is Amber and I'll be visiting Philadelphia for two days. I am 21 years old, 5'4" tall, 120 lbs, and 31C-24-29 with black hair, blue eyes, and a tight ass. I love candy, especially lollipops, and for the right man and lots of roses, I would even travel to Greece and GFE. Maybe BBBJ and CIM, definitely DATY!

Perusing Craigslist in the personal section for casual or erotic relationships, one can easily locate ads that are actually soliciting sex in exchange for money, whether it be the "John" seeking a quick rendezvous while in town or the paid "sex worker" looking for a quick income.

Let's translate. Amber is a call girl, looking for some clients in Philadelphia for the next two days. She is advertising that she will perform oral sex ("lollipop") without a condom ("BBBJ," or "bareback blow job"), allow the client to perform oral sex on her ("DATY," or "dining at the Y") and even allow the client to ejaculate in her mouth ("CIM"). She will provide the "girlfriend experience" ("GFE") and engage in anal sex ("trip to Greece") for the right amount of cash ("roses"). An email or call to Amber will confirm her availability, exactly how many "roses" it will cost, and if she will do in-call or out-call (whether she will go to you or you to her). For clarification, while some like the girlfriend experience (GFE), others prefer "PSE" or the "porn star experience" with a sexually aggressive escort.

You might also see the guy posting in the same personals section of Craigslist seeking part-time office help between 2 p.m. and 5 p.m. a couple of days a week for the girl who has wanted to act out fantasies with her boss. This "boss" suggests that "excellent oral skills would be helpful" and that the job offers $500 per week as a "cash bonus for someone really open-minded." Connecting the dots should be relatively simple here.

Our personal favorite is the following:

> *Exhibitionist. Cross-dresser. Available to entertain you and your girl-friends...retired...you lead me to the bathroom where you have my outfit laid out...wig/makeup or hood me...slave...bondage, CBT...gentleman...clean shaven, hung, D/D free...treat yourself.*

This was from an actual posting in February of 2008 from a "gentleman" who titled his ad "Submissive TV for you and your girlfriends-m4ww." This is a TV (or transvestite) who is into dressing up and being dominated and who is drug and disease free (D/D). Initially we were at a loss for what CBT stood for; however, with the help of Internet search engines, we were easily able to find that this older man is into "c*ck and ball torture." Ouch.

Craigslist ads run daily, so there is never a lack of opportunities from which to choose, at all hours of the day and night. If an ad is reported as violating terms or being offensive, Craigslist will flag and remove it. However, there are so many ads that they are difficult to police. Within minutes, plenty more will take the place of the offensive one just removed. Despite the creative play on words and cutesy descriptors, these ads are exactly what they appear to be—online sex solicitations in exchange for money.

A quick search of the other auction sites, such as eBay, Yahoo!, Amazon, and even Priceline.com, reveal ads for "escort services," some of which are in fact legitimate. However, we know from experience that this is a new venue for male and female sex trade workers to auction their services. In fact, they do actually auction themselves, just like someone would put up for bid a football autographed by an NFL star.

The Emperor's Club

In March of 2008, federal authorities arrested four subjects involved with a prostitution ring that had 50 prostitutes available to travel to cities all over the country, as well as London and Paris, for prices between $1,000 and $5,000 an hour. An unsealed federal affidavit revealed the online prostitution ring to be known as the "Emperor's Club." The business had an application process for the prostitutes as well as booking agents for appointments with clients. The website provided a scale to rate the women, from one to seven "diamonds." The women rating seven diamonds were considered to be the "cream of the crop" and commanded up to $3,000 per hour. An "escort" could be arranged through the agency or chosen directly through the website, with the more elite clients shelling out $5,500 an hour for the coveted "Icon Club" package. The FBI, as well as the Internal Revenue Service, investigated the Emperor's Club. Charges filed included prostitution, conspiracy to violate federal prostitution laws, and money laundering.

SUPALOVER666

In March of 2008, Mark Bedford, a 23-year-old computer science student from Canada, pled guilty to multiple extortion and child pornography charges. Bedford used several screen names, including "supalover666" and "ratemybody." He used several online personas, including that of a 15-year-old female he called "Samantha." He fooled dozens of young girls into performing sexual acts in front of their webcams. In one case, he blackmailed two girls, aged 11 and 13, into performing oral sex on one another, and even made a 12-year-old simulate sexual acts with the family dog.

According to court documents, "In some instances, the chat material discloses a very desperate young female pleading with Mr. Bedford to simply leave her alone or asking him frantically why he is doing this to her. Mr. Bedford cultivated the fear of exposure to parents and friends. He manipulated the young women to either demonstrate his control over them or to exploit them...in order to satisfy his own sexual needs."

Bedford was cunning and used his knowledge of computers to post a series of questions that often elicited vital information—questions such as, What's your favorite color? What bands do you like? Do you have a pet? What's its name? The answers the young women provided often gave Bedford enough information to figure out their online account passwords. With that cyber door unlocked, he would take over the account, change the password to prevent the real owner from getting back in, and then pose as the victim to the hundreds of friends she had online.

Some of Bedford's victims testified in court that they "trust no one" and have attempted suicide. Police identified 63 of Bedford's victims from Canada and Britain. Ontario court judge Judy Beaman called the number of victims "unprecedented." Bedford was sentenced to 23 years in prison.

The Innocence Lost Initiative

In December of 2005, the U.S. Department of Justice announced the results of the Innocence Lost Initiative, a 5-day nationwide sweep targeting criminals involved in trafficking children for prostitution in the United States. The stings, dubbed "Operation Cross Country," spanned 16 cities and resulted in the arrest of 389 people and the recovery of 21 children.

The program was initially launched in 2003 as a joint effort between the FBI, the Department of Justice's Child Exploitation and Obscurity Section (CEOS), and the National Center for Missing & Exploited Children (NCMEC).

Five years later, Innocence Lost ended. More than 400 child victims were rescued and more than 300 individuals were convicted of exploiting children through prostitution. Investigations uncovered schemes that ran the gamut—from prostituting children at truck stops to promoting their services on the Internet.

The initiative pinpointed 14 areas nationwide that had been determined to have a high incidence of child prostitution. Task forces consisting of state, local, and federal agencies were formed in the affected states to investigate the cases.

Among the highlighted cases were the following:

- In Kansas, Don L. Elbert, III, forced three underage sisters—two of whom were 14-year-old twins—into prostitution. He was captured and pled guilty to child sex trafficking in May of 2007. In January, he was sentenced to 8 years in prison.

- In Detroit, Keith Goodwin was sentenced in October of 2007 to 97 months in prison for the production of child pornography. During a search of his residence, three child victims of prostitution were recovered.

- In Atlantic City, a former U.S. Postal Service employee was sentenced in March of 2008 to 23 years in prison for operating a criminal enterprise involving 35–40 females whom he forced into prostitution. His youngest victim was 14 years old.

Mayor Blames Craigslist for Child Prostitution

In August of 2007, Atlanta mayor Shirley Franklin told the *Atlanta Journal Constitution* that Craigslist could do more to prevent being used "as a means of promoting and enabling child prostitution," and she suggested that Craigslist revamp its warnings on erotic services to remove any postings offering sexual services. An Atlanta vice investigator even went as far as to estimate that websites such as Craigslist account for 85% of the arrangements made by men for sexual contact with boys and girls.

An article published in CNN.com in June of 2008 focused on child prostitutes selling services on Craigslist. Investigators in

An Atlanta vice investigator estimated that websites such as Craigslist account for 85% of the arrangements made by men for sexual contact with boys and girls.

Sacramento, California identified 70 girls under the age of 18 who had been offering their services online. This investigation was also part of the FBI's Innocence Lost Initiative.

Teenagers seeking to prostitute themselves post ads on Craigslist's Erotic Services section because it is easy, free, and allows them to place many ads per day.

In July of 2008, two men were arrested in Salt Lake City, Utah for forcing a 16-year-old girl into a hotel room and placing an ad on Craigslist for her services. The two allegedly threatened to harm her family so that she would not quit working for them.

In the CNN.com special report on Craigslist and child prostitution, Craigslist CEO Jim Buckmaster was quoted as saying that the problem would be harder to track if the erotic services category were to be removed, claiming that leaving in this category "makes it all the more easy to track illicit activity; if it's all centralized, you can spot the illegal stuff more easily." Buckmaster did point out that Craigslist does voluntarily work with authorities in helping to track sexual crimes.

THE JUSTIN BERRY STORY

Justin Berry was only 13-years-old when he got his first webcam. Soon after he installed it, the self-proclaimed "shy" young man was immediately befriended online by a number of men from around the country, some of whom "groomed" him with compliments and friendship. The friendships quickly turned to requests that he "take off his shirt," an act for which he would be paid. The acts Berry was asked to perform in front of his bedroom webcam quickly became sexual in exchange for money and gifts.

Within a short time, Berry, a computer geek, began to design and maintain websites where he stripped and performed various sexual acts in exchange for money. These types of underage shows are referred to as "bibcams." Berry encouraged others to take part as well. At the age of 16, Berry left home to be reunited with his estranged father in Mexico. According to Berry, he finally confessed his business to his father. His father's response was that he would assist Berry in growing the business by reestablishing it in Mexico, where prostitutes were plentiful.

Berry's business transactions were intricate. He initially used PayPal (until PayPal stopped servicing adult-oriented websites) and later used credit card merchant accounts. Berry offered subscriptions and webcammed his sexual activities with both male and female prostitutes for payment. Berry became involved with individuals who not only promoted his online activities, but who flew him to Las Vegas so that they could molest him in person.

In 2005, *New York Times* reporter Kurt Eichenwald came across Berry's business and contacted Berry to do a story. Eichenwald researched Berry and the business, and in December of 2005 the *New York Times* published his article, "Through His Webcam, a Boy Joins a Sordid Online World."

Just prior to the article's publication, Berry was granted immunity in 2005 in exchange for his cooperation in prosecuting other individuals who were involved with his sites. Despite numerous death threats, Berry testified before Congress and appeared on several talk shows, including *The Today Show* and *The Oprah Winfrey Show*. He currently works as a paid speaker in the areas of education and safety on the Internet, self-esteem, and alcohol and drug abuse by sharing his experiences as an online child prostitute.

A Nationwide Epidemic—293,000 Children at Risk

In regard to child prostitution, the U.S. Department of Justice's Child Exploitation and Obscenity Section (CEOS) notes that not only does the United States "face an influx of international victims of sex trafficking," but also that the United States "has its own homegrown problem of inter-state trafficking of minors." It is estimated that 293,000 children in the United States are "at risk of becoming victims of commercial sexual exploitation." Many are at risk due to abusive family lives. Some are run-aways or throwaway children, and are susceptible to becoming prostitutes for their own financial support through either forced abduction or their families making arrangements with traffickers. According to CEOS, the numbers of kids living on the streets who find themselves in commercial sex activity is staggering, with an estimated "55% of street girls engage[d] in formal prostitution."

Child prostitution is organized with pimps and involves children in massage services, private dancing, escort services, sporting and recreational events, drinking clubs, conventions, and tourist destinations. CEOS estimates that 20% of these

> It is estimated that 293,000 children in the United States are "at risk of becoming victims of commercial sexual exploitation."

children become a part of organized crime networks and are transported throughout the country via various modes of transportation and assigned fake identification. According to CEOS, an estimated 800,000 to 900,000 human beings are trafficked across the U.S. borders each year for the sex trade, with some of its victims as young as 5 years old. (Source: http://www.usdoj.gov/criminal/ceos.)

Children are essentially sold into sex slavery every day, not just in the U.S., but around the globe. This suggests the sick demand for such a trade. It is not difficult to find men trolling chat rooms and message boards looking for children for sale, sometimes even for sale by their own parents. There are chat rooms in some of the more popular instant messaging sites that are commonly known for certain sexual deviance—whether it be a foot fetish or adults looking to hook up with another parent's kids. As part of an investigation, an agency came across a man whose online profile actually stated that his interests included "incest, moms that share, and young children." Numerous investigations have resulted in men traveling to meet who they thought was a mother interested in providing her children for sexual activity, only to be arrested by the undercover cop waiting for them at the prearranged destination.

Internet Sex and Robbery: "Operation FALCON"

In June of 2008, U.S. Marshals Service Southeast Regional Fugitive Task Force rounded up 1,250 fugitive criminal suspects as part of Operation FALCON (Federal and Local Cops Organized Nationally). One of the arrestees was a 24-year-old suspect that federal and local police had been searching for in Metro Atlanta, who had been using the Internet to search for gay men in chat rooms in order to meet them, have sex with them in their homes, and then rob them at gunpoint. He would gain their trust and convince them to let him come into their homes. He would leave after the first encounter. Then, upon returning a second time, he would bring an accomplice and rob the victims. During one of his crimes, he bound the victims with duct tape and allegedly stole $62,000 from the residence. This is one of many crimes of this type that have received national attention.

Operation FALCON, which focuses on violent felons and sex offenders, has taken more than 36,500 fugitives into custody nationwide since its inception in 2005.

Child Sex Rings: The Darkest Side of the Internet

The concept of prostituting a child is unfathomable to the law-abiding citizen, and yet, it is an evil reality in the darkest corners of the Internet. As we were writing this book, the following story was just unfolding. As parents and members of law enforcement, we followed every detail with baited breath and prayed for a positive outcome.

BROOKE BENNETT GOES MISSING

On June 25, 2008, 12-year-old Brooke Bennett, of Braintree, Vermont, was reported missing, last seen after her uncle, Michael Jacques, a registered sex offender, dropped her off at a convenience store around 9 a.m. The video of the two departing and going separate ways was captured by the store's closed-circuit cameras. Jacques was immediately questioned by police and informed them that Brooke had told him she was meeting a friend to go visit another sick friend at a nearby hospital. With the cooperation of all media, an AMBER Alert was issued for Brooke. Her picture, as well as the video showing her and her uncle walking in opposite directions out the convenience store, was widely distributed throughout the New England area.

Upon further questioning, Jacques informed the authorities that he required his own children and his niece to provide him with passwords to their MySpace accounts for the purpose of parental supervision. He went so far as to log on to Brooke's MySpace account and showed police what appeared to be message from Brooke to a man she was planning to rendezvous with. Forensic examiners and investigators from the Vermont State Police, as well as a member of the Internet Crimes Against Children (ICAC) Task Force, examined the laptop and determined that the message supposedly posted by Brooke was actually posted from Jacques' laptop. It was believed that the posting was created by Jacques to make it appear as though Brooke had been abducted by someone she had met on the Internet.

The investigation revealed that the posting was originally made on June 24th. However, it was edited on two occasions, one of which was on June 25th, more than an hour and a half after Brooke was last seen. During the last edit of the posting, the time was manually changed to make it appear as though the message had been posted earlier in the day. Records from MySpace revealed that there were two logins to Brooke's MySpace account after Jacques' last access and after Brooke's disappearance. These were made from an IP address in San Antonio, Texas, with the time on both of these manually changed as well. This IP address was quickly traced back to the address where Brooke Bennett's stepfather, Raymond Gagnon, rented a room.

SEX RINGS AND TRAGEDY

The police spoke at length to a 14-year-old female friend of Brooke's who gave conflicting stories. When she was confronted, the tragic and gruesome reality of what really happened was finally revealed. The 14-year-old had assisted Michael Jacques by getting Brooke to Jacques's residence after they had visited the convenience store. This was part of a plan to initiate Brooke into an underage sex ring. The female juvenile reported that she herself had been sexually involved with Jacques since she was 9 years old after finding a note under her pillow that she had been chosen for a program for sex called "Breckinridge." Her "trainer" for the program was Jacques, and messages were sent to the child as instructions for the sexual acts she was to perform with Jacques, with the goal of having her reach a standard of proficiency for the "Breckinridge" program. She disclosed having been forced to perform sexual acts on Brooke's stepfather, Raymond Gagnon, in 2007, as well. The juvenile misled Brooke, knowing that she was to be initiated that day into the "Breckinridge" sex program by Jacques.

According to police affidavits, the 14-year-old female watched television with Brooke until Jacques took Brooke upstairs. She never saw Brooke again. Jacques directed the female juvenile to leave and to lie to police if asked about Brooke's whereabouts.

During his interview, Gagnon admitted to accessing Brooke's MySpace page, collecting child pornography, and possessing images of children as young as 5 years old, as well as photos Jacques had e-mailed to him of the 14-year-old having sex with her boyfriend.

Divers searched a lake near an area where clothes belonging to Brooke were found. Many search warrants were executed in the hope of finding Brooke alive. Tragically, this investigation had a heartbreaking end when Brooke's body was found at 4:45 p.m. on July 2, 2008, near her uncle's home. At this time, her uncle and stepfather remain in custody on federal charges.

The AMBER Alert

In 1996, 9-year-old Amber Hagerman was abducted and murdered in Arlington, Texas. She had been riding her bike near a closed Winn-Dixie store when a man pulled her from her bike and threw her into the front seat of his pickup truck. A neighbor heard the little girl scream and witnessed the abduction. Amber's brother Ricky saw it also. The community rallied in search of the little girl; however, 4 days after she went missing, Amber's body was found near a drainage ditch. Amber's parents, Donna and Richard Hagerman, started PASO (People Against Sex Offenders), a grassroots effort to push for stronger laws, and also drafted the Amber Hagerman Child Protection Act. From this, came the idea of the AMBER Alert.

AMBER stands for "America's Missing: Broadcasting Emergency Response." This emergency notification system goes out to the general public by various media outlets in the U.S. and Canada. An AMBER Alert can be issued by law enforcement when they confirm that a child has been abducted. The media sources involved include commercial radio stations, satellite radio, television stations, cable television (through the Emergency Alert Broadcast System), electronic traffic condition signs, emails, and wireless device SMS text messages. Even lottery terminals are used in some states. The AMBER Alert program is a voluntary partnership between law enforcement, broadcasters, transportation agencies, and the wireless industry because time is of the essence whenever a child is abducted.

The Child Alert Foundation created the first automated implementation of the AMBER Alert in 1998, along with the fully automated Alert Notification System to immediately inform the public. In 2002, the National Center for Missing and Exploited Children began promoting the AMBER Alert and the distribution of alerts through media outlets.

The criteria for an AMBER Alert is issued by the U.S. Department of Justice, with specific guidelines for states to follow:

- Law enforcement must confirm that an abduction has taken place.
- The child must be at risk of serious injury or death.
- There must be sufficient descriptive information of the child, the captor, or the captor's vehicle to issue an alert.
- The child must be 17-years-old or younger.

Despite the criteria of the child being at risk of serious injury or death, many law-enforcement agencies are foregoing that and issuing AMBER Alerts in cases of parental abduction.

Sadly, the kidnapping and murder of Amber Hagerman remains unsolved.

AN AMBER ALERT WITH A HAPPIER ENDING

In late June of 2008, a Texas woman went on a crack-smoking and shoplifting spree with a man she had only met a few days earlier. The man, a 55-year-old parolee who had an open warrant for a parole violation, was left to care for the woman's 1-year-old son while the woman went into a nearby Wal-Mart to shoplift. She left the man and the baby in his van in the parking lot.

While in the store, the woman was arrested for shoplifting. She asked Richardson to take the baby to her parents' home; however, when the child did not arrive there, the worried grandparents reported the child missing. An AMBER Alert was issued for the missing baby on June 29, 2008.

At approximately 2:15 p.m. on June 30, 2008, a man bearing resemblance to the paroled man, dropped the child off with a Wal-Mart employee. The child had a note pinned to his shirt identifying him as the missing baby, and he had not been hurt. The man was later arrested in northwest Houston. The AMBER Alert may have been pivotal in the safe return of the child, as the suspect would have wanted to avoid being connected to the child as well as drawing public attention to himself. Regardless of whether the public spots the missing child or the child is anonymously returned, the AMBER Alert can be key in reuniting a child with a loving family.

ANOTHER AMBER ALERT SUCCESS STORY

In 2002, two teenaged girls from California, who were abducted at gunpoint, were rescued 12 hours later, from what would have most certainly been a tragic abduction, because of the AMBER Alert.

Sixteen-year-old Tamara Brooks and 17-year-old Jacqueline Marris were abducted at gunpoint by Roy Ratliff, 37, when the two teens were parked with their boyfriends in separate cars at a local teenage hangout. Ratliff, who was wanted by police for rape charges at the time of the abduction, forced the girls out of the vehicles at gunpoint, bound their dates, and tied them up, and drove off with both girls in one of the boyfriend's cars. An AMBER Alert was immediately issued for the girls, including the vehicle description. Twelve hours later, the vehicle was spotted 100 miles away and police gave chase. The girls were in the vehicle at the time. Ratliff crashed the vehicle and attempted to get away, but police caught up with him. Ratliff refused to surrender and was subsequently shot to death by the sheriff's deputies.

Both of the girls' fathers expressed their joy at hearing the news their daughters were safe. "My little child, Jackie, I can't wait to see her. I love her so much. If you're watching this, honey, I love you. I can't wait for you to get home," said Jacqueline's father, Herb Marris.

Tamara's father, Sammie Brooks, told reporters, "I couldn't be a happier man right now and hope none of you has to go through something like this."

This was California's first AMBER Alert.

THE ELIZABETH SMART STORY

As Internet-based abductions and organized child-sex gangs proliferate, we can't emphasize enough the need for programs like the AMBER Alert. Who can forget the story of Elizabeth Smart, a then-14-year-old teenager from Salt Lake City, Utah, who was abducted from her bedroom in the middle of the night on June 5, 2002? Elizabeth was held hostage for 9 months by Brian David Mitchell and Wanda Ileen Barzee until someone recognized her from an AMBER Alert poster and notified authorities. She was located about 18 miles from her home. Mitchell and Barzee were both found incompetent to stand trial.

Over 2,000 volunteers a day searched for Elizabeth immediately following her abduction. Elizabeth's younger sister, Mary Katherine, who was just 9 years old at the time of the abduction and who witnessed it because the two sisters shared a bedroom, eventually recognized Mitchell's voice the night he told Elizabeth, "You better be quiet and I won't hurt you." She identified him as a homeless man whom the Smart family had hired for just 5 hours to rake leaves. He went by the name of "Emmanuel." Elizabeth, who was disguised with a red wig, sunglasses, and veil, was spotted by an elderly couple who had seen Mitchell's description on the show *America's Most Wanted*, which often highlights AMBER Alert cases. Once taken into police custody, Elizabeth was immediately identified and reunited with her family.

How You Can Help—Please Join In

In 2006, 42 AMBER Alerts were issued for missing children. All 42 were safely recovered. This program works, but it works like it's supposed to when the word can get out. What most people don't realize is that they can receive AMBER Alerts via their cell phones. Almost every carrier has volunteered to issue AMBER Alerts via cell phones, but so far only 400,000 people have subscribed to the free service—mostly because they are not aware they can receive this service. You can help by going to https://www.wirelessamberalerts.org and adding your 10-digit cell phone to the AMBER Alert system. Every set of eyes, every added person looking, will bring these kids home safely. Please consider signing up for wireless AMBER Alerts. They don't happen often, but when they do, time is critical.

More information and active AMBER Alerts can be found at the National Center for Missing & Exploited Children (pronounced *nek-mek*) at www.missingkids.com. For more information on the AMBER Alert program, please visit www.amberalert.gov.

Cellular Porn: The Uglier Side of Cell Phones

Millions of people have cell phones these days. Walk into any crowded area and you're bound to see people finalizing business deals, text-messaging their friends, downloading tunes, chatting with their loved ones, and even surfing the Internet.

But there's another side to cell phones just beginning to emerge in the U.S. that gives us pause—the world of cellular pornography. Yes, the ability to download pornography in between phone calls!

Just to put this burgeoning industry into perspective, consider that the "Mobile Adult Content Conference" was held in Miami in January of 2008. The focus of the entire conference was on enhancing opportunities to expand the adult pornography industry to cell phones and other mobile devices. The adult pornography phone trend is seen as a way for the industry to survive in an age where free online porn sites have taken a chunk out of the profits from DVDs, videotapes, and pay-per-view or subscription websites.

More advanced cell phones with better web browsers that offer higher quality images, combined with phone companies potentially loosening control on their networks, make cell phone pornography a viable business opportunity for the adult porn industry. Other video-based industries recognize this trend. For example, YouTube.com, the video-sharing site, has plans to expand to approximately 100 million advanced cell phones. How far this goes and how quickly this may occur is yet to be seen.

Cell phone pornography in Europe was a $775-million industry in 2007, with expectations that it could grow into a $1.5-billion industry by 2012, as compared to it being only a $26-million industry in North America. New phones with better graphics and advanced web browsers, such as Apple's iPhone (with a sales projection of 10 million units by the end of

2008), may encourage carriers to open their networks for additional revenue. This may be the catalyst for the development of "mobile porn." Some carriers are already talking about providing web filters for the protection of minors. Time will tell how this pans out, but we are keeping a close eye on the emergence of this industry as yet another possible avenue for child pornography to be downloaded, viewed, and traded.

A SHOCKING STORY OF A VICTIM, BUT NO CRIME

Kristyn and Felicia thought they had seen it all until a young woman, whom we'll call "Kallie," came into the police department to report that she had been sexually and physically assaulted by her live-in boyfriend, Tom.

Kallie was quite up front from the beginning that she and Tom had experimented with S&M, or "sadomasochism" sexual practices. She was visibly upset and scared and said that Tom was getting "out of control" and was now hurting her all the time. Kallie told the officer who initially took her report that one day she was late for work, and when she got home, Tom whipped her for every minute she was late. She relayed other incidences where he had burned her, put a choke collar on her, and cut her with a knife. Kallie displayed numerous injuries, cuts, and bruises that were in various stages of healing, as well as old scars. She even reported that Tom had tried to rape her with a flashlight on one occasion.

Kallie was the second victim of this type of incident reported in the area in the same year. The first victim, "Joanie," reported that her husband had put her chest in a vice. Her breasts were mutilated.

Both women wanted charges filed and were seeking protection from their significant others.

Under normal circumstances, the "suspects" would have been arrested for domestic violence, assault, criminal threatening, kidnapping, and sexual assault. However, in these circumstances, when a couple engages in S&M, the issue of consent is a huge legal hurdle to overcome. In Joanie's case, the reports were reviewed by the local DA's office and the case discussed at length. Joanie and her husband had a verbal contract and engaged in the use of "safe words." These "safe words" are the signal to end the act when it has gone too far.

This raised the question of where the line between consent and assault fell, weighed against the horrific disfigurement Joanie endured. Ultimately the case was presented to a jury. An indictment was not issued, and therefore prosecution was not authorized.

Kallie's case was also not prosecuted despite the fact that her injuries were readily apparent, as was her emotional upheaval. It was later discovered that Kallie's boyfriend, Tom, found a website that offered several S&M "contracts." He downloaded a contract that Kallie signed.

By signing this contract, Kallie essentially signed away her rights and gave her boyfriend complete permission to assault her, rape her, and mutilate her. When the responding officer arrived to take her boyfriend's statement, he had a file prepared with copies of the contracts. This egregious crime had just been minimized to a civil contract issue because a naive young woman signed a contract downloaded from the Internet. Her boyfriend's behavior was legal because the contract was a legal agreement between the two parties.

The best that the police department could do was to send her to the court to file a domestic violence petition, in essence a civil restraining order. No other charges could be filed. This was a difficult case for everyone because Kallie will live with these scars forever and because from a law-enforcement standpoint, it was frustrating that anyone could beat, kick, whip, burn, restrain, and sexually violate a young person *legally*. The fact that such sites exist is disturbing, but even more so that there are people out in cyberspace who actively use these sites.

In case you were wondering...http://www.bdsmcircle.net/dslifestyle/contracts.htm.

SWINGING SEX PARTIES IN A QUAINT NEW ENGLAND TOWN

Finally, we'd like to tell you about a bucolic New England seaport town replete with white church steeples dotting the landscape, crispy sea air wafting in from the Atlantic, houses over 200 years old, and white picket fences with sea roses and lilies in bloom.

Now picture that same seaside town as the site of a house that has hosted bi-weekly sex parties for 17 years. The 71-year-old proprietor of this swinging party place has a website advertising alternate Saturday night sex parties "for couples and singles to explore themselves, unleash their passions, discover their sensuality, try something new, watch others enjoy, or take part." The photos of the house online showed a "voyeur" bedroom with a swing hanging over the bed, various adult toys, and even a buffet table.

The site, which is linked to a Yahoo! group that currently boasts over 3,000 group members, contains sexually explicit photos of party goers, and lists party dates, house rules, and the request of a donation (single ladies get in free of charge). Whether or not this "business" could be considered a form of prostitution remains to be seen—money exchanged for sex, regardless of whether it involves a call girl or a swinging couple, is illegal.

The website and parking complaints ultimately resulted in an investigation of the property because it was zoned for residential use only, not as a "social club." Investigators were not able to infiltrate the club, and therefore, the case went nowhere. How ironic that the police department investigated the site based on a zoning violation!

The Danger of Webcams

We want to end with a warning. In our collective and professional opinions, there is very little reason children should ever have a webcam (a camera that attaches to a computer and broadcasts images across the Internet) in their bedroom. We can understand a family wanting to broadcast video to a loved one serving in the military or to family in a distant locale, but allowing a child to have a webcam in the privacy of her bedroom is like inviting child predators to stand in the doorway of your child's room and watch her every move. That is exactly why predators will often send a child a webcam at their own expense as a "gift" in the grooming process. Think about that.

Be smart, be safe, and do *not* let your children use a webcam unless you are there with them. Be mindful, too, that many newer computers have webcams built right into them.

We covered some difficult subject matter in this chapter because we want parents to understand that the Internet removes any distance barriers between the predators who will groom, recruit, and solicit children and your innocent 9-year-old Miley Cyrus fan.

Just as there is no one "profile" of a child predator, there is no "profile" of a victim. They come from all socioeconomic backgrounds and all geographic areas. The common factor is that they are often left unsupervised on the Internet. Please remember that.

> Be smart, be safe, and do *not* let your children use a webcam unless you are there with them. Be mindful, too, that many newer computers have webcams built right into them.

11

Phishing, Pharming, Spam, and Scams

You may not recognize terms like "phishing" or "spam," but we guarantee that you've been a victim of them a thousand times over. Throughout this book, we've covered many different forms of cyber crime, some of which have serious implications to your own personal safety. But there's an entirely different category of cyber crime that can impact you on many other levels—by consuming your time and Internet bandwidth with what is virtually "junk mail"; by scamming innocent victims out of a lifetime of savings; by duping you into visiting misleading websites so your passwords can be stolen. We've become so accustomed to these daily intrusions that we sometimes forget that they are still crimes!

As a consumer, you need to recognize these crimes so you can prevent becoming a victim. These types of "daily nuisance" crimes continue to proliferate

> We've become so accustomed to these daily intrusions that we sometimes forget that they are still crimes!

because there are still plenty of people who will, unwittingly, fall victim to them. The more you know, the better armed you are.

Phishing

Phishing occurs when fraudulent emails that appear to be from a legitimate source are sent in an effort to obtain sensitive information from a user. Phishing is actually a form of online identity theft in which the recipient is "tricked" into providing personal information through a variety of means. Besides the fact that phishing bilks the victim out of money, many indirect losses are also associated with phishing, similar to identity theft—the cost to consumers to repair their credit and replace their accounts, the loss of trust in online financial transactions, and so on.

Phishing targets many kinds of confidential information, including usernames and passwords, bank and credit card account information and passwords, social security numbers, birth dates, as well as "secret question" information, such as your mother's maiden name or a pass phrase.

The costs of phishing to consumers and businesses have been mounting. In the year ending in August 2007, 3.6 million adults in the U.S. were successfully defrauded by phishing emails at a total cost of $3.2 billion, according to Gartner Research. That's a disturbing jump from the 2.3 million users who lost $2.9 billion in 2006.

Phishing attacks are most often perpetrated by organized crime. It is a misconception that these are amateur attacks. It is believed that most phishing attacks come out of Russia. These underground groups have the ability to "virtually" move their operation overnight, thereby thwarting law enforcement's efforts to shut them down.

Call to Action—Danger, Danger

One of the most common forms of phishing is the "call to action" (see Figure 11.1). We've all received those doom emails with "Security Alert— Unauthorized Transaction" emblazoned on them. They advise us that our accounts have somehow been compromised and offer a link within the email itself to log into the account to verify our information.

Other types of "call to action" phishing attempts include the following:

- A claim that a new service is now available at a financial institution with a hyperlink in the message to check it out, but you must hurry because it is a limited-time offer.

- Notice of a fraudulent charge or change to your account with a link within the email.

- An invoice for merchandise not authorized by you with a link in the email to cancel or dispute the order.

- A statement that the account is somehow at risk—"Security Alert" or "Danger, Danger"—with a link to the account to correct the situation.

- A statement that there is some problem with your account and a request for you to visit the account. A link is provided within the email.

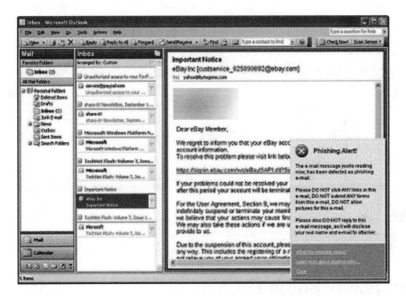

FIGURE 11.1

This is a typical "We regret to inform you that your account has been compromised" type of phishing attempt.

Hyperlinks—Hyper Dangerous!

All "call to action" phishing attempts want you to do the same thing—click the link, or "hyperlink," within the email message. However, the link actually goes to a fake website where the bad guys secretly capture your username and password for their own use.

The link may look legitimate, but you can't go by that. The link itself could read "Children's Fun Time" but really direct you to a porn site. In the case of a bank or credit card, the link could read "USABank" but go to a fake website that looks like the USABank site. The point is never click a link within an email even if it looks absolutely legitimate. If the email is from your bank, eBay, or PayPal, open up a separate Internet session and type the address in the address bar. Do not click the link in the email.

Look at the image in Figure 11.2. It looks like a legitimate link. It even has a "Secure Log On" message as well as a warning about recognizing fake emails. However, it is fake! How do you know? Because the correct Internet address (up on the top line) for AnyBank is www.anybank.com, not http://217.217.... Those numbers before "anybank.com" are a good indicator that this is a phishing attempt. Do *not* click hyperlinks within emails!

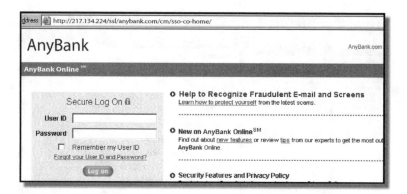

FIGURE 11.2

Spotting a phishing e-mail (Source: www.f-secure.com)

New Twists on Phishing

Here's a new twist on phishing we've seen recently. Imagine getting an email from someone you know advising you that another mutual acquaintance is trapped in a foreign country and urgently needs cash to get back home. That's exactly what happened in Fairbanks, Alaska recently when people began receiving email from the current director of a local council on aging stating that the former director had been in Africa and was in "desperate straits" because she had misplaced her bag with her money, passport, and valuable documents. When the current director tried to access her Yahoo! email account (which had previously been under the former director's name), she realized her password had been changed. That's when the phone began ringing from people asking about the former director's plight and where they could send the money. Her email account had been taken over by the phishers, who used it to send out the fake warnings about the former director.

Someone finally faxed the director a copy of the email they had received, laden with typos and misspellings, along with instructions on where to send money via a MoneyGram or Western Union. The FBI is currently investigating this case, but it points to a much more personalized way of scamming people of their money.

Charity Phishing Scams

Some of the most offensive versions of phishing scams are the ones that disguise themselves as charitable organizations seeking donations for victims of natural disasters. This was huge in the aftermath of 9/11, and we continue to see them crop up in the wake of every other disaster—earthquakes, hurricanes, tsunamis, floods, and so on. Ignore emails that purport to be from charitable organizations and go directly to reputable charity organizations such as the Red Cross (www.redcross.org).

Some of the most offensive versions of phishing scams are the ones that disguise themselves as charitable organizations seeking donations for victims of natural disasters.

How Do Phishers Make Money?

A common misconception is that all phishers gain access to accounts in order to fraudulently run up credit cards and buy expensive merchandise with the account information. This is actually not typical. A phisher can garner access to thousands of credit card and bank account usernames and passwords in a relatively short span of time. They want this information to resell to others in the underworld of cyberspace. That is how they make their money.

Vishing—Cell Phone Phishing

We're always fascinated with how quickly technology evolves. Unfortunately, so are the bad guys. It didn't take them long to figure out if they couldn't scam you online, they could scam you over the phone. Thus began the concept of *vishing*, or *voice phishing*. Vishing is very much like phishing except it uses phones as its medium for carrying messages.

Vishing is no different from phishing in that it is a cleverly disguised method of obtaining your PII (personally identifiable information). Common schemes are to notify you that your bank account was breached, suspended, deactivated, or terminated. You are given a number to call to correct the situation. When you call that number, a legitimate-sounding welcome message is played and then you are prompted to provide your account number and password or PIN.

Many times the vishers either infiltrate messaging services to obtain legitimate phone numbers, hack into financial institutions to obtain phone numbers, or as a last resort, use speed dialers that can dial combinations of numbers very rapidly.

Vishing messages can be sent either by voice or by text message, but they all have the same goal in mind—to get you to cough up your account information. Don't be fooled! If you think your account may be compromised, use the 800-number on the back of your credit card or on your statement as the callback number. That number is legitimate. And as always, remember this: No legitimate business will ever ask you for your password or PIN over the phone!

Recent Trends—Vishing Over Phishing

A recent trend has been to combine both phishing and vishing attacks. We are aware of several recent cases whereby potential victims were sent what appeared to be a legitimate survey by a credit union with the promise of $20 to all those participating. As always, the phishing attempt required a credit card number to credit the $20. The next day, a new email was launched warning that the survey was fraudulent and that the user's account had been temporarily suspended as a result. In order to reactivate their accounts, victims were instructed to call an 800-number. When they called, they were asked to provide their credit card number and PII (personal information such as mother's maiden name, which thieves can use to answer security questions). Having the PII makes the credit card much more valuable because it authenticates the credit card number. It also gives the thieves the ability to open up additional accounts using the victim's information.

We will never cease to be amazed at the creativity these criminals employ in trying to add a sense of legitimacy to their fraudulent schemes. Almost the reverse of the case just mentioned, the FBI recently warned of another scheme whereby text messages were sent to cell phones claiming that the recipient's online bank account had expired. The message instructed recipients to renew their online bank account, and they were given a specific phone number to do that. Of course, when customers called, they were greeted with a welcome message so that everything would appear authentic. They were then asked for their account numbers and PII. The twist on this scheme is that customers also received an email with a stern warning advising them to be careful of fraudulent schemes and reminding them never to provide sensitive information when requested in an email!

There are many forms of vishing, just like there are many forms of phishing, but the one thing that remains consistent is that the perpetrators will always seek out your personal information and account information. Do *not* give it out!

Like any other situation, if you receive a notification from *any* bank that your account has been closed, suspended, or misused, use the 800-number on the back of your credit card or the number on your account statement to verify this information. Always remember that you are only safe if you are initiating the call using what you know is a legitimate number. If you receive a call, it could be from anyone, so act cautiously. We've already shown how easy it is to spoof or fake Caller ID. Any professional business will not mind if you ask to verify the legitimacy of a phone number.

IC3 Name Used in Fraudulent Phishing Scam

In an ironic twist, on June 6, 2008, the IC3 (Internet Crimes Complaint Center), a collaborative program between the FBI and the White Collar Crimes Bureau, released a media alert advising consumers that their own names were being used in an email scheme containing fraudulent refund notifications. The players who thought up this doozey of a scheme sent out emails purporting to be from IC3, claiming that refunds were being made to victims of Internet fraud. They used the IC3 logo while promising thousands of dollars to be sent via the "Bank of England," as long as the victim signs a "fund release order," which of course would require bank account information. IC3 asks that victims of this email scam file a report at—you guessed it—www.ic3.gov.

Pharming—Fake Websites

Pharming occurs when a fake website is set up that appears identical to a real website, but carries a payload of malware (malicious software). The malware could be used to deliver a computer virus, capture every keystroke you type, or install software that will allow someone else to have remote access and control over your computer.

This type of attack used to appear only on the seamier side of the Internet—porn sites and the like—but recent studies show a proliferation of pharming attacks on even very legitimate websites, including government sites.

We have experienced this phenomenon ourselves when following legitimate web links through a browser to municipal and government websites.

With as fast as everyone clicks the results of a search engine, it's almost impossible to verify that every link is legitimate. However, one way to tell is to hover the mouse over the website link. If the link is to Sears, for example, the address that pops up should be www.sears.com.

When you hover your mouse over any search engine result (such as the result of a search for "Sears, Roebuck and Co."), look down at the very bottom of your screen (see Figure 11.3). The Internet address, or URL (Universal Resource Locator), should go to http://www.sears.com (see Figure 11.4). It should not go to http://123.sears.com, for example. If it does, this may be a pharmed site!

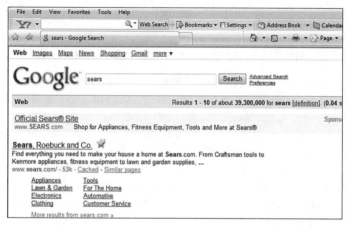

(© 2008 Google)

FIGURE 11.3

Search results for "Sears, Roebuck and Co."

FIGURE 11.4

The URL at the bottom of the screen

Your best bet for avoiding pharmed sites is to type the address for the location to which you want to go (such as www.sears.com) directly in the browser address bar. Use the hover technique and verify that the link is actually legitimate. "AnyBank" should be www.anybank.com, not www.secure.anybank.com. Be suspicious of any link that begins with a prefix other than the actual name of the site you are visiting. It's not unusual to have different things appear *after* the name, but the general naming convention should be www.*companyorsitename*.com.

Spam, Spam, Spam

Spam is that annoying email that clutters your inbox offering great deals at Canadian pharmacies, "enhancement" drugs, and access to porn sites, among many other variants. It's more than just annoying—sometimes it's a veiled phishing attempt, and other times it contains nasty malware that will infect your system. The technical term for spam is *unsolicited commercial bulk email*. The frequently used term is *junk email*.

Where Did Spam Come From?

The first known spam was actually sent back in the spring of 1978 by an energetic marketing specialist from a technology company when the Internet was still in its infancy. In his zest to tell everyone about a new computer system his company had developed, the marketing man, named Gary, turned to what was then known as ARPAnet, the Internet in its earliest stages. So small was the Internet then that only a few thousand people were active on it. All of their names were conveniently kept in a single directory, if you can imagine that. Gary selected about six hundred of those names and sent a message: "We invite you to come see our new system...." The reaction was strong, immediate, and nearly all hostile. "This was a flagrant violation of the ARPAnet," one recipient wrote. Gary was harshly reprimanded by the system administrator. Nevertheless, his company sold more than 20 of the million-dollar computer systems. Thus the first spam was launched.

Now fast-forward 30 years later: Current estimates are that a staggering 120 billion spam messages are sent out each and every day (source: The 2008 Internet Security Trends Report). From 600 annoying emails to 120 billion in 30 years—that's how fast spam has grown.

> Current estimates are that a staggering 120 billion spam messages are sent out every day.

Who Profits from Spam?

People understand what spam is. They understand how annoying it is, but few understand how anyone could profit from spam. "I always delete spam," everyone says. So how do they make money from it?

For every million people who delete spam, many open it and respond. Consider the sheer volume of 120 billion spam emails a day. It doesn't take much to realize that given the enormity of that number, several thousand people could reply a day. When someone does respond, their email address and personal information is recorded and resold—for a very nice profit—to other companies. For example, someone who has expressed an interest in a mortgage is likely to have their information resold as a lead to other mortgage companies. The people who pass the information along are called "leads generators" or "affiliate marketers," and they make a tidy profit from it. For each final lead that includes the interested party's information as well as contact information, a leads generator can earn anywhere from $10 to $20.

Although many companies that use marketing information say they have a "zero-tolerance" policy for spam, they mean they don't actively send spam. It does not mean they do not profit from spam, as long as they purchase your name and information from a leads generator whose source is spam. That is not to say that there aren't legitimate leads generation companies, because there are, but many times the leads from spam travel through so many layers that it's impossible to tell the legitimate ones from the not-so-legitimate ones. It is not uncommon for someone on the bottom of the leads generation food chain to receive less than a dollar to forward along someone's email, but again, the sheer volume of spam means that even these bottom feeders are making a tidy profit.

Why Spam Is Dangerous

Spam has moved beyond being a simple annoyance to being a potential threat, considering that in 2007, more than 83% of spam contained a URL or web address within the body of the spam message (source: 2008 Internet Security Trends Report). This means that more and more spam contains malware (malicious software) that can install keystroke loggers and spyware on your system.

Not only can spam carry a payload of malware, it wastes an enormous amount of network bandwidth that could go for much more valuable pursuits. It is not unusual for corporations to block 95%–99% of all incoming mail because it is identified as spam. That's a lot of wasted network bandwidth.

Beyond those dangers, think about how much time is wasted just going through hundreds of email getting rid of the spam. Commercial products are available that can block spam, and many corporations employ them. However, spam-blocking lists literally change overnight, and it's almost impossible to keep up on all the sources of spam. The end result is that thousands of hours are wasted every year by consumers and workers trying to wade through the list of junk mail that fills their inboxes.

Spam has also been linked with many dangerous scams, such as tainted prescription drugs sold on the black market.

MAN CHARGED WITH CHILD PORN WAS SPAM VICTIM

Want one more reason why you need to protect your computer from viruses and spam? Consider the plight of Michael Fiola, a former investigator at the Massachusetts Department of Industrial Accidents. Fiola, a former firefighter with no criminal record, was issued a Dell laptop by his employer in November of 2006.

IT staffers began to examine Fiola's laptop in March of 2007, because Fiola was using four times the normal amount of Internet access. Upon examining Fiola's laptop, workers discovered pornographic material, including child pornography, in the temporary Internet folder. Fiola was fired that same month. The case was turned over to authorities, who charged Fiola with possession of child pornography, an offense that had him facing 2 1/2 years in prison.

Insisting he was innocent, Fiola hired a computer forensics expert to do an examination. The expert, Tami Loehrs, concluded that the antivirus software on Fiola's laptop was not working, the system was not properly updating, and that it was more than likely already infected with malicious software (or "malware") when Fiola got it. "He was handed a ticking time bomb," Loehrs concluded.

Based on the computer forensics expert's report, the District Attorney dropped the charges stating they could not "meet our burden of reasonable doubt."

Spam Vigilantes

Groups such as APEWS (Anonymous Postmaster Early Warning System; www.apews.org), Spamhaus (www.spamhaus.org), and SpamCop (www.spamcop.net) actively attempt to catalog known sources of spam and block them. These spam vigilantes work independently not only to reduce spam but identify sources of spam.

Spam Spiders

People often scratch their heads when trying to figure out how spammers got hold of their email address in the first place. Did you know that computer programs called "spiders" sweep the Internet and automatically cull through millions of web pages looking for email addresses? Because most email addresses use the format *name@webprovider*.com, it is easy for these spiders to know when they have a hit and to harvest that address.

How to Reduce Spam

Notice we said "reduce." It is virtually impossible to rid yourself entirely of all spam, but you can certainly limit the amount you get by following these steps:

- **Never reply to spam.** Before you fire off that nasty email to the spammer to tell him to stuff it, stop before you press Send. All you will accomplish by doing this is to confirm that your email address is valid. That's what he wanted in the first place. Just delete the email.

- **Turn off your "preview" feature in your email account.** Microsoft Outlook, by default, opens up all email in a preview pane. Shut off this feature so you don't open any emails until you've had a chance to screen them. Just opening an email can deliver a payload of a virus onto your computer system. Instead, just delete the spam email.

- **Never click any links contained within spam.** It is very possible they contain malware. Just delete the spam.

- **Disguise your email address on the Web.** Those spam spiders will have a much harder time if your email address is written out as "user at anywhere dot com" rather than user@anywhere.com.

- **Stop forwarding emails to your friends.** "If you send this back and to eight other friends, something wonderful will happen within the next hour," says the email from your best friend. If you reply and forward the email along, you've just managed to harvest eight more email addresses on behalf of spammers. We know, these emails are often entertaining, but by forwarded them you're just giving up your friends' email addresses to spammers. Just delete the spam instead.

New Twist—Death Threats via Spam

It's bad enough that your inbox is filled with spam and junk email, but in a recent twist, users are getting death threats delivered via spam. As you know, spam can be customized to include your last name, first name, even your address. These emails, which often have the subject line "BE MORE CAREFUL," contain frightening language. Oftentimes, the sender claims that they have been solicited to kill the recipient. As we said, it's not unusual for the recipient's name and address to be included to add veracity to the claim.

Anyone would be frightened to receive this type of email. The sender may claim they have been watching the victim for some time or that they even have photos of him or her. The message "We have watched you go in and out of 123 Main Street" would be disturbing to anyone. The email usually goes on to say that the sender is willing to "spare" the recipient's life for a price, or sell a recorded copy of the actual "murder for hire" solicitation to the recipient. Of course, the recipient is warned not to contact authorities. The entire scam is an attempt to extort not only your money, but your private bank and credit card account information.

Is Spam Illegal?

It most certainly is. Ask Robert Alan Soloway, dubbed one of the "Top Ten Spammers." He just recently plead guilty to charges of fraud, email fraud (under the CAN-SPAM Act), and failure to file an income tax return. Prosecutors claim that Soloway sent more than 90 million emails in 3 months from just two of the many servers he used around the world. Soloway is purported to have made over a million dollars by sending out millions of junk emails. He faces a maximum sentence of 20 years for fraud, 5 years for email fraud, and 1 year for not filing an income tax return.

The CAN-SPAM Act

The acronym CAN-SPAM stands for "Controlling the Assault of Non-Solicited Pornography and Marketing Act," which belies its roots. The law became effective on January 1, 2004. It had several purposes, one of which was to prevent pornography from being disguised in email with the subject line "Family Photos" or "News from Tom." The CAN-SPAM Act requires that any solicitations with adult content be clearly marked as such in the subject line.

The act has been controversial in that it does not seem to have done much to curtail the threat of spam. Although the CAN-SPAM Act has undergone periodic revisions as recently as July 2008, its effectiveness remains to be seen.

New Twist—Text Spam on Your Cell Phone

Ever get a text message on your cell phone telling you to apply for a job or that you've been selected for a special promotion? If so, then you've been "text spammed." What makes these messages so bothersome is that they are lengthy and try to install downloads. What's more, if you pay per text message, then you have to pay to be spammed! And by the way, phone spam is illegal as well.

Cell phone companies claim they are trying to combat this latest annoyance. Verizon Wireless says they block more than 200 million spam messages per month. In fact, the FCC voted to ban all unauthorized commercial text messages to cell phones and pagers, and the Telephone Consumer Protection Act prohibits autodialed and prerecorded calls to cell phones. This Act also applies to text messages—but good luck trying to report a text spam to the local police.

The best recourse you have when you do get text spam is to report the violation to your cell phone carrier. They may reverse the charge when you report it, but even more important, they'll want to know about it in order to put in better blocks. Some cell phone providers also allow you to block text messages that are generated by computers—the source of most cell phone spam.

$234 Million Spam Judgment

In May of 2008, the social networking site MySpace won a $234 million judgment against two prominent spammers in what may be the largest anti-spam award ever.

MySpace went up against Sanford Wallace and Walter Rines, two notorious spammers. Wallace has the nicknames "Spamford" and "SpamKing" for his role as the head of a company that has sent as many as 30 million junk emails per day. Walter Rines is a local resident of Seacoast, New Hampshire, and both have been in hot water in the past due to their spam activities. Back in 2006, 2 years prior to their 2008 judgment, Wallace and Rines settled with the FTC on charges of distributing spyware. They agreed to stop doing it and pay a slap-on-the-wrist $50,000 fine.

Under the 2003 Federal CAN-SPAM law, each violation entitles the victim to $100 in damages, which can be tripled if the act was conducted "willfully and knowingly." According to court records, Wallace and Rines worked together to create MySpace accounts and then emailed other MySpace members, asking them to watch a video in which they attempted to sell items.

MySpace told LA District Court Judge Audrey B Collins that some of the spam distributed by Wallace and Rines—much of it sent to teenagers—included links to third-party websites containing pornographic material. They then attempted to take over other accounts by stealing passwords.

This ruling is important because it sets a tone that spam will not be tolerated and reminds people that spam is, in fact, illegal. However, it's not likely to stop the deluge of junk email in our inboxes every day.

Report Spam to spam@uce.gov

Most people delete spam as an annoyance, but you can actually report spam to the Federal Trade Commission at http://www.ftc.gov/bcp/conline/edcams/spam/report.html, or you can forward it to spam@uce.gov.

What will this do? It will *not* stop the deluge of spam into your inbox, but it might give investigators more power to stop spammers as well as give them a better understanding of how prevalent the problem is and what the source is. A quick tip: Add spam@uce.gov to your email address book to make it easier to forward spam.

Yahoo! Sues Unknown Spammers in Lottery Scheme

In May of 2008, Yahoo! filed a lawsuit against an unknown group of individuals for allegedly sending out email messages to Internet users claiming they had won a lottery from Yahoo!. The suit targets individuals who sent out emails that read "Yahoo! Lottery!" in the subject line.

The fake lottery scam is a well-established hoax designed to trick unsuspecting email users into revealing valuable personal data such as passwords, credit card information, and social security numbers, but in this case the thieves made the mistake of using a well-known company to try and dupe customers, and Yahoo! took notice.

Why would Yahoo! file a lawsuit against unknown people? First of all, these spam messages were genuine-looking enough to fool a lot of people, and that does not bode well for Yahoo!. With over 260 million users, Yahoo! cannot afford to have their corporate reputation tarnished by people thinking the company has duped them. Secondly, Yahoo! is hoping that the actual identity of the spam scammers will be revealed in the court discovery process. We will be watching this case with great interest.

RESOURCES

- The Spamhaus Project (www.spamhaus.com) is an international, nonprofit effort to track spammers, work with law enforcement in identifying spammers, and introduce legislation that will further protect consumers against spam.

- The Federal Trade Commission (www.ftc.gov) is the primary enforcing arm when it comes to spam.

The Nigerian Letter Advance Fee or "419" Scam

People like to think they are above falling for fraudulent schemes, particularly from emails that are misspelled and have offers that are simply too good to be true. However, the reality is that many people *do* buy into these scams because they *want* to believe they are true or they don't have the capacity or knowledge to question such offers. When people do get duped, their anger and embarrassment often prevents them from reporting the crime.

One such scam is the "Nigerian letter" or "419" scam. Although there are many different names for this scam, it's basically an "advance fee" scam, which we'll explain shortly. The name is derived from the fact that the bulk of these scams have been traced back to Nigeria. The number "419" is a reference to the Nigerian penal code, which designates the crime of fraud as "Section 4-1-9."

The "advanced fee" part comes from the fact that the sender, who often purports to be a Nigerian government official, sends the letter or email looking for someone willing to accept a large sum of money (often in the millions) but requires an advanced fee to ensure the transaction as a "show of honesty" on the victim's part. The intended victim is reassured of the authenticity of the arrangement by forged or false documents bearing apparently official Nigerian government letterhead, seals, as well as false letters of credit, payment schedules, and bank drafts. The scam artist may even establish the credibility of his contacts, and thereby his influence, by arranging a meeting between the victim and "government officials" in real or fake government offices.

These Nigerian cases are extremely difficult to prosecute because they often are generated from overseas, and whenever you cross international boundaries, another layer is added to the investigation. More importantly, the cooperation of government officials in that country is required to prosecute and assist the criminals.

Recent Arrests

There have been several arrests recently in Nigerian scams. In June of 2008, Edna Fielder of Washington State was sentenced to 2 years in prison and 5 years of supervised release for her role in a Nigerian scam.

Fiedler was working with Nigerian accomplices and agreed to send fake checks to people in the U.S. The victims, duped into thinking this was an official transaction, agreed to cash the fake checks with the promise that they could keep part of the money for themselves as a "transaction" fee. Fiedler was the go-between for the Nigerians. She would receive the fake check packages, including phony Wal-Mart money orders, Bank of America checks, U.S. Postal checks, and American Express traveler's checks, and then forward the packages onto the potential victims, keeping a piece of the cut for herself. In total, Fiedler has sent out around $600,000 in fake checks to victims. When the FBI searched her house, they found another $1.1 million in fake checks she was prepared to send out.

What we find most interesting about this particular case is that the U.S. Postal Service recently sent 15 investigators to Lagos and Nigeria to follow the trail of these letters. That means the Nigerian government had to sanction the actions of these inspectors, which is a dramatic change from just a few years ago. We're not venturing a guess as to whether the officials were cooperative, but even allowing U.S. inspectors into their country to work the case is significant.

The "Lottery" Version

Recently, the FBI, working with the Spanish police, arrested 87 Nigerians suspected of the Nigerian 419 advanced fee scam. In this particular case, the suspects were accused of defrauding at least 1,500 people in a postal and

Internet lottery scam. The Spanish police said millions of dollars were taken from the victims, most of them in the United States and European Union. The twist on this case is that the victims were told they had won a substantial amount of money in a lottery and then were asked to send a payment before the prize money could be sent. Thousands of letters and emails, most in ungrammatical English, were sent out to prospective victims every day. The faked documents asked them to make an initial payment of $1,400 in "taxes or administrative costs." The scam is estimated to have netted around $24 million.

How Can They Profit?

It is estimated that only one in 1,000 recipients of the letters needed to fall for the fraud for it to make a profit. One in 1,000, yet over 1,500 people were willing to come forward and admit to being victimized. There's no telling how many did *not* come forward. Among those duped in this particular scheme was an Anglican bishop.

In April of 2008, police in Newport Beach, California sent out a press release indicating that an 80-year-old resident had fallen victim to an "advanced fee" (419) scam in which he received an email claiming he had won an overseas lottery and was required to pay a processing fee to have the funds released. This is the typical scenario, but in this case, the victim was defrauded over the course of 2 years and duped out of $700,000. That amount may seem astronomical, but bear in mind that many of these types of scams are specifically targeted toward senior citizens, who might not be as aware of them.

These scams embarrass people, bilk them out of their money, and wreak havoc on their financial accounts. Recently, we were saddened to hear of the suicide of one of the victims. A young university student, who had recently emigrated from China to Britain, was taken in by one of these scammers to the tune of around $11,000. She hung herself when she discovered she had been defrauded.

Here are some facts about the Nigerian 419 scam:

- The U.S. Postal Inspection Service estimates that U.S. consumers have been duped to the tune of $120 million a year.

- IC3, the Internet Crimes Complaint Center, estimates the average loss for victims of Nigerian scams to be $1,922 per victim.

- The Financial Crimes Division of the Secret Service receives approximately 100 telephone calls from victims and potential victims and receives 300 to 500 pieces of related correspondence about this scam per day!

Sample Nigerian Letter

Here's an example of a typical Nigerian advance fee letter, which can be received via email, fax, or post office mail. Note that there are many varieties of this type of letter in existence:

Lagos, Nigeria.
Attention: The President/CEO

Dear Sir,

Confidential Business Proposal

Having consulted with my colleagues and based on the information gathered from the Nigerian Chambers of Commerce and Industry, I have the privilege to request your assistance to transfer the sum of $47,500,000.00 (forty seven million, five hundred thousand United States dollars) into your accounts. The above sum resulted from an over-invoiced contract, executed, commissioned, and paid for about five years (5) ago by a foreign contractor. This action was however intentional and since then the fund has been in a suspense account at The Central Bank Of Nigeria Apex Bank.

We are now ready to transfer the fund overseas and that is where you come in. It is important to inform you that as civil servants, we are forbidden to operate a foreign account; that is why we require your assistance. The total sum will be shared as follows: 70% for us, 25% for you, and 5% for local and international expenses incidental to the transfer.

The transfer is risk free on both sides. I am an accountant with the Nigerian National Petroleum Corporation (NNPC). If you find this proposal acceptable, we shall require the following documents:

(a) your banker's name, telephone, account, and fax numbers.

(b) your private telephone and fax numbers—for confidentiality and easy communication.

(c) your letter-headed paper stamped and signed.

Alternatively we will furnish you with the text of what to type into your letter-headed paper, along with a breakdown explaining, comprehensively what we require of you. The business will take us thirty (30) working days to accomplish.

Please reply urgently.

Best regards,

Howgul Abul Arhu

Where to Report a Nigerian (419) Advance Fee Letter

This scam is one of the reasons we advocate for centralized reporting of cyber crime. Here's what the FBI website (http://www.fbi.gov/majcases/fraud/fraudschemes.htm) says about reporting Nigerian 419 letters:

> *If you receive a letter from Nigeria asking you to send personal or banking information, do not reply in any manner. Send the letter to the U.S. Secret Service, your local FBI office, or the U.S. Postal Inspection Service. You can also register a complaint with the Federal Trade Commission's Consumer Sentinel (http://www.consumer.gov/sentinel/).*

The Cyber Crime Melting Pot

Historically, one telltale sign of a potential scam has been the poor spelling and grammar present in many spam and phishing attempts. Messages that read, "You to can be of great luck please," and other awkward grammatical formations quickly belie their roots. To overcome this hurdle, malware authors are quietly recruiting people fluent in foreign languages on underground bulletin boards and list servers.

Data Breaches—When Your Data Is Stolen

Have you ever swiped your credit card at a store or filled out a detailed form outlining your personal medical history, only to wonder where that information goes? Imagine if your most private information—your medical history, your financial profile, your adoption records, your credit card numbers—were compromised. Unfortunately, this happens to millions of people every year, many of whom become victims of credit card fraud, identity theft, and sometimes even blackmail.

Data breaches have largely been a result of a combination of poor security policies, out-of-date programs, and inattention. Here's a list of just a few data breaches that have been reported:

- In March of 2008, Harvard University apologized for allowing their computer files to be hacked, resulting in the potential exposure of about 10,000 graduate students and student applicants.

- In March of 2008, a Broward County, Florida high school senior broke into his school district's computer system and stole personal information about district employees.

- In June of 2008, Stanford University acknowledged that a laptop containing confidential personnel data of many Stanford employees was stolen. The laptop contained employee's names, dates of birth, social security numbers, addresses, and phone numbers.

- In June of 2008, AT&T reported that a laptop containing unencrypted employee names, social security numbers, salaries, and bonus information was stolen out of an employee's car.

- In June of 2008, Walter Reed Army Hospital confirmed that "sensitive information" on their patients was exposed in a breach.

- In April of 2008, Helping Homeless Veterans and Families of Indianapolis, Indiana reported that hundreds of files containing sensitive medical information, medical histories, and social security numbers were found in the trash on the east side of Indianapolis. The records were those of homeless veterans.

THE TJ MAXX DATA BREACH—LARGEST IN HISTORY

In January of 2006, retailer TJ Maxx announced that they had suffered a serious hacker attack. TJX, the parent company, oversees 2,500 stores, including TJ Maxx, Bob's Stores, and Marshalls. First reports indicated that nearly 50 million credit and debit cards holders were put at risk by this incident, but later court filings suggested that number was closer to 94 million. When it comes to data breaches, TJ Maxx is the poster child, having earned the dubious distinction of having the largest data breach on record.

Ever have to show a driver's license or some other form of ID when you return something without a receipt? In addition to the millions of credit cards being exposed, over 455,000 people who returned items without a receipt at a TJX store had their credit card and PII (personal identifying information) breached, including driver's license information, military identification, and state identification numbers. The breach lasted for more than a year before the company discovered the problem. According to TJX's own filing, the data was stored "together with related names and addresses, and in

> When it comes to data breaches, TJ Maxx is the poster child, having earned the dubious distinction of having the largest data breach on record.

some of those cases, we believe those personal ID numbers were the same as the customers' social security numbers."

Up until the TJX breach, the typical data breach consisted of a laptop with personal data being stolen.

LAWSUITS FILED

As was expected, lawsuits started flying everywhere. State Attorney Generals sued. Credit card companies sued. Credit card transaction companies sued. Banks sued. And, yes, customers sued.

In one settlement, TJX agreed to pay Visa $40 million and Mastercard $24 million to help defray the costs of replacing their customers' cards, which can cost as much as $20 each, including processing, handling, and recovery. Customers who were affected were given free credit monitoring for 3 years and some reimbursement costs.

Total costs for recovering from this debacle are estimated to be around $256 million. That cost includes fixing the company's computer system and dealing with lawsuits, investigations, and other claims stemming from the breach. Who do you think will ultimately pay this cost?

IT ALL STARTED WITH WIRELESS

According to statements filed in court, it is believed that this breach began because of an unsecured wireless connection at two stores in Miami, Florida.

Not only did TJX use a nonsecure method of encryption (WEP), they also broadcast their identities (SSID), which enabled hackers to know their target.

Once the open door was located, there was no stopping the thieves. With an open access point, they could easily install malware to determine administrative passwords. With that information, they could easily take over servers.

PCI COMPLIANCE

Any store or retailer that processes credit card transactions is required to be PCI (Payment Card Industry) compliant to ensure the security and integrity of account information. The PCI rules took effect in June 2005 and mandate a dozen security controls for protecting consumer data. To this day, not all retailers are compliant. Court documents filed in the case indicate that TJX was deficient in meeting PCI standards.

Eleven Charged

In August of 2008, the U.S. Secret Service filed charges against 11 individuals in the TJ Maxx breach as well as several other breaches affecting TJX stores, BJ Wholesalers, and OfficeMax.

Albert "Segvec" Gonzalez of Miami is being charged as the mastermind behind the plot, along with two other men from Miami. The others charged came from Estonia, China, and Belarus.

Following the trail of a data breach is complex and can lead in many directions, but the indictment alleges that Gonzalez and his co-conspirators were able to gain entry into the networks of retailers via "wardriving" (that is, driving around with equipment to find open entry points and security vulnerabilities in wireless networks). See Chapter 16, "Your Online Safety Checkup," for more information.

Once they gained access into the system, they installed "sniffer" programs like we describe in Chapter 3, "Cyber Crime Tools You Won't Believe." These sniffer programs captured card numbers, passwords, and account information as the cards were being processed. According to the indictment, some of the credit and debit card numbers were sold on the Internet. Others were "cashed out," meaning fake credit cards were created by placing the real card information on a blank card with a magnetic strip. As long as the card is encoded properly, it can be swiped at a terminal and used. Whatever the limit on the cash available was, that amount was cashed out. This resulted in tens of thousands of dollars of ready cash.

Gonzalez is alleged to have been working as a confidential informant for the Secret Service when they discovered he was involved in the case. He faces maximum penalties of life in prison.

TJ Maxx Employee Fired for Disclosing Security Problems

On a side note, we have to mention the story of Nick Benson, a 23-year-old college student from the University of Kansas, who worked in the Lawrence, Kansas TJ Maxx outlet. Benson claims that as many as 18 months after the TJX breach was discovered, employees were still able to log onto TJX servers using blank passwords and that at first his password was the same as his username. Store managers left their usernames and passwords on sticky notes near computers. Benson claims to have brought his concerns to TJX management, but the problems went unfixed.

Frustrated with his attempts to point out lax security at his store, in August of 2007, Benson began posting his concerns to the security online forum, www.sla.ckers.org.

Here's one of Benson's postings using the anonymous name of CrYpTiC_MauleR:

> Re: TJX Still Lacks Security
>
> Posted by: CrYpTiC_MauleR (IP Logged)
>
> Date: May 08, 2008 10:27AM
>
> UPDATE to anyone interested: So the store I work at the password to remotely desktop to the store server before the breach was the same as the username, then after the breach it was changed to a variation of the old password. Today I learn that the password has been changed to a blank password. WTF?? You would think they would learn from their mistakes, I assume they must think now that they have the above mentioned firewall in place they don't need a strong password or they are just lazy. I am not sure if this is just an isolated incident within this specific store, but it goes to show that you can't trust a company to protect your information, esepcailly TJX. Today was a very sad day for me =o(

In May of 2008, Benson was summoned to the general manager's office and greeted by the regional loss prevention manager who advised Benson he was being fired for disclosing confidential corporate information. Apparently, TJX had hired a firm to monitor all postings about the company online.

THE HANNAFORD BROTHERS DATA BREACH

While we're talking about data breaches, in March of 2008, Maine-based supermarket chain Hannaford Brothers announced their data had been breached. Up to 4.2 million credit card numbers were compromised. Hannaford Brothers is a New England–based chain, and we're sorry to say that even some of our coworkers became victims. Police officers are not immune to credit card fraud and identity theft. The sensitive data was exposed when shoppers swiped their cards at checkout line machines and the information was transmitted to banks for approval.

At first, this seemed like a run-of-the-mill data breach, which typically infiltrates and steals databases full of credit card information, but as more and more details emerged, security analysts were stunned to discover that the credit card breach occurred while the data was "in transit," meaning during the time the customer swiped the card and the information was being transmitted for approval. This "upped the ante" of sophistication because this is not an easy thing to do. It's akin to robbing a truck full of TVs while the truck is rolling down the highway.

Soon after the breach was announced, the company also revealed that malware (malicious software) had been discovered on over 300 store servers across the country. Some industry experts felt this had to have been an inside job.

At the time of this writing, a class action suit has been filed.

PFIZER PHARMACEUTICALS BREACH

Data breaches don't just happen with financial data. In May of 2007, a Pfizer Pharmaceuticals employee took a laptop home from work. Her husband proceeded to install P2P software on it and inadvertently began to share the computer's contents—including sensitive data.

According to a letter sent to New Hampshire Attorney General Kelly Ayotte, the breach affected "approximately 17,000 of Pfizer's current and former employees," including 98 New Hampshire residents. Pfizer's attorney qualified that number further to say that "the affected employees can be grouped into two categories—approximately 15,700 who actually had their data accessed and copied, and approximately 1,250 who may have had their data accessed and copied." This data included the names and social security numbers of employees, which could lead to identity theft.

Verizon Report: 87% of Breaches Were Avoidable

In June of 2008, Verizon Business Security Solutions released a "Data Breach Investigation Report" that made 500 forensic examinations of data breaches involving 230 million records. The conclusion of the study was that 87% (nearly nine out of ten) data breaches could have been prevented by "taking reasonable security measures." Whereas 59% of "deliberate" breaches were the result of hacking and intrusions, some 90% of known security vulnerabilities that were exploited had patches available that would have taken care of the security holes at least 6 months prior.

In other words, the bucket was leaking and the plug that would have shored up the hole was available for at least 6 months, but nothing was done to stop it up. That's just a bad security policy.

Unfortunately, it's very hard to regulate that the hospital, university, government agency, or store where you swipe your credit card keep their systems up to date with the latest patches. There are mandates for industries regarding compliance and there are certainly plenty of lawsuits after the data is breached (as well as fingers pointed in every direction), but all this does not protect the consumers whose information is stolen and whose lives are often turned upside down as they attempt to recover from their data being breached.

> The conclusion of the study was that 87% (nearly nine out of ten) data breaches could have been prevented by "taking reasonable security measures."

Verizon Business also concluded that although three-fourths of all data breaches led to compromised data within days, 63% of businesses didn't know the data was breached for months afterward. Even more significant is that 70% of data breaches are uncovered by third parties, such as consumers. The most popular method of breaching data? Good old-fashioned hacking (59%).

Data Breach Laws

It may surprise you to learn that as of February, 2008, only 38 states had enacted data breach laws. California led the way over 5 years ago by enacting the landmark SB 1386 Data Breach Law. Other states have followed suit, but it still concerns us that 10 states still have no mandates requiring companies to notify customers when their data is compromised. These states are South Dakota, New Mexico, Iowa, Missouri, Kentucky, Mississippi, Alabama, South Carolina, Virginia, and West Virginia. (Oklahoma has a breach law, but it only requires notification when a governmental agency experiences a data breach.)

The data breach laws have several components, including how much time an organization has to notify their customers of a breach, what the penalties are for failure to notify, whether or not customers can take private action against a company, and what kinds of exemptions might apply. For example, data that is encrypted is not likely to be discernable, so often it is exempt from data breach laws.

As of this writing, no federal data breach law is on the books. Several have been proposed, but none has been passed yet. Federal law would trump any state law, and as we understand it, although there is bipartisan consensus that a federal data breach law is needed, one of the sticking points is whether or not notification to consumers should be required. Another issue is that the state laws keep changing. For example, California just amended its laws to include mandatory notification of patients when their health information is breached. Other state changes have addressed the length of time credit card information can be stored.

Are Data Breach Laws Ineffective?

In June of 2008, Carnegie Mellon University released an interesting study based on U.S. Federal Trade Commission data that stated that the data breach disclosure laws—the same laws put in place that require organizations to reveal when personal information has been compromised—have been ineffective in reducing identity theft.

The problem with this study is that it addresses the wrong issue. The data breach laws were not put into place as a means of deterring identity theft. The laws were meant to minimize the damage once the theft occurred. Victims of identity theft are often unaware their identities have been stolen—sometimes for years. As in the Hannaford Brothers and TJ Maxx data breaches, as soon as customers were advised of the breach, they could be on guard to prevent any further fraud. That is where the data breach laws do their work. They were not meant to stop the crime, but to make sure the damage is as minimal as possible.

Privacy Rights Clearinghouse

The Privacy Rights Clearinghouse (www.privacyrights.org) is a nonprofit consumer information and privacy advocacy website. One of the most interesting features of this site is its chronological listing of all reported data breaches. The numbers and volume are staggering, and it is constantly updated with the latest news about stolen data. Just click "A Chronology of Data Breaches" under the Consumer tab to read about the most recent breaches.

Online Auction Fraud

According to the FBI's "2006 Internet Crime Report," over 200,000 complaints of cyber crime were filed in 2006 (the highest yet), with a total loss of $198.4 million. The number-one cyber crime complaint was auction fraud, which accounted for nearly 45% of all complaints. Product misrepresentation was the primary reason stated, followed by nondelivery of an item. About 70% of the fraud victims were scammed through online auctions, and about 30% of the victims were scammed via email. The average median loss per auction fraud complaint was $602.50.

Auction fraud is particularly upsetting because it relies on trust. No one wants to think they've been duped.

Escrow Services

Before you bid on that French Louis XV commode for $35,000 (yes, we saw one at the time of this writing), you might want to consider using an escrow service. An escrow service holds your payment to the seller until the item is authenticated. Obviously the seller has to agree to this, but it would seem fair to say that any legitimate seller dealing in high-end items such as antiques would be willing to participate in this process. Think of it like a "contingency clause" pending house inspection.

Oddly enough, there have been numerous cases of fraudulent escrow services that took the buyer's money and never released it to the seller. As a result, eBay is very clear that the only escrow service they will endorse is Escrow.com (www.escrow.com).

Pay by Credit Card

Although some people are afraid to use their credit card for online transactions, we actually encourage it because most credit cards companies will work with you to get your money back in case you are a victim of fraud. A credit card also limits your liability for how much you are personally responsible for if you do not receive an item. Do not use your debit card because your personal bank account could get wiped out.

Learn As Much As You Can About the Seller

eBay and other auction sites almost always have a rating system. Heed it. Look at the rating and read the negative ones first. What percentage of feedback is positive? Even if there have been a few legitimate problems, such as a delay in shipping and goods arriving damaged, most sellers will still have a good rating. If they do not, this is a red flag that something could be wrong.

How long has the seller been online? If a seller has a brand-new account and is offering a deal that seems too good to be true, it probably is.

Is the seller located in the United States? If not, it could be more difficult to resolve any issues that arise.

Google the seller's online name. If the seller does a lot of business, you might find him or her mentioned elsewhere. Be informed.

Secure Versus Nonsecure Transactions

Figures 11.5 and 11.6 show a secure transaction. Instead of "http," the URL or address reads "https" to designate a "secure" site that is encrypted. The padlock on the bottom also indicates a secure site. Whenever you are at a site that requires any kind of credit card or financial account information, make sure you see "https" and a padlock icon. If you don't, you could be at a fraudulent website!

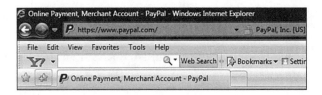

FIGURE 11.5

Address line in Internet Explorer showing a "secure" site because of the "https" designation

FIGURE 11.6

Padlock icon that appears at the lower-left corner of an Internet Explorer screen indicating a secure site

If It Sounds Too Good to Be True, It Is

We've all received one—the email in your inbox that reads, "I don't usually forward these things, but my friend, who is a real attorney, sent me this." It goes on to say that Microsoft founder Bill Gates is "sharing his good fortune" and "if you forward the email, Microsoft will pay you $245." Not really. This is one of a thousand different hoaxes that fill our inboxes and prey on our vulnerabilities. Some of these hoaxes have been circling the Internet for years, because it only takes one person to believe them and pass them along.

Trust your gut instinct. If it sounds too good to be true, it is. Remember that. Better yet, take the keywords in the email, add the word "hoax," and Google the entire phrase, as shown in Figure 11.7.

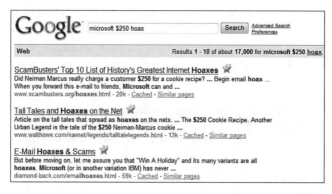

(© 2008 Google)

FIGURE 11.7

This email has been identified as a hoax on numerous sites.

RESOURCES

The following websites keep track of known hoaxes and are a good resource for determining whether an email's story is legitimate:

- Snopes (www.snopes.com)
- HoaxBusters (http://hoaxbusters.ciac.org/)
- UrbanLegends (www.urbanlegends.com)
- VMyths (www.vmyths.com)

Work-at-Home Scams

Many people who apply for work-at-home positions are struggling to balance family care with trying to make ends meet. Some people who apply for positions are disabled. We find these types of scams, which prey on people who need the extra money the most, particularly reprehensible.

Staffcentrix, a work-at-home advocacy organization, did a study in 2006 that revealed that only one of every 42 work-at-home offers was legitimate (source: www.staffcentrix.com).

Here's a list of some of the "typical" offers made by work-at-home scammers:

- "Work part time in your own home and make $500 to $1,500 your first month! It couldn't be any easier!"
- "A genuine opportunity! Guaranteed income!"
- "Work minutes a day at home and earn enough to make your dreams come true."

Remember that con artists pitching work-at-home schemes rake in $427 billion dollars a year. These scams are a favorite way for con artists to exploit people.

How to Spot a Scam

First, and most important, legitimate jobs that allow "telecommuting" rarely post their positions with a title of "Work at Home." That, in and of itself, is a good tipoff that the job may not be legitimate. "Medical transcriptionist" is a legitimate job title. "Work at Home—Easy Typing" is not.

Second, be wary if the offer is too good to be true. We don't mean to burst anyone's dreams, but an offer of "$1,500 a week for just 15 hours a week" should make you think twice.

Third, if the offer arrives in your inbox and you didn't ask for it, consider it spam. Delete it.

And finally, if the job offer does not have a legitimate job description and is deliberately vague, consider it a hoax.

Think about what a legitimate company would offer and expect nothing less. If a real company is behind the offer, they should have a legitimate company website, Human Resources department, phone numbers that can be authenticated, and so on. Remember that lots of money can be made from work-at-home scams, and sometimes they can be fronts for other scams that could land you in a world of trouble, so proceed cautiously whenever you consider any of these offers.

For every 42 offers, only one is legitimate. Keep that number in mind and act accordingly. We want to emphasize that there are some legitimate work-at-home offers, but you really need to do your research before you commit to one of these offers.

Mystery Shopper Scams

Earn $500 a week as a mystery shopper? Not likely. The only mystery about this scam is how they can keep coming up with more and more clever ways to bilk hard-working people out of their money.

Secret shopper or "mystery shopper" scams pretty much work the same way as other shop-at-home scams. A potential victim responds to an ad and receives information back from what appears to be a legitimate company. Often, this company even has a telephone number to call to verify its credentials. They may even send out an "employment packet" with training materials, training schedule, and so on. There's nothing like the human touch to bilk someone out of thousands of dollars.

Once the victim is convinced the company is legitimate and she can make money simply by shopping—something she may already love to do—the company sends her their first package with instructions and a check, usually a cashier's check, for several thousand dollars with the orders to cash the check right away. There's usually a stipulation that the check-cashing task must be completed "within 48 hours" or she will be fired. The cashier's check is really counterfeit, but it clears the bank because of the delay in notification that it is actually a counterfeit.

The victim is told that her "secret mission" is to test the effectiveness of a money-wiring service. Sometimes it's Western Union. We've heard of several that work with MoneyGram, which is a money-wiring service in Wal-Mart stores. The victim is instructed to test the effectiveness of the money-wiring service or is actually given shopping tasks at local chain stores and then asked to wire the remaining money—which can be several thousand dollars—back to the company. The victim is told to carefully document and evaluate the entire process to give it authenticity. It takes only a matter of time before the victim is notified by her bank that the check she cashed was a fake and she is now responsible for making up that amount.

Use Common Sense

No legitimate company would ever ask someone to wire money to someone they didn't know. Know that it can take up to a week or more to determine whether a check is good, especially if the check, even a cashier's check (which is supposed to be more "legitimate"), is from a foreign country. If you are asked to front any money, told you must pay fees, or have any suspicions, don't follow through with the task. There are legitimate mystery shopper programs, but read up about them first. Google the company name and see if anyone has written anything about them—good or bad. In other words, use common sense!

Money Mules

These types of scams, many of which masquerade as work-at-home jobs, rely on people to become "money mules." Basically, victims are being asked to launder cyber crime money. Many of these scam artists comb employment sites such as Monster.com and Careerbuilder.com to find resumes of people seeking employment. The offer is often to make a few hundred dollars a week, and it almost always involves money transfer transactions either online via PayPal or directly in person. These scams almost always involve a payment with money being wired somewhere, but the results are almost always the same—the victim finds out that the transaction was fraudulent and is left holding the bag for the amount of the damage—which can often run in the thousands of dollars. In addition, the victim has often handed over his own personal account information to the scammers in the process of completing the transaction. Be smart and do your homework.

The Power of Google—Turn the Tables

Whenever we are approached about a possible hoax, we turn to Google and run a search using the company's name and the word *hoax* or *scam* as the keywords. If we're lucky and the offer is indeed a scam, someone may very well have posted about it somewhere on the Internet. Use the power of the Internet to try and debunk these scammers! They can hide behind fake websites and legitimate-looking documents, but they can't hide behind powerful search engines that reveal what they really are. Just be aware that many of these scam artists are incredibly good at mimicking legitimate companies, even building fake "virtual" store fronts by copying the websites of legitimate businesses and posting them.

Social Engineering Scams

One of the most interesting facets of cyber crime is the technique of *social engineering*, which means the cyber crime is perpetrated by playing on the vulnerabilities of people.

Social engineering can involve a big red box that suddenly pops up on your computer monitor announcing "Security Alert—Click here." It might be an email that appears to come from your bank and states, "Critical Warning—Your Account Has Been Compromised. Click here to log in." See Figure 11.8 for an example.

FIGURE 11.8

Screenshot using scare tactics to try and get you to download spyware software. Note that many times the supposed "spyware" actually installs malicious software on your computer!

Ever had a warning pop up indicating your computer was infected? The thieves that develop these programs are very good at preying on our vulnerabilities, fears, and trust. For someone who is not computer savvy, these pop-ups appear to be legitimate warnings. They are designed to scare you into clicking them so more malware can be installed on your computer. Once installed, the

Once installed, the malware could be used to log your keystrokes, send your personal data to another computer, or hijack your computer for use in perpetuating spam or phishing scams, or worse.

malware could be used to log your keystrokes, send your personal data to another computer, or hijack your computer for use in perpetuating spam or phishing scams, or worse. The rule of thumb is to install a solid virus-protection program (see Chapter 16 for information on antivirus programs) and respond only when that program say there's a problem.

400 People Click to Get a Computer Virus

In an interesting experiment on social engineering, an IT security professional, Didier Stevens, placed the Google ad you see in Figure 11.9 on a website he purchased called www.drive-by-download.com. The ad offered to infect the user's computer by simply clicking it. Stevens ran the ad for 6 months. The results? Four hundred and nine people clicked the ad. Of course, Stevens did not actually infect anyone's computer, but it points to the fact that even with the best protections in place, software companies cannot control what people will do.

> **Drive-By Download**
> Is your PC virus-free?
> Get it infected here!
> drive-by-download.info

FIGURE 11.9

Actual ad asking people to click to get a virus on their computer

Women Versus Men—Who Gets Scammed More?

We couldn't resist citing some recent statistics just released in April of 2008 by the FBI based on data from the Internet Crime Complaint Center (www.ic3.gov). The statistics showed that "men lost more than women on average to Internet scams—$765 for men versus $552 for women."

And to be fair, we'll also cite another study conducted in the UK that asked 576 office workers in London to fill out a survey in return for a chocolate bar. The survey asked for a lot of personal information, including name, address, birthdate, and computer passwords. Only 10% percent of men gave up their passwords, whereas 45% of women gave up theirs (source: InfoSecurity Europe). It's chocolate, for heaven's sake!

The Easiest Way *Not* to Get Scammed

We can't say it enough—use common sense! Check everything out. Google all potential offers. You should always assume that email, job offer, or the promise of "riches beyond your wildest dreams" is not legitimate. On that note, we need to say that there are many legitimate mail order, direct marketing, and work-at-home businesses. Do your research and trust that inner voice that says, "This is too good to be true." It's usually right!

12

Peer-to-Peer Network Dangers

Your teen seems to have a never-ending playlist of music on his iPod or MP3 player. You assume he is just trading songs with his friends. You don't listen to that kind of music anyway, so you assume they are swapping CDs just like you and your friends used to swap albums. There's no harm in that, right? Wrong.

The Record Industry Association of America (www.riaa.com) is the trade group that represents the recording industry. The RIAA has, in recent years, emerged as the "piracy police" for any recorded audio.

Know that while your college student is ignoring you because she has her earbuds firmly implanted, she could also be opening up you and herself to some pretty hefty fines. In fact, the legal limit to which someone can be penalized for music piracy is 5 years in jail and $250,000.

Is it realistic to think these kinds of fines will be instituted against your child? Not really, but the RIAA has become much more aggressive in recent years fighting the battle against music piracy.

The RIAA cites an Institute for Policy Innovation study that concluded global

> Know that while your college student is ignoring you because she has her earbuds firmly implanted, she could also be opening up you and herself to some pretty hefty fines.

music piracy accounts for $12.5 billion of economic losses every year; 71,060 jobs lost; a loss of $2.7 billion in workers' earnings, $291 million in personal income tax, and $131 million in corporate income and production taxes (source: www.ipi.org).

P2P Networks

Peer-to-peer (or "P2P") networks allow multiple users to share files readily. They have many uses that are legitimate and allow easy file exchange via the Internet, but they have gained tremendous popularity as a means of sharing music. Some common P2P applications are LimeWire, DC++, BearShare, Warez, Morpheus, BitTorrent, and iMesh.

P2P and Music Piracy

It didn't take long for the RIAA to realize that these P2P networks were more often being used to share music collections, particularly among college and university students. Because P2P networks have user data records that are retrievable and resolvable, it also didn't take long for RIAA to target these networks as a major source for music piracy.

The RIAA openly acknowledges this targeting. Here's a statement from its website (www.riaa.com/faq.php):

> *That said, the piracy habits of college students remain especially and disproportionately problematic—despite real progress by the music industry on other fronts. According to some recent surveys, more than half of the nation's college students frequently download music and movies illegally from unlicensed P2P networks. That's a statistic we just cannot ignore.*
>
> *As a result, we have stepped up our efforts to address college piracy across the board by significantly expanding our deterrence and education programs, continuing our push for legal music offerings on campuses, and advocating technological measures that block or curb piracy on college networks.*

Actual Cases

In 2003, the RIAA began a crackdown against music piracy. To date, the RIAA has sued around 18,000 people. The figure includes 1,062 computer users at 130 universities. In 2007, the RIAA began a campaign specifically targeted at colleges and universities across the U.S. offering students caught in illegal downloading or trading the opportunity to avoid a potential lawsuit by settling out of court for a reduced fee. As of February of 2008, over 5,000 letters have been sent to students. These "prelitigation" offers gave the students the opportunity to pay up or face a lawsuit. Students who do not take the offer face lawsuits and minimum damages of $750 for each copyrighted recording they shared if they lose. That's $750 per song! The RIAA has engaged in formal lawsuits against 2,465 students who either ignored the initial offer or never received it.

The RIAA Investigation

How does the RIAA know which students to target? They don't. The following is from an October 24, 2007 article that appeared in the *Portsmouth Herald* newspaper interviewing an RIAA representative, Carol Duckworth:

> *"We have an active online investigative team," said Duckworth. "They log on to illegal peer-to-peer networks and monitor for copyright infringement. When they capture evidence of distribution, they get the IP address, a representative sampling of files shared, and a time stamp of the activity."*

There's that old IP address again. You'll hear us say this over and over: An IP address is like a homing beacon that can eventually end up on your doorstep. In this case, once the IP address is established, the RIAA sends out Digital Millennium Copyright Act letters. These letters inform the university's Internet service provider that an IP address on the network is illegally sharing copyrighted material. "From there we have no identifications, but the university network can send letters to the appropriate users," Duckworth explained.

University Cooperation?

Do universities, among the most liberal backdrops of America on issues of protecting privacy, cooperate with these requests? You bet they do. Among the many schools targeted was the University of New Hampshire, which we're most familiar with. A university spokeswoman, Kim Billings, was quoted in that same article as saying that the school passes the letters on to students. "They contact RIAA and get things worked out." At student orientation, the campus population is advised that UNH has a policy recommending students don't download illegal content. "We cooperate with anyone who issues the subpoenas," said Billings. "We say, 'We told you; here it comes.'"

That has been the case with most of the universities.

Challenges to the Lawsuit

Just recently, the RIAA suffered a legal setback when a judge ruled that the sole act of making a music file available in a "shared folder" does not violate copyright laws (Atlantic v. Howell). This ruling has tremendous significance to the RIAA's remaining lawsuits.

How P2P Works

To understand the significance of the ruling, it is important to understand how P2P networks work. Let's say you want to make certain files available to others over the Internet. There are many ways to share files, but one easy way is to install file-sharing software. Generally, these programs designate a particular folder as the public "shared" folder. P2P software is commonly used to share music, video, and software files. It also comes with some very inherent dangers, however.

P2P Dangers

The most common problem with P2P software is malware—malicious software that can easily be installed on your computer because, basically, you've left the front door open. P2P software manufacturers can make claims about protecting your computer all they want, but the reality is that P2P software is a huge source of nasty stuff that can wreak havoc on your system.

Another real danger is that by joining a P2P network, the potential exists that others could access, pilfer, or corrupt your private documents. These programs are not always intuitive, and some unskilled users have been known to share their entire hard drive, including their financial information, their family photos, their emails, and so on. The interface on some of these programs is very awkward to navigate and can lead to users sharing far more than they ever thought.

What the Experts Say

The SANS Institute, a nonprofit computer security organization, has identified file-sharing applications as one of the most crucial Internet security vulnerabilities.

Kids & Digital Content reports that 70% of kids ages 9 through 14 are downloading digital music. The NPD Group, a marketing research firm, has stated, "high levels of illegal peer-to-peer (P2P) file sharing" are attributed as the source of those downloads.

According to the Identity Theft Assistance Center, throughout 2008 "criminals will continue to exploit new technologies to commit identity theft." At the top of their list of "major event" security breaches from 2007 is a case involving a peer-to-peer file-sharing network.

SHARING KIDDIE PORN

In June of 2008, 44-year-old Scott Carpenter of Maryland was sentenced to 5 years in federal prison after pleading guilty to one count of receiving child pornography. Carpenter was apprehended when an undercover FBI agent signed onto a LimeWire account and entered search terms that were affiliated with child pornography images. Remember that many of these images are readily traded and that the people who are "regulars" know exactly what filenames to search for because they come up over and over again. Using the computer's IP address, the FBI was able to track the images back to Carpenter's computer. The agent had downloaded 14 images.

Supreme Court Justice's Data Breached

Think P2P problems only impact college students? Think again. In July of 2008, Supreme Court Justice Stephen Breyer's birth date and social security number, as well as records for about 2,000 other clients of an investment firm, ended up on the Internet when an employee of that investment firm who had LimeWire installed on his computer used it to swap personal files at the company's office—but company records were swapped as well. The breach went on for 6 months until a reader of *The Washington Post* discovered it and alerted the paper.

We'll say this over and over again: You need to be especially careful that, when you install a P2P program, you know exactly what files you are sharing and how the program works. Companies with sensitive data need to employ strong management practices by prohibiting this type of software on their corporate networks. It's a recipe for disaster.

> You need to be especially careful that, when you install a P2P program, you know exactly what files you are sharing and how the program works.

13

Crimes on Camera

The proliferation of social networks such as YouTube, Xanga, Facebook, and Technorati, just to name a few, have opened up a new avenue for criminals as well, not to only share their nasty deeds, but to do it in living color through streaming video. You wouldn't think that criminals would be so stupid as to put evidence of their crimes on the Internet for all to see, but they do—a *lot*. Law enforcement is finally catching on.

THE FLORIDA TEEN BEATING

As law enforcement veterans, we're exposed on a daily basis to things that would disturb most reasonable people, but one recent case left us horrified both as parents and women—the video of the 16-year-old Lakeland, Florida teen who was repeatedly beaten and harassed by six of her female classmates, all teenagers, even as young as 14 years old (see Figure 13.1).

(Courtesy Polk County Sheriff's Office)

FIGURE 13.1

Still image from Florida teen beating video in which a 16-year-old tries to defend herself from her attackers.

According to the Polk County Sheriff's Office, the victim was staying at the home of one of her attackers during spring break. On March 30, 2008, at approximately 8:00 p.m., the victim arrived at the residence and was met by two classmates, who both began yelling at the victim and threatening her.

The victim retreated to a bedroom and was met by another young teen hiding in the bedroom, who began insulting and threatening her. This young woman allegedly struck the victim several times in the face, and slammed the victim's head into the bedroom wall, knocking the victim unconscious.

When the victim came to, she was on the couch in the living room surrounded by six girls. According to the victim, the suspects held her down and began to beat her again and yell at her while one of the attackers videotaped the assault. At one point in the video, the suspects block the victim from leaving the residence.

Two teenage boys waited outside the home as lookouts.

After the attack was over, three of the suspects forced the victim into a vehicle and drove her to another location where she was finally released with a threat from the suspects warning her not to contact law enforcement or she would be beaten even worse.

Once at a friend's home, the victim called law enforcement and was transported to Lakeland Regional Medical Center by ambulance for injuries sustained as a result of the beating. She was treated for a concussion, damage to her left eye and left ear, and numerous bruises.

The six girls involved in the beating were charged with felony battery and false imprisonment. They are being charged as adults. The two boys who acted as lookouts are also being charged. Although it is doubtful the sentence would be this severe, felony kidnapping is punishable up to life imprisonment.

Polk County Sheriff Grady Judd called the attack "animalistic." He said, "I've been involved in law enforcement for 35 years, and I've seen a lot of extremely violent events, but I've never seen children, 14 to 18 years of age, engage in this conduct for a 30-minute period of time and then make these video clips."

The victim's father said the teens' motivation for the attack was to produce a video that would become popular on YouTube. The mother of one of the suspects said the victim had provoked the other teens by threatening and insulting them on MySpace.

OUR REACTION

We don't know what the real motivation was behind this brutal attack. As law-enforcement professionals and as parents, we understand that teenagers don't always act rationally. It's hard to even express how vile and sickening this whole episode was to hear about and view. We couldn't decide what was worse: the fact that these young women resorted to brutal violence in what was a "gang-like" assault to resolve a conflict, the fact that they thought it appropriate to videotape the assault, or the fact that they laughed and encouraged each other to continue to beat the victim. It's a sad commentary that does not reflect what most teens are about, but we mention it here because it illustrates the mindset of a generation that thinks in terms of videos and posting on the Internet as a normal course of their social lives—good or bad.

In an ironic twist, a couple from Lakeland who do not even have children have been repeatedly harassed by callers from as far away as Brooklyn,

New York, because their phone number was mistakenly associated with the teen beatings on YouTube. The couple, who has had the number for years and uses it for business purposes, has tolerated phone call after threatening phone call. "I'm calling from Brooklyn you f__ piece of s__," one caller said. "Let me tell you something. Look out your f__ window. I'll slit your throat and beat the s__ out of you." The phone rings approximately every 3 minutes. Police have increased patrols in their area since their address was also disclosed.

The Beating of an Art Teacher

Unfortunately, this is not the only episode of assault being captured on videotape for later posting on the Internet. In April of 2008, a 30-year-old art teacher from a high school in Baltimore was sucker punched by a female tenth-grade student and then beaten while another student recorded the incident on her cell phone camera. The video begins with the teacher on the floor trying to defend herself while other students cheered on the attacker. The video was later posted by the students on MySpace. The teacher, whose name we are withholding, told news reporters that she is "petrified to go back to that building. I miss the good students that I have. I love them dearly, but I can't do it." The teacher subsequently filed criminal charges against the student.

Caught in a Trap

A recently aired story from a local news station shows a man in a bathrobe who strips and starts dancing to the theme from *Rocky* around a set mouse trap. We all know where this is headed—he places his penis on the trap, which then snaps on the family jewels. His reaction is also caught on film.

Dozens of news stations as well as online forums picked up the story. Needless to say, the clip can be accessed on the Internet, and as disturbing as people claim the whole behavior (and subsequent public airing) is, it has generated a considerable amount on online attention. Not only can you chat about it, comment about it, and blog about it, you can view it on several sites. This is not the first such incident that has hit the Internet— one teen actually did the same act for $20 and a pack of cigarettes. However, this incident was intended to be viewed over public cable access on television. The reaction over the public television episode locally hit the

Internet and the word spread. Twenty years ago, a childish stunt like this would not have garnered much attention. However, in today's world, millions can now view this type of infamous idiocy almost instantaneously.

Ten Hours of Video Uploaded Every Minute

It used to be that people would videotape their families and send in their funny home videos to television shows for a shot at seeing themselves on primetime TV or even for some prize money. However, YouTube and other video sites have changed the nature of sharing video. Although the funny clips can still be found, it is just as common to find kids daring each other to perform reckless and dangerous stunts, or for criminals to video themselves committing crimes.

YouTube, an independent subsidiary of Google, allows people to post videos online with free registration. One can post videos for private or public viewing. According to their own policies, YouTube does not allow nudity, graphic violence, or hate crimes to be posted. However, YouTube often depends upon their own members to police what is uploaded and for viewers to flag such videos in order to have them removed. It is estimated that approximately 10 hours of video is uploaded onto YouTube every single minute, making for a considerable amount of material to censor. YouTube does have a division dedicated to working with law enforcement to investigate crimes memorialized on their site. Despite their efforts, though, there is little control over the material uploaded onto the site until someone finds it offensive enough to report it.

It is very common to find clips of people performing idiotic stunts for a shot at fame. Remember the guy who stuck his genitals in the mousetrap? A quick search of YouTube will confirm this was not an "original" act. Other stunts include fire, bicycles, vehicles, skateboards, and taunting animals, much like what appeared in the popular *Jackass* series and movies.

> Despite their efforts, there is little control over the material uploaded onto the site until someone finds it offensive enough to report it.

Then there are the videos that document victimizing others, sometimes violently. Some of these crimes include burglaries, rape, homicide, and gang violence. For example, Twin Falls, Idaho police were seeking information on a video posted in which a male is apparently feeding beer to an infant. In the clip, other young children are also allegedly drinking. In another investigation in July of 2007, the FBI and Jackson County, Texas police tracked down individuals who allegedly gave a toddler the drug ecstasy while the young child was unsecured laying unresponsive on the floor of a van. The video uploaded to YouTube showed the toddler's eyes rolled back so that only the whites showed. Comments could be heard in the video about how the child may have been given ecstasy. There were reportedly three adults and four teens in the video as well, with the 21-year-old mother of the child driving the van. The people involved in this horrific example of child abuse were tracked down through the YouTube and MySpace accounts connected to the video.

In July of 2008, teens videotaped their crime spree through Shawnee and Lawrence, Kansas and broadcast it on YouTube. They spray-painted a logo around skate parks and lit an M-80 firecracker attached to a spray paint can behind a local business. A Shawnee officer found the videos on YouTube, which provided very important clues.

Utilizing websites such as Facebook, MySpace, and YouTube as investigative tools is becoming more and more common for police, because the videos are documentation of actual crimes and therefore excellent evidence. Searching YouTube has become a regular duty of many local school resource officers and detectives. Investigators can find many clues about crimes and who may have perpetrated them within these videos. The account information connected with such as video, such as email, user ID, and even the IP address at the time of the posting, are also important clues for police and can provide strong leads to track the criminals involved.

In May of 2008, the Royal Canadian Mounted Police investigated the assault of two teenagers with a weapon outside of a night club. A video of the incident was located, and the RCMP posted a link on their website, asking for community assistance in identifying the perpetrators. This is becoming a common investigative technique, in addition to the use of such programs as Crimeline and Crime Stoppers, where images captured of crimes are posted and individuals can leave tips if they have information on a particular crime.

In November of 2007, authorities in New Jersey placed a video clip on YouTube with the hope of tracking down the suspect in the beating death of a Rowan University student. The clip showed the suspect inside a convenience store on the night of the murder. The victim was approached by several men in a vehicle who asked for directions to a party, then proceeded to punch and kick the victim leaving him on the ground. The victim succumbed to his injuries the following day. Investigators hoped that this video tip, along with a reward, would bring some important leads their way. As of July 2008, this murder is still unsolved. As of this writing, this unsolved case is also among the "Fugitive Data Files" on the website for *America's Most Wanted*, which aired the story in January of 2008.

The Dallas Police Department has launched their own YouTube page where surveillance videos are posted in the hope that viewers will provide some leads. In July, Dallas PD solved their first case using the YouTube site when they arrested two suspects who had stolen flat-screen televisions off a wall in an upscale hotel for pets called "Pet Ritz."

British police are posting audio clips of hoax emergency calls and calls to the British emergency line 999 (akin to 911 in the States) with the hope of shaming people into stop wasting emergency dispatch and emergency service resources. Examples include one woman calling the emergency line to ask what year the Internet was started and a man complaining that his wife refused to make him anything other than salmon sandwiches for lunch. This initiative was started because the Avon and Somerset police were receiving more than 400 prank calls per month on the emergency line.

Even residents are taking matters into their own hands. Residents of a neighborhood in downtown Madrid, Spain became aggravated at the prostitution occurring in their streets at night, so they began filming the activity using webcams. Neighbors claimed that there were upwards of 100 girls working the streets at night as well as activity in a building they claimed was used as a brothel. They felt their many complaints to the local police were being ignored, so they broadcast the clips of prostitutes negotiating with their clients and even arguing with their pimps in the hope of shaming the johns and deterring the activity. Ironically enough, an association that defends the rights of prostitutes in Spain, called Heteria, made a formal complaint that the neighbors had violated the prostitutes' right to privacy by videotaping the activity. Residents were ordered to stop filming and fined for broadcasting the images of people without their consent. The Spanish Data Protection Agency reported that this was the first time that action had been taken against private citizens for invading people's privacy. On a more positive note, local authorities have now installed cameras on that neighborhood street.

The most notorious example of YouTube use was in the recent arrest of Radovan Karadzic. Karadzic was the leader of the Bosnian Serbs during the Bosnian civil war in 1992–1995 in the former Yugoslavia. Regarded as the "Osama Bin Laden of Europe," Karadzic was the chief architect behind the slaughter of an estimated 8,000 Muslim men in Bosnia during that time. Wanted for these atrocious war crimes, Karadzic went into hiding in 1997 and eluded capture for 11 years. Upon his arrest in July of 2008, it was discovered that Karadzic had been hiding in plain sight for all those years as Dr. Dragan Dabic. As Dr. Dabic, Karadzic was a practicing homeopathic physician who lectured in community centers, wrote articles for medical journals, and composed poetry. He had dramatically changed his appearance by growing his gray hair very long, wearing it in a ponytail, and covering his facial features with an overgrown mustache and beard. He also wore large framed glasses and obtained false papers for his new identity. He had been living in an apartment in the Serb capital of New Belgrade, and had openly lectured and attended conventions. Dr. Dragan Dabic had an official website advertising his philosophies and how to contact him for television appearances, private consultations, seminars, and public forum invitations (www.dragandabic.com).

Video clips of his appearances and lectures can be seen on YouTube, and as of this writing, the official website is still accessible.

Of course, it should be no surprise that YouTube is not only used by criminals bragging about their misdeeds and cops looking to solve cases, but also by aspiring miscreants of society looking for a little video instruction. The wanna-be methamphetamine maker can find a how-to video on YouTube, and now even the child porn collector can learn how to best hide his illegal collection thanks to a 4-minute demonstration of how to use a new program to hide videos, programs, and photographs on the ever popular iPhone (http://www.youtube.com/watch?v=HhJs9XQEF44&feature= related). The software, called HidePod, can be purchased by using PayPal directly through the developer and installed on a "jailbroken" iPhone. *Jailbreaking* allows unauthorized software to be added to an iPhone and is reportedly easy (and free) to do. There's even a site that gives users instructions for jailbreaking in 45 seconds (http://lifehacker.com/370532/ jailbreak-any-iphone-or-ipod-touch-in-45-seconds). The HidePod software appears on the iPhone touch screen as a calculator, and when the user enters a password, hidden programs and media can be accessed. This is yet one more hurdle for law enforcement to keep an eye out for when investigating crimes on video.

Using a Digital Camera or Cell Phone to Determine Coordinates

Did you know that many new digital cameras can put a location stamp and a timestamp on your picture that will reveal the latitude and longitude where the picture was taken as well as the exact time? From the user's standpoint, this makes it easier to find the dozen pictures you took in Rome out of thousands of images from your European vacation. From a law-enforcement standpoint, it presents a unique investigative tool.

Consider the child pornographer who snaps exploitive photos of a child with a digital camera at his apartment on a particular date. The perpetrator can assert all he wants that the child never came to his apartment, but via this software, the digital "location stamp" could present keen evidence to the contrary.

What You Put Out There, Stays Out There

Video-hosting sites such as YouTube are self-regulating. Although they may state that their policies prohibit videos of criminal acts, given the volume of videos uploaded on an hourly basis, these social networks remain "self-policing." These videos can be captured and saved in perpetuity even if they are flagged as offensive or in violation of policy. Too many young people do not realize that the Internet is archived, and a thoughtless act as a teen could very well come back to haunt them later on. In Chapter 2, "Two Bedrooms Up, One Bedroom Down—What Someone Can Find Out About You on the Internet," we discussed The Wayback Machine, a joint effort between the Library of Congress and The Smithsonian to archive everything on the Internet (www.archive.org). Remember, what you put out there, stays out there.

14

Computers and Drugs

For some, combining the topics of the Internet, computers, and drugs will make them immediately think about their email in-boxes being filled with unsolicited ads for Viagra and other male-enhancement drugs. Although annoying, this barrage of sales pitches for little blue penile-enlargement drugs is not all one can find online. In regard to harmful drugs, the Internet has truly become a tremendous resource for all kinds of information related to substance abuse, including sites about recognizing the symptoms of drug addiction, warnings about drug interaction, drug treatment resources, and substance abuse support. This information is invaluable, and the resources are nearly endless. However, what many do not realize is that the Internet has also become a gateway of easy access for information on illegal drug activities. This is the darker side of drugs and computers we will explore.

Techie Dealers

Think for a moment about how computers and the Internet have transformed the way you do business—you have instant communication, secure private networks, easy file transfer, and a plethora of information all at your fingertips. Think now about what all this means to a drug dealer—encrypted business ledgers, private emails, easily shared customer databases, arranged meeting points, anonymous communications, and so on. Trust us, this has not escaped the notice of investigators.

Rave Parties

We'd like to take you back in time to the 1950s in London, where the term *rave* was first used to describe wild bohemian parties. The band The Yardbirds coined the phrase *rave up* in the 1960s, and those who were hard partiers quickly became referred to as *ravers*.

In the 1980s, youths were attending large parties where "acid house" music and techno electronic music was played in a setting of laser light shows. The repetitive electronic beats created an almost hypnotic background for partygoers.

These parties were held in warehouses, clubs, and outdoors, and they attracted thousands of partygoers. The parties would often last for days and were marked by the use of club drugs such as Ecstasy, speed, methamphetamine, GHB (the date rape drug), Rohypnol, LSD, and Ketamine (an animal tranquilizer). These parties caught on in major urban areas across the United States, where they were largely held "underground."

Aware of their presence, law enforcement investigated these rave parties in the late 1990s and early 2000s because of the common and widespread use of club drugs. Rave parties were a place to buy drugs for the partier and a place to cash in for the party promoter and drug dealer. Typically a cover fee would be assessed, and once inside, partygoers would pack into the space, dancing and hugging to loud techno music. Drug use was out in the open, and the partying and drugging would occur all night and even for days.

These parties were huge moneymakers for promoters. People were packed into locations like herded animals. The parties were loud and hot. Ironically, no alcohol was served because of the common attendance of underage partiers, although that did not stop the sale of illicit substances, which were sold by the dose and could cost anywhere from $5 to $50 per hit. On the other hand, bottles of water went for $5 or $10 because the combination of the ecstasy and wild dancing in closed quarters could send a partier's body temperature skyrocketing.

Dust Masks and Glo-Sticks

Ecstasy, a popular club or "designer" drug, is a form of hallucinogen (MDMA [3,4-methylenedioxy- N-methylamphetamine]) that impacts the five senses. Under the influence of the drug, an individual's hearing, smell, sight, taste, and emotional feelings are amplified by outside stimulus. Bizarre behavior could be witnessed at these parties, such as attendees dancing around with glo-sticks on their heads, wrists, or even pierced onto parts of their bodies. It was common to see kids sucking on pacifiers and wearing dust masks. The glo-sticks and the laser light shows helped enhance the visual high, while the loud music provided an auditory stimulus. The dust masks often contained Vicks Vapor Rub, because the smell was enhanced by the drug use and aided in the euphoria of the partier. The baby pacifiers were not for a high but rather to prevent the partier's teeth from grinding, a side effect of ecstasy. People would be hugging and friendly, touting the philosophy that they believed in PLURR (Peace, Love, Unity, Respect, and Responsibility). The effect of ecstasy was often one of feeling affectionate, and therefore it was not uncommon to see people hugging and kissing, regardless of whether they knew each other. In the restrooms or in the corner of the room, one could find the dealers peddling their wares, one hit at a time. Kids would shell out cash for any substance purported to make them high, often buying and ingesting substances unknown even to themselves. During one raid, arrestees admitted to putting unknown substances in their bodies, not giving any thought to what they were ingesting or how it might harm them.

> Kids would shell out cash for any substance purported to make them high, often buying and ingesting substances unknown even to themselves.

A Different Dose Each Time

Because club drugs are often cooked up in clandestine laboratories, there are no standards. Two different dealers selling a dose of ecstasy could actually be selling two entirely different substances. The strength of the hit, the way it is manufactured, and the cut used for the drug could be different and even deadly. The term "cut" refers to the additives that dealers use when packaging their drug for sale. The purity of a drug is actually cut by the additive. Inostitol, a supplement that can be purchased at any vitamin store, is the common cut for cocaine dealers. When a dealer wants to get more mileage from the product, he will use almost any available substance to do so. In terms of club or designer drugs, these drugs are often made by a basement chemist who mixes at will and cuts with agents such as lye or Draino in filthy conditions. Labs have been found in barns, hotel rooms, trailers, and in the woods. The process is volatile and dangerous, and has resulted in the deaths of chemists as well as law enforcement officers.

There are well-documented cases of kids dying after using Ecstasy (or XTC, one of its street slang names) just one time, often because their bodies were unable to regulate their internal body temperature and they cooked to death from the inside. In trainings we conducted for law enforcement and parents' information, we showed a popular television news segment that went undercover at rave parties and interviewed partygoers. The reaction from the crowds, regardless of whether they were seasoned law-enforcement veterans or parents of new teenagers, was shock at the behavior exhibited in front of the cameras. Some youths were behaving with delayed reflexes, slurred speech, and almost trance-like actions. Others were off the wall, dancing, jumping, and hugging and kissing everyone, even complete strangers. Some were actively snorting lines of Ketamine or drinking bottle caps of clear GHB. There were even kids who had passed out, were having difficulty breathing, or were unconscious, possibly from the body overheating or from the reaction of the combinations of drugs in their bodies. The youths who agreed to be interviewed behaved in a dopey, drug-induced manner. Some talked about being in this state for a couple of days or even looking forward to the next party. One female talked about the risk of taking some of the club drugs and how she was aware she could die; however, it just didn't matter. These kids put anything in their systems regardless of the consequences just to experience the "high."

Rave Parties and the World Wide Web

Whereas it used to be that fliers were the primary way of spreading the word about upcoming rave parties, more and more party organizers have turned to the World Wide Web. Ravers can go to promoters' websites to find out the next party location, sometimes getting the information cryptically somewhere on the site. Party attendees are sometimes given a password that allows them access to websites that promote the next party location, date, and time. Many times, social networking sites are used to distribute the word about large rave parties. Just go to YouTube and put in "Rave Party" as a search term or visit one of the many online rave stores, where you can purchase all your party favors and supplies. If that's not enough, go to www.ravelinks.com, the underground rave party site. This site has links for the partygoer looking to find a party, purchase supplies, or find music for their own party, and they can even blog about their raving. The site has ads and information about all things rave.

Online Recipes

We're not talking about Martha Stewart's dessert of the month or Emeril's newest creation. We're talking about how to mix up the latest batch of GHB or methamphetamine. It's downright frightening how quickly one can find the recipe for a lot of very scary, illegal substances. For example, enquiring about making GHB resulted in over 679,000 search results for the infamous clear liquid, which is commonly referred to as the "date rape drug."

Not only can you whip up the recipe, but you can find many links to the sites where you can purchase any necessary ingredients you can't find under your bathroom sink. If reading the recipe is too difficult, there are plenty of "how-to" videos available on popular video sites.

Typing the words "make ecstasy" into a search engine returns over 9 million results.

Typing the words "make ecstasy" into a search engine returns over 9 million results. One of the sites talks about using common household items and how the "lab" can be moved from place to place easily in a small container. Another advertises making ecstasy at home.

Remember when you could walk into your local drugstore and purchase Sudafed and other similar nasal decongestants in bulk without being interrogated? Now many over-the-counter cold remedies must be requested at the pharmacy counter and are sold in limited quantities because aspiring chemists were buying cold medication in bulk in order to make their own Ecstasy in their basement labs.

How Many Colds Can One Man Have?

During one case, we set up surveillance on a subject who had ordered 10,000 pills containing ephedrine from a large chain pharmacy. (Obviously, the pharmacy had dropped a dime to law enforcement following the unusually large and suspect order.)

We followed the suspect out of the parking lot and onto the interstate, where a carefully orchestrated motor vehicle stop was conducted by a uniformed state trooper. The suspect gave the officer consent to look in the trunk, and upon seeing the bags of pills, he asked the suspect what he was doing with the medicine. The suspect responded that he was sending the pills overseas to family members to treat their colds. That's a lot of colds....

The Exploding Kitchen

An Internet search for "How to make methamphetamine" returns 473,000 results. One site even advertises making methamphetamine "the proper way." In this search, you can also find the how-to video if you are unsure in the kitchen. We found one very complete recipe that not only outlined ingredients and equipment, but also had a list of over-the-counter medication to steer clear of because they do not contain the coveted ingredients. The site also encouraged the use of distilled water so as to "do things right." This site very courteously pointed out the flammable hazards of the process and other precautions, such as the fact that Ethyl Ether is very flammable and is heavier than air—and that it is also an anesthetic and can cause respiratory collapse if you inhale too much. It then very clearly outlines every step in the entire procedure so well that we believe anyone could give it a shot. Needless to say, this drug is made in the same clandestine laboratories utilized in the making of Ecstasy, and therefore it's just as dangerous.

Scam Cannabis—One-Stop Marijuana Shopping

What discussion about drugs would be complete without covering the topic of marijuana, a controversial substance in regard to legislation? We will mention up front that we are adamantly opposed to the legalization of marijuana for a number of reasons, so as far as we are concerned, the following information is in the category of "illegal," just like all the others mentioned.

The pro-marijuana site www.scamcannabis.com purports itself to be a free service "that seeks ways to expose the truth about real marijuana cannabis websites." It's entirely devoted to marijuana information, message boards, cannabis search engines, seed bank ratings, how to make an online purchase, and even tips to avoid getting caught by the police and defense strategies in the event one does get caught. It claims to help visitors prevent getting scammed by imposter sites and from purchasing seeds with fake seed ratings, as well as educating its visitors about falling for sites that are not selling real marijuana but rather marijuana alternatives. Obviously from a law-enforcement standpoint, this site simply seeks to justify the illegal use and sale of marijuana.

According to the website, "It's a smart practice to start off small and find a reliable cannabis vendor by placing a few small orders with different companies. You'll always find someone willing to deliver to anywhere in the world. Privacy should be #1 on your mind at all times." The site then gives some warning signs, such as a vendor who brags about how long they have been in business, and advises never to buy an item through bulk email. It even warns the visitor about unauthorized credit card transactions. Reading the information on the site, it would appear as though the site was giving advice about making online shopping purchases of vitamins.

This site is accessible to anyone who can type the word "marijuana" into a search engine, even children. A search for "marijuana seeds for sale" brings up plenty of options for anyone with access to a credit card number or online account. There are also many other sites that encourage marijuana use and offer justifications for it.

It goes without saying that anyone who wants to justify their illegal drug use can certainly find others with a common interest through many avenues. Newspapers, news programs, periodicals, and other media sensationalize drug use by celebrities and politicians—not to mention movies and music. And then there is the Internet. YouTube, MySpace, newsgroups, informational sites, blogs, and chat rooms are plentiful and accessible to both adults and children. This is the only place where one can type in a drug-related search phrase and get the immediate gratification of a response within seconds. For that matter, the Internet actually provides thousands of results for a query in seconds. Is it no wonder that "marijuana" is one of the most frequently searched-for phrases online?

Steroids

The phrase "buy steroids online" produced 398,000 results. With steroids being such a hot topic these days, we thought we'd point out sites such as www.buysteroids.com, which advertises "buy steroids online.... We ship discreetly, internationally, no prescription required, secure checkout, trusted vendor." And then there's www.steroidsexpress.com, where you can acquire European anabolic steroids "from a real online pharmacy."

The purchase or possession of anabolic steroids in the United States is illegal without a valid prescription. It is also essentially illegal to import steroids from other countries unless the buyer is a DEA-registered importer. Many countries control anabolic steroids; however, in Thailand and Mexico steroids are available over the counter.

In September of 2007, the Drug Enforcement Administration announced the arrests of 124 subjects in 27 states as a result of an international investigation into illicit anabolic steroid use. Four days of raids shut down 26 underground steroid labs across the country, with a total of 56 labs closed over the 18-month investigation. Chinese companies were targeted in "Operation Raw Deal" for supplying raw materials for these labs to produce the illegal substance. Several other countries were also identified as being involved. Six and a half million dollars and over 500 pounds of raw steroid powder were seized. During the investigation, investigators targeted online message boards where steroid use advice was given and websites that promoted the sale of the finished product. Hundreds of thousands of emails were also intercepted and compiled into databases and analyzed as part of the investigation.

Drug Dealers Love Technology, Too

Narcotics investigators may use the Internet to gather information from social networking sites, video-sharing sties, chat rooms, message boards, and emails, but they are also keenly aware that drug dealers use computers, too.

It is not uncommon for drug dealers to keep meticulous records online, so investigators know to include all computer equipment in search warrants. The drug business is a very mobile one, so home phones and cell phones also become part of the puzzle. Wire taps, which were once done with landlines (home phones) hooked up to tape recorders, are now managed completely on the computer. Software enables investigators to monitor pertinent calls in real time, date and timestamp the call, rewind for clarification, transcribe the recordings right on the computer, and manage and organize the information collected from the wiretap. Long gone are the tedious days of handing a tape recording to the administrative assistant to transcribe and logging an endless number of cassette tapes into evidence.

Tools of the Drug Dealers

For the dealer, text messaging, disposable cell phones, email, and social networking are tools of the trade. For the advanced dealer, encrypted ledgers and pertinent information are stored on the computer. Larger-scale dealers use high-tech equipment for alarms and surveillance of their homes or places where business is conducted. Some dealers have equipment that will detect a body wire on an informant or undercover officer. And don't think that a larger-scale dealer doesn't check up on the background of new customers to verify that they are legit—search engines, reverse directories, white pages, and other information databases are employed to build a dossier on a subject. Counter-surveillance techniques are also commonly used by suppliers as a means to protect themselves from getting caught by law enforcement or being "ganked"—that is, cheated on by another dealer or customer with either fake money or bogus drugs. Remember, too, that competition between larger dealers can be very territorial and sometimes violent.

Who's a Rat?

One website in particular, www.whosarat.com, boasts of being the largest online database of "rats"—that is, cooperating informants and law-enforcement agents. This site has a "rat of the week" section and a lawyer referral. Although the site is now accessible only to paid subscribers, once a member, you can access agent and informant profiles and even pertinent case law. Currently the site has over 5,000 "rat" profiles, although the accuracy and timeliness of the information is not known. From our standpoint, this type of site can be construed as having the intention of intimidating cooperating individuals, as well as being a safety issue for informants and undercover officers as well.

> Remember that if the drug dealers can access the information, so can your kids. If they can spell the name of a drug, they can find sources for it.

Once again, computer technology and the Internet is a double-edged sword, providing tools both for those involved in illegal drug activity as well as for those seeking justice.

The key here is to remember that if the drug dealers can access the information, so can your kids. If they can spell the name of a drug, they can find sources for it.

In her earlier career, Felicia was a teacher in an elementary school. One day, her students were given the assignment of searching for biographical information about children's authors. One of the more popular authors goes by the name of "Avi," which also happens to be a standard video format. It was all Felicia could do to shut monitors off as quickly as possible when adult videos started popping up everywhere. The school did not have any blocking software in place at the time, but the lesson was that even children who don't intend to look up inappropriate material can easily stumble upon it. Just one more reason why parental oversight is so critical whenever kids are using computers.

15

Who Is Tracking Your Online Activities?

If a serial killer is on the loose, law enforcement may use a "criminal profiler"—someone who is trained to analyze all facets of the crime, including the modus operandi, frequency, habits, and psychology of the prospective killer. With enough information and evidence, a hauntingly accurate portrait of the killer can be drawn—for example, "repressed, white male, approximately 30 to 40 years of age, who has narcissistic tendencies, may have served in the military, and is now living in the South."

You've Been Profiled—Data Aggregators

Profiling is also used in many ways to monitor some of your daily activities without you even realizing it. It can include what items get scanned at the checkout when you sweep your store discount card, what magazines you subscribe to, what car loans you have, and so on. Instead of a criminal profiler, marketing specialists target your personal habits. They want to know as much as they can about you to target you for potential sales.

Privacy advocates often vent about how much information the FBI has in its files, but that's nothing compared to what your online profile says about you. Think for a minute about what your online habits can tell a marketing company:

- You prefer foreign cars over domestic because you visit eBay autos and go to the foreign car section.
- You are gay because you frequently visit *The Advocate* online.
- You are a Christian because you visit online bible study groups.
- You have a dog because you visit online pet stores. (Then again, marketers might already know if you have a dog if your town has published your pet registration information online.)
- You love country music because you stream country channels.
- You have fibromyalgia because you frequent online support groups.
- You prefer fine wine because you have an online subscription to notify you when a new vintage is released.

Cookies—Not the Sugar Kind

We cannot emphasize this enough—the Internet, despite everything you think of it as being, is really just a product. It has, perhaps, the largest customer base of any conceivable product. Millions of people want to take advantage of this potential customer base. Anyone who knows anything about marketing knows that information is invaluable to direct sales. The more a company knows about its customers, the easier it is to steer sales their way. This is why top sales executives always approach a sales meeting with a "profile" portfolio containing as much information about their potential customers as they can. The more they know about their customers, the easier it will be to sell to them.

> No one wants to think that what they do in the privacy of their own home can be disseminated, but the truth is, it can and it does.

The Internet presents a unique challenge to marketers because an expectation of privacy is attached to it. No one wants to think that what they do in the privacy of their own home can be disseminated, but the truth is, it can and it does.

A *cookie*, in computing terms, is a tiny bit of text sent by a "big" computer or server to your computer's web browser (such as Internet Explorer or Firefox). This text is subsequently sent back to the server whenever you visit the website. For example, if you go to www.nytimes.com, a cookie will be downloaded to your computer. You won't know it's there unless you specifically look for it, but it is there.

What Kind of Information Do Cookies Track?

Cookies are sometimes used for authentication—in other words, if you log into a social networking site that requires a username and password, a cookie can verify that you are legitimate and will allow you back in without requiring you to reenter that information.

Cookies can be used to personalize the websites you visit. For example, you might want to customize what you see on a newspaper's website so that you see all the local news, but not the sports page. A cookie can be used to customize your view and retain that information each time you visit the site.

Cookies can also track your web history—where you've gone, what sites you've visited. This is where privacy advocates have issues. Although the cookie returned to the server is not supposed to include personally identifying information, it could. It could easily include your email address or, in the case of a form-based cookie such as an online shopping cart, your name and address—whatever you provide to the site.

Because cookies are like mini scratch pads, different websites can share tracking cookies, and each website with the same tracking cookie can read the information and write new information into it.

Preventing Cookies

It is possible to set your browser settings to reject cookies, but guess what? You may not be able to get to many of the sites you regularly visit unless you allow their cookies to be set. If you're so inclined to not allow any cookies, here's how to set that in Internet Explorer:

1. Go to Tools, Internet Options.
2. Select the Privacy and then click the Advanced button.
3. Check the Override Automatic Cookie Handling option in the resulting dialog box.
4. Select Third Party Cookies.
5. Check the Block option.
6. Click OK and then click OK again.

Our Take on Cookies

Many people are split on the issue of cookies, but the reality is that they've been around for a long time, and most people don't even realize they're there. We operate under the premise that everything you do on a computer is traceable, not just what sites you've visited, but what emails you've sent, what online chats you've had while instant messaging, what images you've viewed, what files you've downloaded, and so on. From a computer forensic standpoint, this is generally true, so unless you're conducting some untoward business that is going to cause your computer to end up being dissected and analyzed by a computer forensic analyst, you shouldn't worry that much about the cookie that gets dropped onto your computer because you went to a medical site. That information is being tracked along with the golf clubs you just bought and the hotel and flight you reserved with your credit card.

What's a EULA?

You've probably seen a EULA dozens of times and didn't realize what it was. A EULA (or End User License Agreement) is the pop-up box of legalese that appears whenever you install software on a computer. Sometimes you have to actually scroll through the box and then click I Agree, but most times you can just click I Agree and keep the installation going.

EULAs are the legal backbone for companies to do all sorts of things, and it behooves everyone to at least be aware of what some of those potential things are. Primarily, a EULA controls the license of the software on your computer. It usually has language stating that the software can only be installed on one machine, and to install it on other machines requires additional licenses. When you click I Agree, you're basically signing an electronic contract stating that you will abide by the terms of the agreement.

What many people don't realize is that a EULA will often specify rights related to privacy and the protection of your computer. For example, many EULAs will clearly state that in the future, they may install software on your computer without your consent. They may install tracking software to get better demographics on who is using their programs. A EULA may also stipulate that it will automatically patch your computer with software updates, and, yes, if something goes wrong, you can guarantee that the EULA will stipulate it is not responsible for any damage as a result.

Does this mean that people are not going to install software they need or want because of what is stipulated in the EULA? Probably not, but it's a smart idea to at least read the EULA before you click I Agree to know what the potential for problems is, especially if you have privacy concerns.

Even Hackers Have EULAs

In an ironic twist, Symantec Corporation, producer of a suite of antivirus programs, recently announced on its blog that it had noticed a Russian posting that essentially was a EULA for hackers. It read as follows:

> *The customer can't resell the product, examine its underlying coding, use it to control other bot nets, or submit it to antivirus companies and agrees to pay the seller a fee for product updates.*

The punishment if other hackers don't comply with this rule?

> *Violate the terms, and we'll report you ourselves to the antivirus companies by giving them information about how to dismantle your bot network or prevent it from growing bigger.*

A Symantec Corporation senior principal security researcher described this EULA as "humorous."

You Need to Know About Bots and Botnets

It is estimated that millions of computers are being used unwittingly to propagate cyber crime. Your computer could very well be part of it. A *bot attack* happens when your computer is hijacked via malicious software (called "malware") installed on it. This allows remote control of your computer to spread viruses, send spam, or even commit fraud. Once your computer is infected, it becomes part of a "botnet," or network of remotely controlled computers. The people who launch these attacks are called "bot herders." They use your computer to perform all kinds of criminal activity, including launching spam, viruses, phishing schemes, and DDoS (Distributed Denial of Service) attacks, where they basically tie up a network to render it useless.

> It is estimated that millions of computers are being used unwittingly to propagate cyber crime.

Beginning in 2007, millions of computers were infected with an email Trojan-horse program called "Storm Worm." Computers infected with the Storm Worm Trojan became botnets that were used almost exclusively to send out spam. Machines infected with the Storm Worm have also been affiliated with money mule recruitment emails.

Think about it for a moment: How else could cyber crime propagate across the Internet so quickly if it weren't for the fact that millions of computers act as a pass-through gateway and actually aid in the propagation unbeknownst to their owners? That's what bot herders are counting on—quick, pervasive attacks and launches using your computer as a part of their network so they can wreak as much havoc in the shortest amount of time. Your computer is used solely as a "resender" of spam, without you knowing it, through backdoor programs. If someone tapped into your electrical circuit to steal electricity to tape illicit videos of children, you'd be furious, wouldn't you? Yet every day, computers are "tapped" into to send spam and phishing attempts, and you may not even know that your computer is part of it.

Bot herders are so clever at what they do that they can "virtually" change locations overnight by infiltrating thousands of computers at a time. It is not unusual for a bot herder to completely shift operations within a matter of days. This is why it is so difficult for law enforcement to shut down these operations. And you may inadvertently be helping them. Fortunately for you, those who are trained to detect herding operations also know that the bot attacks happen unbeknownst to the computer's owner.

Commtouch Report: 10 Million Infected Computers

In July of 2008, Commtouch, a cyber security vendor, released a report based on the automated analysis of billions of email messages weekly. The company concluded that 10 million "zombie" (infected) computers are online each day around the world contributing to the propagation of spam (source: www.commtouch.com).

That's 10 million computers under someone else's control. We will confess that we are often dubious of claims made by vendors, especially security vendors, because the darker the picture they can portray, the better the chances they have of selling their product, but in this case, we don't doubt these figures. The report goes on to say that by the time analysis systems have identified compromised PCs, most botnets will have shifted to new machines. We'd have a better chance at chasing the wind.

Operation Bot Roast

In June of 2007, the FBI announced "Operation Bot Roast" (no comment on the name choice), a joint effort with the Department of Justice to "disrupt and dismantle" botnet operations whose specific target is to phish account information from victims. We'll talk more later on about botnets and what they are, but in this first phase, the FBI was able to identify over one million infected computers by their IP (Internet Protocol) addresses. In November of 2007, they launched phase two. In May of 2008, the U.S. Department of Justice (DOJ) charged 33 individuals in a 65-count indictment for their alleged participation in an international racketeering scheme that used the Internet to defraud thousands of individual victims and hundreds of financial institutions. Thus far, they've uncovered more than $20 million in economic losses, but what makes this case unusual is how the criminals operated in real time across multiple countries using multiple technologies in a very organized manner—all through the use of botnets and machines that were compromised (one of which could have been yours).

How They Did It

According to the DOJ, thousands of credit and ATM cards were phished when mobile phone users received a text message that said, "We're confirming that you've signed up for our service. You will be charged $2 per day unless you cancel your order at this website: [omitted]."

The website was a ploy to gather specific account details such as account numbers and so on. That information was quickly passed to the U.S.-based part of the operations, which used this information to manufacture fake cards with the stolen credit and ATM card details imprinted on the magnetic strip.

Understand that these card printers are readily available from a variety of sources for under $1,000. The cards were then turned over to "runners" who would drain the accounts at ATMs and POS (point of sale) terminals in stores. The FBI worked this case in conjunction with Romanian law-enforcement officials. The 33 individuals indicted included U.S. citizens, Canadians, and foreign nationals (Romanian, Mexican, Vietnamese, Cambodian) who operated from the U.S., Canada, Romania, and Portugal.

This was a sophisticated operation that clearly crossed international boundaries. We know how comprehensive these types of investigations are, particularly when they cross jurisdictional lines (let alone international lines), so it is encouraging to know that these types of criminal enterprises can be shut down. Unfortunately, for every one that does get shut down, hundreds are still in operation.

Trends in Botnet Operations

We've been hearing through the cyber grapevine that bot herders are scaling down their operations significantly, not in terms of their attack, but in terms of the number of computers they will infect at the same time. Apparently, they now realize that massive botnet operations are much easier to detect than smaller-scaled operations that only control a thousand computers at the same time. This "downsizing" also makes shifting operations much easier.

Is Your Computer Part of a Botnet?

The difficulty with this type of infection is that the software code that allows the bot herder to take control of your computer is extremely hard to detect. Just like a virus, the bot code can be part of a web link you clicked, an email you opened, or a file you downloaded.

Symptoms of a Bot

The botnet code is very difficult to detect and remove, so you need to be alert to specific symptoms that can be indicative of your computer being a "bot" (but bear in mind that these symptoms can be from other causes as well):

- **Your computer becomes unusually slow.** We'll assume (please say "yes") that you have adequate virus protection and you're keeping your computer up to date with patches. Is your machine slow only when you're on the Internet, or is it slow in general? The first thing we recommend if your machine is slow when accessing the Internet is to unplug your Internet router for about 5 minutes (make sure it's completely powered off because many have internal backup batteries) and then plug it back in. This will reset the router and sometimes clear up any speed issues.

- **Your hard drive runs even when you're not active on the computer.** Bear in mind that this could also be the result of built-in services running or programs performing automatic updates. It's just another symptom to be aware of.

- **You have items in your Sent mail folder that you know you did not send.** This is a big warning sign that you need to get your computer reviewed by a professional.

- **Someone sends you a nasty email accusing you of sending them spam.**

- **Your software programs suddenly don't run.** Again, there could be a multitude of reasons for this, but anything that has suddenly changed should raise a red flag and you need to determine why.

If You Think Your Computer Is Part of a Botnet

If there's any doubt in your mind, we recommend you seek professional computer help. As we said, trying to remove botware is difficult and can cause even more problems. Your best bet is to go to a computer professional and ask him or her to run the necessary scans on your computer to make sure it's clean.

In the meantime, if you think your computer is clean, keep it so by always applying virus and operating system patches. Shut off your computer when not in use! The bot herders will scan for computers that are on and have vulnerabilities. Shut off your computer when you're not using it to keep it further at bay. Also, make sure your firewall is turned on—always.

The "Gift" That Keeps on Giving

We'll give you one more reason to be concerned about all this. Consider what gift you are giving to the bad guys by not minding the state of your computer's system security. Let's say all you do is pay your utility bill online—many people do. If your computer is compromised, you've first of all given someone access to your bank account information. With that, the bad guys may very well either steal directly from your account or pass your account information on for a few dollars to someone else, who will then steal you blind.

Because we know that many of these bot herders are made up of highly organized groups that operate under the radar and are sometimes linked to countries we don't trust, consider that you've now potentially given them an access point into the utility company as well. We already know that public utilities are a cyber terrorist's dream target. Why give them anymore to work with?

Read on, because the next chapter outlines the three most important steps you can take to protect your system.

16

Your Online Safety Checkup

No matter what computer you use to access the Internet, here are the three most important steps you need to take to ensure protection:

1. Always keep your system up to date with automatic updates and patches to the operating system.
2. Install virus protection and make sure it is updated.
3. Install a spyware and/or malware detection program and run it frequently.

Keep Your System Updated

When your system alerts you that updates are available, install them immediately. They often contain important security patches. Every day, software companies such as Microsoft are notified of security vulnerabilities. Depending on the severity of the vulnerability, they generally package all the updates and fixes into one update and release it, usually on what has come to be known in the industry as "Patch Tuesday." It is imperative that you keep your system and any other software you use up to date on security patches.

If you use a Windows-based computer, you should have Automatic Updates running. If you don't, go to Control Panel, Security Center and turn on this feature. For nontechnical users, set this feature to automatically update the patches at a time you know your computer will be on. If

When your system alerts you that updates are available, install them immediately.

you'd prefer, you can manually install the patches, but the important point is to make sure you install a patch whenever a new release is available. The 5 minutes or so it takes to install a patch and reboot your computer is time well spent if it shores up a security hole. Remember that cyber criminals are counting on you not staying current with the updates. Malware and viruses can propagate across the Internet in a matter of hours. It takes the same amount of time for malicious code to attempt to access your computer by identifying security vulnerabilities. Keep the system patched!

Install Virus Protection

According to a 2005 study, 81% of home computers lacked "core" protection (source: National Cyber Security Alliance 2005 Online Safety Study). We hope that number has since improved.

Computers are often shipped with a demonstration (30-day free trial) virus protection program. After the 30 days, you need to subscribe to continue receiving the protection. Most of these programs average $30 to $50 a year. This money is well spent to ensure against computer viruses that can completely wipe out your system or make you vulnerable to credit card fraud or identity theft. A single virus that attacks the system can render it useless. It's not worth the risk when the cost of prevention is relatively inexpensive.

We recommend Symantec AntiVirus (www.symantec.com) or McAfee Antivirus (www.mcafee.com) for baseline protection. These are the industry-standard programs.

If you cannot afford either of these programs, you can install AVG Anti-Virus (www.grisoft.com) for free, but get something on your computer to protect it against basic viruses.

An antivirus program is only effective if its files are kept updated. New viruses are introduced every day that propagate across the Internet rapidly. It's almost pointless to have a virus protection program installed if you don't keep it updated. Each virus has a "signature"—a small line of code that identifies it—and that's what the virus protection program looks for. Make sure your virus program is set to automatically update itself whenever a new release is available.

New viruses are introduced every day that propagate across the Internet rapidly. It's almost pointless to have a virus protection program installed if you don't keep it updated.

Install Spyware and Malware Detection Programs

Two of the most effective tools at combating spyware and malware remain free of charge. We highly recommend you install SpyBot Search & Destroy (http://www.safer-networking.org) and/or Ad-Aware (www.lavasoft.com) and run them regularly. These programs will search for keystroke loggers and malware, remove unnecessary cookies, and alert you to any suspect programs. When running the free versions, we recommend you clear all your cookies first to speed it up (in Internet Explorer select Tools, Internet Options and click Delete Cookies.) Run these programs on a regular basis—weekly if you can.

Malware City

We recently came across Malware City (www.malwarecity.com), which is a portal on software producer BitDefender's website (www.bitdefender.com). It looks like a game, but is actually filled with the latest information and news related to malware. We mention it because it is not only entertaining, but rather informative. We're not advocating software, just suggesting its interesting features could help keep users wanting to learn more. The site is meant to appeal to the young popular gaming culture and offers opportunities to join the site as a contributor to the "wise warriors fighting malware."

StopBadware Report

StopBadware.org is a partnership between academic institutions, technology industry leaders, and volunteers that aims to educate and reduce the amount of malware, or what they refer to as "badware."

A May 2008 report issued by StopBadware.org found that almost half the websites that "push" malware are hosted by just 10 networks. This means that most of this malware is coming from just a few highly organized places. The report also indicated that six of the 10 hosting networks were based in China.

Passwords

We cannot emphasize enough the importance of using *strong* passwords, which means at least eight alphanumeric characters (that is, a combination of letters and numbers).

Here's a list of what you should *never* use for a password:

- Blank (no password)
- The word *password, passcode, admin,* or a derivation
- Your name or login name
- The name of your significant other or another person
- Your birthplace or date of birth
- A pet's name
- A dictionary word in any language
- Your automobile's license plate number

Programs are freely available on the Internet for download that can be run against a password list and crack a password in a matter of minutes. When doing forensic examinations of computers, we sometimes come up against password-protected files or folders. These programs have a special feature that allows the investigator to build a potential password cracker.

The investigator "feeds" the program with potential passwords, such as birthdates, kids' names, dog names—whatever can be gleaned during the course of the investigation. The same types of tools are, unfortunately, available to the bad guys as well. So, please, never use a "real" word as a password.

Creating Strong Passwords

How can you create a secure password? It's actually much easier than you think.

Think of a phrase you can remember. We'll use "Mary had a little lamb whose fleece was white as snow" as an example. Now take the first letter of each word—MHALLWFWWAS. That's 11 characters, which is a good length for a strong password. Note that some passwords are restricted to eight characters, so this would have to be truncated. Using MHALL-WFWWAS, substitute some numbers for letters. We'll use the number 1 for the letter *L*. Now the phrase reads MHA11WFWWAS. We could also use upper and lowercase letters because many password programs are case-sensitive: mha11wfwWAS. Hum the song in your mind a few times and emphasize the last three words to remind yourself they are uppercase. Do it a few times and you'll quickly remember which ones are uppercase. That's a pretty good password, and because you know the original phrase, it's easy to remember.

Multiple Accounts, Multiple Passwords?

It's not atypical to have half a dozen or more accounts to log into these days. Between professional and personal email, bank accounts, credit card accounts, college accounts—the list is endless. However, you should never use the same password for more than one account!

If your password is inadvertently gleaned in one application, you could be giving data thieves access to all your accounts. It's always better to use different passwords, but then how do you remember eight different passwords for eight different accounts? That's easy. Change your base password up. Let's go back to our final passphrase (remember it?): mha11wfwWAS. If you want to use it for eBay, you could change the first letters to "EB," so the password would be "EBha11wfwWAS." If the password is for American Bank, it would be "ABha11wfwWAS." The important thing is that each password is slightly different. That's pretty easy if you think about it. Just change up one important keyword in the phrase and you'll remember to substitute each time.

Table 16.1 is an interesting chart showing examples of passwords and the time it would take to crack them.

Table 16.1 Time to Crack Passwords

Sample Password	Darren	Land3rz	B33r&Mug
Combinations	308.9 million	3.5 trillion	7.2 quadrillion
Class A	8.5 hrs	11 yrs	22,875 yrs
Class B	51.5 mins	1 yr	2,287 yrs
Class C	5 mins	41 days	229 yrs
Class D	30 secs	4 days	23 yrs
Class E	3 secs	10 hrs	2.25 yrs
Class F	Instant	58 mins	83.5 days

(Source: http://www.lockdown.co.uk)

Note that most personal computers these days are fast, with dual processors, and could perform a Class D attack. A more organized group would have Class E capabilities. A supercomputer would be categorized as having the capability to perform a Class F attack.

Password Management Tools

A number of online tools are available for maintaining your passwords in encrypted form, some of which are free from download sites. We're not particularly keen on these types of programs, but they're probably better than using the feature in Internet Explorer called "AutoComplete," which stores passwords, including those for your bank and credit accounts, so you don't have to reenter them when you go to their websites. We always shut off this feature on any computer because we do not want anyone who might gain access to the computer, either directly or remotely, to be able to access private account data without being prompted for a password.

Hacking—The New High School Curriculum

When we think of passwords being discerned and people getting unauthorized access, it's natural to think of potential crimes such as identity theft and credit card fraud, but there are many other instances where access to passwords has led to more "juvenile" crimes.

There have been many cases in which either individual schools or entire school districts have been hacked into by students. In fact, if you visit www.youtube.com and search for "school hacked," you'll see several videos documenting this. In Santa Clara County, California, students hacked into their school system to get a sneak peek at their upcoming final examinations. In April of 2008, six students from a San Diego area high school were suspended for hacking into their school's computers, changing their grades, and obtaining advanced copies of exams. The students allegedly used software downloadable from the Internet (likely a keystroke logger) to obtain passwords from teachers, which then gave them access to restricted files and programs. The files were stored on a flash drive, which was discovered by a teacher when left in one of the computers.

Would You Leave Your Door Unlocked? Unsecured Wi-Fi

Wireless routers have become quite popular for home use, but they continue to present a security vulnerability if they are not configured properly.

Every day we read cases about people who set up their wireless access point (Wi-Fi router) with the factory-default settings. This is like leaving your doors unlocked at night and allowing someone to come into your house and steal your possessions!

If you leave your Wi-Fi connection unsecured, the criminals using it can be long gone but the records will still point back to your account.

"I don't mind if my neighbor's kid borrows my connection to play online games," you may say. That's what one neighbor in Delaware County thought until the police showed up at his door, search warrant in hand. What was the offense? Possession of child pornography—a serious offense with even more serious consequences. Little did this neighbor know that a suspect who had been on the run for over a year was "borrowing" his unsecured wireless network to download 100 images of child and adult pornography. The warrant was based on the account holder information of the Internet service provider. If you leave your Wi-Fi connection unsecured, the criminals using it can be long gone but the records will still point back to your account. In apartment complexes or streets where houses are close together, it's not unusual for an unsecured Wi-Fi signal to be available several houses down—up to 200 feet away on average, depending on building features.

Piggybacking

Criminals love to access unprotected Wi-Fi, a practice known as *piggybacking*. And it's no different than splitting into your cable line and stealing your cable access. It is still considered theft of services. Many just want the free Internet access without having to pay for it, but some deliberately seek it out to cover their tracks and thwart law enforcement's efforts to find them.

Many times, we travel with a Wi-Fi-enabled laptop and are amazed at the number of unprotected networks we find. Unless you are offering a public Wi-Fi network, do you really want your neighbor across the street to be able to browse the Internet at your expense or to download kiddie porn on your account?

Unprotected Wi-Fi also means that the neighbor may be hogging a great deal of the bandwidth you're paying for, which can cause your Internet access to bog down. Interestingly, the United Kingdom takes piggybacking very seriously. Offenders there can face up to 5 years in prison and a fine of about $1,900.

Think it's hard to detect Wi-Fi connections? Think again. Figure 16.1 shows a $30 t-shirt available from Think Geek (www.thinkgeek.com) that can do just that. The glowing bars on the front of the shirt dynamically change as the surrounding Wi-Fi signal strength fluctuates.

(Courtesy of thinkgeek.com)

FIGURE 16.1

Wi-Fi t-shirt from Think Geek

Wardriving

In 1983, the movie *War Games* was released about a teenager who, thinking he was playing an online game, accidentally hacked into a military computer network and nearly launched World War III. The expression "wardriving" is based on that movie. Wardriving is when someone drives around and attempts to hack into open, wireless networks. Using readily available and free software such as NetStumbler, people involved in wardriving find open, unsecured networks that are quickly tagged, identified, and mapped on the Internet for others to take advantage of. Many wardrivers use GPS (Global Positioning System) units for quick reference to their location and provide that to others on the Internet.

Using readily available and free software such as NetStumbler, people involved in wardriving find open, unsecured networks that are quickly tagged, identified, and mapped on the Internet for others to take advantage of.

Wi-Fi and "Evil Twin" Spoofing

You're sitting in a local café sipping your latte and surfing the Internet, knowing that you're using the café's free Wi-Fi account. A good idea? Not if you're careless. It's possible that the person sitting across the way you've witnessed with his head buried in his laptop is actually gathering every single word you type. How is this possible? Through Wi-Fi spoofing, also called *evil twin spoofing*. Here's how Wi-Fi spoofing works: You go into a place with a free wireless account and think you're logging onto their wireless network, when in fact you're actually connected to BadGuy's laptop, which is pretending to be the coffee shop's wireless account.

There are an estimated 68,000 Wi-Fi "hot spots" in the U.S. alone, and that's a conservative number. Unlike wired network systems that use cables to transport information through the Internet, Wi-Fi uses radio waves, which are inherently more vulnerable because many laptops are configured to automatically connect to the wireless network with the strongest signal. If a hacker is sitting two tables away, he can easily override the local Wi-Fi signal and have you connected to his laptop, where he'll happily collect your account usernames and passwords, your credit card information, every keystroke you type.

To avoid Wi-Fi spoofing, change the settings under Control Panel, Networks, Wireless to not automatically connect to the strongest signal. Watch for the name of the wireless network. If you're sitting at Los Angeles Airport and always connect to "LAX-Wi-Fi," don't assume that "LAX2-Wi-Fi" is valid. Be aware and leery in public Wi-Fi spots. They may be okay to check the local news or weather, but we would not advise logging into your bank account to check your balance.

> If a hacker is sitting two tables away, he can easily override the local Wi-Fi signal and have you connected to his laptop, where he'll happily collect your account usernames and passwords, your credit card information, every keystroke you type.

How to Secure Your Home Wi-Fi Connection

Several methods can be used to secure an open Wi-Fi connection. We recommend you do as many as you can and enlist the aid of someone knowledgeable to help you if needed. Note that in order to secure a wireless connection, a password is usually involved, so only give the password to those you trust. Professional technical support people should always be willing to hand over the keyboard for you to enter the password out of their view.

Change the SSID

The first part of any wireless setup is establishing the SSID, or *Service Set Identifier*. This is the name given to the router to be broadcast out to everyone else. Typically, when you take the wireless router out of the box, the default SSID is set to the manufacturer's name (for example, Linksys or Belkin). If you leave it set up with the manufacturer's name, hackers are more prone to try and penetrate it because this shows there is minimal security and may even give them a heads up that no password is set. Use something obscure for the SSID, not anything that would identify it as yours. Don't call it "Smith Family Network" or "Jones Avenue." The instructions to change the SSID are usually included in the setup software.

Turn On Encryption

All routers use some basic level of encryption, typically either WEP or WPA. Without it, it's like leaving your front door wide open all day long.

The two wireless encryption standards are WEP (Wireless Equivalency Protocol) and WPA (Wi-Fi Protected Access). Of these two standards, WPA is the more recent and the more secure. These encryption standards usually require either a password or a passphrase to connect a computer to your network. WEP is much less secure and can be quickly hacked in less than 20 minutes using readily available software on the Internet. Once the network is penetrated, the data being passed between the hacked computer and the Internet can be seen in clear text and can even be used to gain access to the computer's files. When it comes to Wi-Fi equipment, it pays to spend extra money to get the most recent devices because they will employ the newer standards, such as WPA, which is far more secure (but make sure your computer can still connect to the device if it's brand-new technology). If you're unsure whether your computer's network card will run on a newer router, write down the make and model number and take it with you. Most qualified salespeople will be able to assist you with this.

Change the Default Administrative Username and Password

"Administrator" is commonly used as the default username for wireless routers. This means you're giving a hacker half the work of penetrating your network. If possible, change the username and password under the security settings to something obscure that you can remember.

Place Equipment Where It's Accessible

One common mistake people often make in installing their Internet connection and Wi-Fi equipment is to place it in an area that is not easily accessible, such as the basement. There are several reasons for placing the equipment where you have better access it. First of all, you can easily see the device to ensure it is properly functioning. Many times the wireless router is connected to an integrated modem, where you receive phone, cable television, and Internet service all from the same company. It's going to be a whole lot easier to troubleshoot everything if you can see which lights are on and which are not. Secondly, there are many times when you will want to shut off the router by pulling its power source to refresh it, as discussed next.

Shut Off Your Wi-Fi Router When Not in Use

In order to have the most security, consider shutting off your wireless router when not in use. Install it in an easily accessible location and consider unplugging the power chord when you're not at home. This serves two purposes: It reduces the chance of someone hacking into your network because there is no network for them to hack into, and more importantly, it resets the IP address of the router, making it more difficult to trace. This can enhance your privacy if your Internet service provider is tracking your web access history.

Protecting Your Cell Phone

Cell phones are vulnerable to hackers, sometimes also called *phreakers*. A phreaker can hack into your cell phone and listen in on your calls or steal personal information simply by exploiting a short-range Bluetooth wireless connection. A hacker can do even more damage by stealing a cell phone or finding one lost by its owner.

Cell Phone Safety Tips

We highly recommend the following tips for anyone with a cell phone, particularly since, with the newer phones, you can do much more than make a call or send a text. Cell phone Internet and email service make you and your phone even more vulnerable to a hacker.

- Always keep a close watch on your cell phone. Don't leave it in public unattended, even for a minute!
- Lock your cell phone calling availability by password-protecting it.
- Disable the Bluetooth wireless connection when you're not using your cell phone.
- Consider using antivirus software to block hackers, and keep it updated.
- Never accept text messages or files from a stranger.
- Notify your cell phone provider immediately if you lose a cell phone or suspect it has been hacked. Discontinue service right away to prevent a thief from running up a bill.

Getting Rid of That Old Computer

With technology practically changing overnight and the price of computers dropping rapidly, it's not unusual for people to upgrade their computers. The question is, what do you do with that old system?

Many people, with very good intentions, donate their old systems to non-profit organizations such as local schools or churches. It sounds like a reasonable, charitable thing to do. Unfortunately, without taking the proper steps, it's also a very dangerous thing to do.

Deleted Files Are Not Deleted!

Just because you've deleted all your personal files before you donated a computer doesn't mean you've really deleted them. Deleting a file just means that the index to that particular file is removed. The actual file is likely still residing on the hard drive, and while one may argue that a church isn't going to actively attempt to recover your deleted files, you really have no say what happens to that computer after you make the donation. It *is* possible that it could fall into less-than-honest hands.

If you are thinking about donating your computer to a local school, remember that there are some very savvy students who would quickly run one of the many file-recovery programs that exist on the Internet and thus be able to retrieve your data.

Would You Hand Over Your Checkbook?

Once that computer leaves your possession with your data still on it, you might as well be handing over your checkbook. You run the risk of having the following data exposed and/or compromised:

- Your personal financial information, including your checking account information if you do online banking.

- Your social security number, which could lead to identity theft, if you've ever filed taxes online or applied for credit online.

- Your credit card information, including account numbers and/or passwords.

- Your personal medical information, if you've ever used the Internet to research a specific medical topic.

- Your email address list and any other personal contact information you stored.

We could go on and on, but the point is that once you hand over a hard drive, even if you think you have deleted the files, you're taking a huge risk. There are many ways to minimize this risk. One is to simply run a "clean wipe" program on your hard drive before you turn it over.

Go to any of the shareware websites, such as www.download.com or www.tucows.com, and enter the search term "secure wipe." You'll find many listings for utility programs (some for free) that will perform a secure wipe of your hard drive. Just remember that a secure wipe is just that—a secure wipe. Whatever you've "wiped" is *not* recoverable, so proceed only when you know you will never need that data again.

Secure Wipe Versus Reformat

When a hard drive is reformatted, the process does not usually securely clean the hard drive—it merely prepares the hard drive for the installation of a new operating system. Felicia assisted on a case a few years ago in which a computer was stolen from a local restaurant. The computer was later recovered, but upon examination had been renamed and appeared to not contain any traceable files.

The perpetrators mistakenly thought that by reformatting the hard drive, they would remove all evidence of the computer's prior ownership. It only took a few rudimentary tools for Felicia to "undelete" the hard drive. Suddenly, numerous documents, including menus, suppliers, and customer lists, began reappearing.

Note that when you run a secure wipe, the operating system can also be deleted, rendering the computer useless until this is restored. Many charitable organizations will accept computers without the operating system installed because often they will install their own, but check with the organization first. Be especially aware that the place where you donate your computer is not necessarily where the computer will end up.

Assume Whatever You Did on the Computer Is Still There

This is the best rule-of-thumb to use with computers. They are, by nature, "memory machines," and what they can capture and store is unfathomable. Every chat, email, image viewed, website visited—all of this can potentially be recovered and restored. Use your computer wisely and dispose of it thoughtfully.

Electronic Depots

Many organizations will now take computers regardless of whether they have the hard drives in them. You can find many of these organizations on the Web. Computer components contain precious metals that have value. Some companies actually melt certain components down and resell them. Don't think that the hard drive couldn't be put into some other computer and viewed, because hard drives can easily be swapped from one computer to another for examination. If you go this route, pull the hard drive and smash it with a hammer, shoot it up on the range, or drive over it if your tires are strong, but make sure you have rendered it useless. Otherwise, someone else may find it quite useful for unsavory purposes.

How to Recover Your Stolen Laptop

We recently had a case where a laptop was stolen from a business. In this case, the business was relatively small, so they outsourced their IT work to a local technology group. Weren't we pleasantly surprised to find out that the IT company had installed "locator" software on the laptop, as well as remote access. Within a few hours, they were able to provide us enough detailed information about the laptop's "new" owner that officers were able to knock on their door in a relatively short amount of time. Charges are forthcoming.

Stolen Laptop Locator Services

Many different programs are available that, depending on the configuration of your laptop, can either send out its location or at least give remote control access back to the original owner.

One interesting program is Retriever, by Front Door Software. Once the laptop is stolen, this program sends out the message "This computer is reported stolen." It then prompts for a pass code. If the pass code isn't entered in a timely manner, the laptop's location is displayed on a Google map to allow the original owner to locate it.

Dozens of similar programs are available. Just Google "anti-theft laptop" and pick one. It could result in the safe return of your laptop! In the meantime, back up, back up, back up.

And while we're at it, given the enormous popularity of iPods, we couldn't help but mention the iPod disguise, available for around $10 from www.iDisguise.com. It looks like a mint container but is actually used to store your iPod.

If disguising your iPod doesn't work for you, try a special case that comes with a combination lock and a steel cable. The one shown in Figure 16.2 is available for around $50 from www.audiocubes.com.

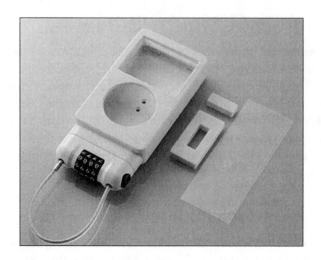

FIGURE 16.2

iPod anti-theft case

Lock Your Car, Please!

On a final note: We must say that we are constantly amazed at the staggering number of electronic devices stolen from unlocked vehicles within our jurisdiction. This includes iPods, cell phones, laptop computers, GPS units, and so on. Thieves who steal from cars are usually down-and-out folks who are looking for items they can quickly resell or pawn. The best way to prevent your electronic gear from being stolen is to *lock your vehicle*. It would shock people to know just how often cars are left unlocked with valuables left inside, often in clear sight. Use common sense.

Consider what you're giving to thieves the next time you walk away from your unlocked car. Do you really want them to have your entire music library in which you've invested thousands of dollars? Do you want them to have your social security number from the taxes you filed last year online on your laptop, your entire email contact list, your resumes, and your bank statements? Do you want them to have your GPS with "Home" already programmed in, or your child's cell phone number, which is programmed into your cell phone? Probably not. So, please, lock your car.

> Consider what you're giving to thieves the next time you walk away from your unlocked car.

17

How We Would Combat Cyber Crime

Having spent many years studying, researching, investigating, and testifying in cases, we want to assure you that law enforcement is as frustrated about the lack of progress combating cyber crime as victims are. Every month the number of reported cases of identity theft, online sexual solicitation of children, credit card fraud, and cyber stalking and harassment rises. Some days it truly feels like we are swimming against the tide. And because we keep a close eye on national trends and maintain ties in the law-enforcement community with other specialized units, we know that cyber crime is not going away.

At a local level, it is especially frustrating. Municipal law-enforcement agencies struggle with budgets that are bare-boned to begin with, and certainly don't allow new programs such as specialized cyber crime units to flourish. What used to be a budgetary boon to agencies—federal grant dollars—has largely been diverted to antiterrorist efforts to the detriment of departments across the nation that just want to be able to combat crime in their neighborhoods and on their streets.

The Victim's Perspective

Victims have a right to expect that justice will, if at all possible, be served. They do not want to hear "Contact your insurance company and file a claim" when someone has run up $1,000 on their credit cards. They do not want to hear "All we can do is file a report for you to take to your bank" when their identity is stolen or "If this man is bothering you, stay off the computer" when they feel their lives are in danger.

Unfortunately, that's exactly what is still happening across the country due to law enforcement's lack of resources, personnel, training, and funding. At some point, we hope that cyber crime is recognized as the pervasive, invasive crime that it is and resources are allocated for hiring and training, as well as education and prevention programs. That is what we hope to have accomplished with this book, but there's a lot more work to be done.

The Anonymity of the Internet

It's hard to fight what you can't see. The Internet is like a large black hole for law enforcement that allows strangers to become perpetrators and victims. This is not the kind of crime law enforcement is used to investigating, and the fact that there are so many ways to stay anonymous on the Internet presents a unique challenge to law enforcement, who, traditionally, could drag suspects into the police station and either interview them or fingerprint them to get their real identity.

From the victim's perspective, this same anonymity shakes at the very foundation of a person's fear. If you were home alone and your neighbor was persistently staring at you from his window or the same car kept driving by your house, you would be well within your rights to notify the police about such "suspicious activity."

In these two situations, you would at least be armed with tangible details to provide to the police for their report. When the stalking happens from an unknown person across the Internet who seems to know about you, it is that much more frightening because you have no idea where that person is or to what lengths he'll go to reach you.

Crimes Are Often Multijurisdictional

Let's face it, police officers are generally used to investigating crime that has occurred within their city or town. Granted, sometimes a case crosses jurisdictional lines, but it tends to be regionalized. Enter the challenge of cyber crime, where crimes could be committed thousands of miles away in other states, and very likely in other countries. Does the foreign country have the same laws forbidding online solicitation of minors? Some don't still. Does that police department 3,000 miles away have the manpower to track down the closed-circuit security video from the store in Kansas where your credit card was used to purchase a new television? Do the authorities in Africa have the incentive to try and locate who sent you the 419 letter that duped you out of $2,000?

Although most law-enforcement agencies work cooperatively to solve crime, the reality is that some agencies simply don't have the manpower to do a whole lot of investigating on what they might consider to be a "minor" crime. Once the case slips beyond the boundaries of the local town or jurisdiction, which much of cyber crime does, it is generally up to the good will and cooperation of another agency to knock on that business's door and ask for the video surveillance tape. If that agency is understaffed and doesn't consider your type of crime a high priority, the case will come to a dead end.

How We Would Fight Cyber Crime

Given our frustration in trying to deal with cyber crime, we put our collective blonde heads together to come up with this list of recommendations based on our personal knowledge, training, and experience. Please note that these ideas do not necessarily reflect the views of any law-enforcement agency. They are our personal recommendations only, but we would hope that law-enforcement agencies across the country would consider them carefully.

Recognize That Cyber Crime Is a Business!

Excluding the predator who travels 3 hours in an attempt to have sex with who he thinks is a 13-year-old, the majority of cyber crime is perpetrated for financial gain. A new study has put a price tag of more than $7 billion on the financial suffering experienced by victims of Internet fraud and attacks (source: *Consumer Reports'* 2007 State of the Net).

A new study has put a price tag of more than $7 billion on the financial suffering experienced by victims of Internet fraud and attacks.

There really is no finite number on what the true cost of cyber crime is. It doesn't matter. It's huge, and it's growing because it *is* a business—and a booming one at that. It's time to start approaching cyber crime as a competitive business that needs to be shut down by looking at the overall model of cyber crime and using a multitiered approach through education and enforcement.

Develop Greater Cooperation with Financial Institutions

The trail of payments to kiddie porn sites, fraudulent auctions, and identity theft has to end somewhere. Although we are encouraged by recent collaborative efforts between law enforcement and financial institutions in following the money trail of cyber crime, it's not enough. A greater effort has to be made to locate those who are profiting from the exploitation of children in particular, and follow the money trail back to the bad guys. This can only be done through cooperative efforts with major leading financial institutions. Although we understand that banks and credit cards companies have an obligation to protect their customers' privacy, they also have a societal responsibility to protect our children. Tracking the monetary trail of those who pay by credit card to watch children perform sex acts online or who order videos such as "Baby Rape" is the key to putting a stop to these heinous crimes.

Change Law Enforcement's Paradigm of Cyber Crime

Traditional investigative techniques are predicated on investigating a crime perpetrated by a single person against another person. In the case of cyber crime, a highly organized and well-trained group or organization may perpetrate a crime using thousands of computers in 5 minutes, stealing credit card data, usernames, and passwords. This crime is not committed with a knife that can be dusted for fingerprints, but by malware programs and Trojan horses that execute commands and find the next thousand computers to penetrate. It takes a very different mindset and a very different set of skills to combat this type of crime. Law enforcement has to recognize that this requires people with a new skill set—those who are analytical, detailed, technical, and methodical.

Along these lines, law enforcement needs to acknowledge the overall impact of cyber crime on their community—from the text message that is sent to the teen at the high school telling her that she is ugly, to the spam mails that tie up the city's mail server, to the senior citizen who is bilked out of his life savings by a spam email. Collectively, we would venture to bet that there is no other form of crime so prevalent when all is taken into account.

Create a Single Reporting Site for Cyber Crime

When law-enforcement agencies aren't even sure where to report cyber crime, how can victims be expected to know? Right now, depending on the type of cyber crime that has been perpetrated, it may be appropriate to report it to any number of agencies, including your local police department, the FBI, the Secret Service, and the U.S. Postal Service. It's no wonder that so many cyber crimes go unreported.

We need to create one single point of submission for reporting cyber crime. This is not meant to supersede your local police department, but it is meant to make it easier for victims to make complaints. For simplicity's sake, we'll call this the "Cyber Crime Agency." Make cyber crime reporting of any kind a click away on a designated website or a toll-free phone number. That central reporting agency will then be responsible for disseminating the case to the appropriate agency for follow-up.

Some may say this already exists with IC3, the Internet Crime Complaint Center (www.ic3.gov), but IC3 is primarily for fraud complaints. We're talking about a centralized agency for *all* types of complaints, including cyber harassment, cyber stalking, voyeurism, identity theft, sexual solicitation, and any other type of cyber crime, that could then be funneled to the appropriate agency for follow-up. Why burden the victims even further by making them fret over where to report their crime to? Keep it simple and create a single entry point. Maybe if everyone knew how and where to report cyber crime, we could, at the very least, get a better handle on just how serious this issue is, and perhaps the money that is being diverted to other federal programs could be channeled back to keeping our children safe from sexual predators.

Collect Better Statistics

It may shock the public to know that there really is no hard data that truly represents the magnitude of how pervasive cyber crime is. Many studies have been released, but these are largely funded by corporations that specialize in cyber security and therefore have to be taken with that subjective viewpoint in mind. The reality is that most forms of cyber crime still remain unreported. Think about it: How many phishing emails and spam emails do you receive in a given day? Do you report them to the authorities? Probably not, yet these are still crimes.

Crime Statistics and NIBRS (National Incident-Based Reporting System)

Here's the reality of crime statistics: Some police departments report general crime statistics on a monthly basis to their states, which in turn report this information to the FBI for national collection, analysis, and dissemination. Contributing agencies tend to be medium- to large-sized police departments because for the average officer, trying to meet all the requirements for crime reporting is painful. Just mention the word "NIBRS" to any street cop and see what kind of reaction you get.

For the agencies that do comply with NIBRS submissions standards, the FBI then collects and analyzes this data to produce annual crime statistics. Unfortunately, the reporting elements are "generalized," meaning one overall heading can account for many different types of crimes.

For example, many cyber crimes such as identity theft are reported under the category of "Impersonation," which could also mean someone impersonating a police officer or impersonating someone else.

It's hard to tackle a problem as big as cyber crime when no one really knows just how big the problem actually is. Add to this problem the fact that many of the reporting criteria are horribly outdated. Here's an example taken right out of the NIBRS manual to demonstrate how outdated it is:

> *Example 4: A computer "hacker" used his personal computer and a telephone modem to gain access to a company's computer and steal proprietary data. "C" = Computer Equipment should be entered.*

"Telephone modem?" What about spam via cell phones? What about the child who is sexually exploited via an Xbox? Most of these crimes leave officers scratching their heads as to how to fill out the correct information required by NIBRS because the language is so outdated and the reporting is so cumbersome.

How would NIBRS categorize a man who has upskirted a woman with a mirror in a bookstore? Right now, voyeurism is categorized under NIBRS standards as "Peeping Tom," which is considered a "Crime Against

Society." The actual definition is "...to secretly look through a window, doorway, keyhole, or other aperture for the purpose of voyeurism." That's not exactly upskirting, and it's a crime against a person, not society, in our book.

Only 25% of the Population Is Covered

Here's the latest statistical data (as of the time of this writing) taken directly from the Justice Research and Statistics Association's "IBR Resource Center" website about how much of the population is represented in NIBRS data (source: www.jrsa.org/ibrrc/index.html):

> As of September 2007, 31 states have been certified to report NIBRS to the FBI, and four additional states and the District of Columbia have individual agencies submitting NIBRS data. Approximately 25% of the population is covered by NIBRS reporting....

Only 25% of the population is covered? How can anyone get a handle on cyber crime when only 25% of the population is represented? How can cyber crime trends be targeted when new technologies emerge every day and the collection elements don't capture that? If officers on the street, who are the primary source of this data, are not trained in how to correctly code a case where thousands of victims are swindled in a phishing scam via their cell phones, how can law enforcement deploy their resources to go after the criminals?

It's time for a total revamp in collecting crime data to focus on the problem of cyber crime. New technologies such as gaming systems and cell phones, and new crimes such as cyber stalking and phishing, need to be clearly spelled out for police departments to be able to report them. It's hard to fix what we can't collectively see.

Parents Need to Take Control

Would you, as a parent, hand over your car keys to your 10-year-old and let her take it for a spin? We hope not! Yet that same frightening scenario happens every minute of the day as parents let their kids drive unsupervised down the "information superhighway," where danger lurks on so many streets. It's time for parents to acknowledge that the Internet is inherent with **You are just as responsible for monitoring what your children do on the Internet as you are what they do anywhere else.**

dangers. Hear us? It's fraught with bad people who want to hurt your kids. Trust us. It is. And who is responsible for keeping kids safe? You are! We're parents, too, so we'll get in everyone's face a bit about this. You are just as responsible for monitoring what your children do on the Internet as you are what they do anywhere else.

Want the easiest way to do this? Put the computer in a centralized location so you see exactly what your child is doing on it. And watch. Talk to your child and ask questions about who he is chatting with. Take control. That's not only your right, it's your responsibility!

Develop Partnerships and Share Information

We've made the statement that cyber crime is actually *far* more pervasive than any researcher has been able to prove and that it may, in fact, be the most prevalent form of crime our nation sees today. We base that on the collective knowledge that every day hundreds of millions of spam emails and phishing attempts are circulated around the Internet. These are, for the most part, "nuisance" crimes that most people have come to accept as the normal course of daily business, but they are petty crimes that often have catastrophic results for the small percentage of people who fall victim to them. A simple crime such as email spam also has a "trickle down" effect in lost time and the cost of trying to prevent them to begin with. The problem is, law enforcement hasn't developed partnerships with all the industry leaders who could help thwart these types of nuisance crimes, or there is still a reluctance to work cooperatively with corporations to understand the source of these crimes.

There have been some successful partnerships, but at some point, trusts have to be better established between law enforcement and industry leaders to work cooperatively and collaboratively on putting a stop to cyber crime.

It may surprise people to know that even law-enforcement agencies sometimes have a tough time sharing information among themselves, so it's no wonder there is reluctance to share information beyond the boundaries of the police world.

In addition, law-enforcement agencies are often reluctant to share information because they fear the data will be misused or inappropriately released, but at some point, this paradigm needs to shift for the greater good of protecting citizens and taking action against the criminals who prey on them.

Cops on the Cyber Beat

In 2007, Indiana State Police Lt. Charles Cohen garnered a great deal of attention with his talks to law-enforcement officers around the country asking simple questions such as, "How many of you have heard of *Second Life?*" (in reference to the online game that has its own virtual community with millions of players). Lt. Cohen's premise is that police departments often overlook cyberspace as an important investigatory tool. He mentioned the case of a New Jersey detective who tracked the alleged killers of three college students by mining MySpace pages maintained by the suspects and their friends.

Based on our own experiences in investigating cyber crime, we agree. Law enforcement has largely overlooked this new "patrol zone." Too many departments rely on their "cyber crime" investigators—officers who are specially trained in computer forensic investigations—for everything computer related. The reality these days is that routine investigations often cross the cyber barrier, particularly if younger people are involved, so regular law enforcement cannot overlook this area as an important resource in investigations.

Every department should be training at least their general investigators or juvenile investigators on how to mine information from social networking sites such as MySpace and Facebook, how to collect and permanently catalog videos on YouTube, how to develop a presence on popular online game sites such as *World of Warcraft* and *Second Life*. Investigators whose specialty is computer forensic examinations are often so swamped these days that they don't have the time to stay on top of all these social venues, but these social networking sites have become the cyber playground and hangout for many of our youth, and to overlook that is wrong.

"Virtual" Policing and Cyber Patrols

Community policing has been a law-enforcement term for well over a decade. The main premise behind the concept of community policing is that police officers should maintain a proactive presence in the community rather than just showing up after a crime has been committed.

In our dream world, agencies would also practice "virtual policing" by maintaining a proactive presence online—a cyber patrol, if you will. We know from many studies that a police presence is a deterrent. It's not enough anymore for police departments to say they maintain a cyber presence just because they have a website. Websites are a dime a dozen and for the most part are flat. There's no real interaction with the community other than to typically provide a generic email address for sending questions or comments. That's not a virtual presence.

The "New" Community

We would go so far as to suggest that an officer be assigned cyberspace just like any other beat. It takes little time to develop a presence on social networking sites, but it does take time to view profiles and comments. We think this would be well worth it, especially because our experience is that many parents aren't even aware of their children's online presence. If a 14-year-old girl suddenly develops an online friendship with a 45-year-old man she does not know, or a young man comments on his website about "getting wasted at Tom's party," someone needs to intervene before these risky behaviors become disastrous.

We understand that officers are supposed to be out on patrol on the street in the community, but the paradigm of what the "community" is has to change to include the "virtual" community—to include school sites, individual home pages, social networks, and popular interactive gaming sites. Until law enforcement acknowledges the concept of "virtual policing," it will continue to shut the door on an entire community where so much proactive policing could occur.

Offer More Education Programs for Parents

Our children live in a very different world from what we grew up in—a world in which technology pervades their lives. It is not enough to think that just because you raise good kids, they'll be safe. Parents have a responsibility to understand the dangers the online world presents. We can find any number of online safety programs, but too often they are offered by individuals who have no real-world experience dealing with real cyber crime. In fact, many parents still don't know that "ASL" means "age, sex, location."

We'd like to see enhanced funding programs for parents to educate them about online dangers, including child exploitation, cyber stalking, and cyber bullying, by qualified professionals. Although many parents are aware, too many are not. How do you reach parents who are juggling work schedules, soccer games, piano lessons, and so on? Many corporations allow their employees to take a few hours out each month to volunteer in their community. Why not let employees take an hour to attend a presentation by qualified professionals who can teach them about these dangers they may not know about. Seriously, think about it: Did you know there were specialized websites dedicated to cannibalism or supporting suicide before reading this book? We don't mean to frighten you, but this is the world we work in, and you owe it to yourself and your children to be educated about it.

Eliminate Territorial Boundaries

Law enforcement is inherently territorial. Besides the issues with sharing information, agencies compete fiercely against each other for federal grant money to try and supplement their miniscule municipal budgets. At major crime scenes, disparate agencies fight over who has jurisdiction.

If we're ever going to make a dent against cyber crime, this has to stop because so much of cyber crime crosses "territories."

Use Police Civilians as Experts

Different forms of cyber crime require technical expertise in many areas. One officer who may be highly trained in conducting computer forensic examinations is not necessarily going to be trained to investigate identity theft cases or know how to gauge whether a corporate network has been compromised in an embezzlement case.

Add to that the fact that technology is ever-changing, often overnight. It's hard enough for anyone who knows anything about information technology (IT) to keep up with new products, new operating systems, and new devices. Police officers already have a plethora of duties, and few departments can afford to limit Detective Smith's duties to just one task. Although she may be the "cyber crime wizard," she may very well have to work extra shifts on patrol if manpower is short, or have to respond to a major crime that has nothing to do with cyber crime, or be tied up testifying in court.

We're not suggesting that any investigations be "outsourced" beyond the walls of the department, though some agencies do use qualified and vetted experts at times. We are suggesting that more departments consider the use of civilians in assisting with cyber crime cases. The reasons are many fold:

- Civilians who are employed with law-enforcement agencies are usually governed by the same rules and regulations regarding confidentiality and often have to follow the same policies and procedures as sworn personnel.

- When hired, police civilians often undergo the same vigorous background checks as police officers to ensure they are of good character and are trustworthy.

- By allowing civilians to conduct some of the more technical aspects of these investigations, investigators would be freed up to follow leads on the case.

- Police officers are often promoted out of their positions to a higher rank. In our department, we've seen no less than three highly trained police officers who received years of specialized training in cyber crime, at a huge expense, get promoted out of their positions. This leaves a gap that takes a great deal of time, training, and money to fill. Civilians are less likely to be promoted out of their positions and can maintain the much-needed consistency that is necessary to develop expertise in the area of cyber crime.

- Civilians could also be assigned to monitoring and maintaining a virtual presence.

- Just like civilian dispatchers monitor phone lines and alert police officers whenever their response is needed, civilian employees could monitor cyberspace and alert police officers whenever their response is needed. It just makes sense.

Many larger agencies already use civilians, but unfortunately there are still too many agencies who feel that only police officers can do these jobs. We think that's very wrong, especially when taxpayers are shelling out thousands of dollars for training, only to have that police officer leave that position after just a few years because she was promoted.

Adopt Tougher and More Consistent Cyber Crime Laws

The penalty for a crime such as cyber stalking still varies widely from state to state, if it exists at all. Federal laws are still haphazard in addressing many cyber crime issues. Lawmakers are still woefully uneducated about cyber crime. We're encouraged by some of the more recent federal laws being introduced, but remember that cyber crime is largely a multijurisdictional crime. It becomes a prosecutorial nightmare when laws are inconsistent and penalties are drastically different from one state to the next. It comes as no surprise that sexual predators are very well versed in what states are more lenient than others and that they tend to migrate toward those states in case they get caught. That's pretty sad. Let's shore up this loophole and make cyber crime laws consistent across all states so these miscreants don't think they can find safe harbor in our neighborhoods.

Standardize Forms

When someone becomes a victim of identity theft, this person is usually required to fill out an affidavit, or a sworn statement indicating he was not the one who conducted the fraudulent transactions. The problem is that every institution seems to have its own forms and requirements; therefore, the victim ends up being revictimized every time by having to spend so much time and energy, both physical and emotional, filling them all out.

There is no reason banks, credit card companies, motor vehicle departments, and other organizations could not accept one standardized affidavit that would contain all the pertinent details of the alleged crime. We understand that different databases require different fields and in a different order, but let's give the victim a break by adopting standardized forms like those found at the Federal Trade Commission (FTC) website (www.ftc.gov).

Provide More Training on Cyber Crime to Law Enforcement

We don't just mean specialized training for those that will become the cyber crime investigators, but to all police officers, especially first responders—the police officer who shows up at your door when you realize your bank account has been bled dry. Too often, valuable evidence is lost because first responders do not know the proper procedure when technology is potentially involved in the commission of a crime. Computers that were turned off get turned back on, thereby changing files that are needed as evidence. Peripherals such as digital cameras are unplugged without being catalogued, recorded, or photographed. Accounts are logged into without appropriate records being taken.

This all starts at the very basic level—the police academy. We're happy to report that more and more police academies are incorporating basic cyber crime training in their curricula, but this needs to be broadened to include the 15-year-veteran cop as well. This training is critical to be able to prosecute cyber crime. A forensics expert can't testify in court that a file is original and untainted if Officer Smith went on the computer at the scene to see if it had any illegal pictures on it.

Understand the Changing Nature of Cyber Crime

One of the most difficult aspects of writing this book was deciding what *not* to include. Every single day we were barraged with more cases, new security alerts, new vulnerabilities and methods to exploit those vulnerabilities, and changes in laws state by state. It became more and more difficult to decide what to keep and what to exclude because the reality is that cyber crime changes almost on a weekly basis.

> The reality is that cyber crime changes almost on a weekly basis.

Just when we thought we'd seen and heard it all, we'd either be directly exposed to or learn about another method of exploiting children, your bank account, or your identity. It changes that quickly, and we've endeavored to give you the most recent and accurate information we could find so you would be well educated. However, all this will have changed yet again by the time you finish reading this book.

Cyber Crime and Cyber Terrorism

We've focused most of our efforts on talking about how cyber crime impacts people on an individual basis, but we would be remiss if we did not mention the concerns we have about cyber terrorist initiatives. It is well known and widely reported that highly skilled terrorist organizations are focusing more and more efforts on trying to penetrate vulnerable cyber infrastructures. This has prompted large-scale "cyber war" simulations in many countries in which governments try to gauge the impact of their critical infrastructures—power grids, financial markets, water supplies, nuclear strongholds, communication systems—being knocked out due to cyber threats. The weaker a country's cyber infrastructure, the more susceptible it is to attack. This was highlighted in a recent quote from *ZDNet Australia* by David Vaile, Executive Director of the Cyberspace Law and Policy Centre at the University of New South Wales:

> *Why would you bother with flying a plane into a skyscraper when you could cause a crisis of confidence in the financial sector with an internet-based attack? You don't even need to rob the banks, just cause a run on them. ("Is the World Ready to Fight Cyber Crime?" ZDNet Australia, July 10, 2008.)*

Because the punishment for cyber crime varies so greatly from country to country and is largely inconsistent, cyber terrorists have hunkered down in countries that have weak laws, but their threat is no less serious. We occasionally receive "law-enforcement-sensitive" alerts and bulletins describing suspected cyber terrorism activities, but the information contained in these alerts is almost always already widely reported across the Internet.

The reality is that the damage someone can do from a computer with an Internet connection tucked away in a cyber café in a third-world country is no different than if they were sitting in a cyber café within the boundaries of the United States.

New technologies, new methods of exploitation, new vulnerabilities—staying on top of it all is truly a full-time task, but we hope this book has educated you so you and your loved ones can be better protected. That is our goal in writing this book.

A

Toys They Don't Want You to Know About

This section highlights products that are readily available online. Although everything we discuss can be used for legitimate purposes, it's a bit frightening to think about what happens when these items are used for illegal purposes.

The small device shown in Figure A.1 is a keystroke logger. It can be purchased on the Internet for as little as $50. This device is placed on the back of the computer between the keyboard and where the keyboard plugs in. There are many varieties of keystroke loggers; prices generally vary based on how many keystrokes the device can record. Keystrokes can also be logged via software that allows retrieval from anywhere. However, these devices usually require the user to retrieve the recorded data using the same computer on which the device was installed. This $50 device can record around 131,000 keystrokes, enough to easily obtain passwords to email and financial accounts. Other devices can record volumes of data.

FIGURE A.1

Keystroke logger

The following products can be found at www.PIMall.com:

- A high-resolution covert camera can be hidden in a book's spine so that someone can appear to be reading, but actually be recording. The book can be placed on a shelf and set to automatically record whenever motion is detected.

- A digital clock with covert camera is widely available on the Internet. The camera records to an internal memory card, and is available in black and white ($500) or full color ($600).

- What looks like a children's boom box of a popular children's character is actually a full-color covert camera that sells online for about $600. It is sold as a "nanny spy."

- A pen can actually conceal a hidden camera and is widely available on the Internet.

The site, www.chatcheaters.com, is just one of several sites designed to give suspicious partners easy access to surveillance equipment and online spying resources. It was begun by John LaSage of California, whose wife of 23 years left him to join a New Zealand man she met online. According to site statistics, ChatCheaters averages 400 visitors a day.

The site, InfidelityCheck.org, offers even more tools and resources for suspicious partners.

A cell phone SIM card extractor and can be purchased for about $150 on the Internet at www.dynaspy.com. The SIM card is where much of a cell phone's data is stored. In a matter of minutes, the SIM card can be removed from a cell phone, attached to this portable device, plugged into a computer's USB port, and the data extracted.

A tiny device called a credit card skimmer is used by thieves to sweep the barcode information from credit cards for later fraudulent use. (It's no bigger than a cigarette lighter.) These skimmers are extremely portable and cheap to come by. Some states have begun to introduce legislation making the possession of a credit card skimmer illegal. These devices can capture data at several different points. Also, some skimmer devices are designed specifically to fit over ATM and credit card machines. These are difficult to spot. You should look for anything mounted near where you would type in your PIN in case there is a hidden camera in it (a brochure holder, for example). Also, always look at the device you are skimming your card through. If anything looks unusual, notify the police and ask them to check it out. It is not uncommon for employees to be involved in the skimming operation, so be careful who you report it to.

Be especially aware when using standalone ATMs at convenience stores. These are especially prone to skimming devices, as are gas pumps. Be alert!

Many credit card companies are now issuing "smart cards" that can be "swiped" just by holding them up against an RFID (radio frequency identification) reader. (This device is no bigger than a walkie-talkie.) Despite the credit card companies' assertions that they have used the highest level of encryption allowed by the U.S. Government, questions continue to be raised about how secure these smart cards really are.

In March of 2008, a video began circulating around the Internet that originated on BoingBoingTV. It showed an episode about a device that can be purchased from eBay for $8 that's used to read the RFID information on credit cards. We looked and were able to find RFID readers in the range of $20 for standard readers ($300 for ones that come with a boost antenna).

Granted, you're more likely to have your credit card information stolen from an online transaction than someone bumping up against your wallet with a remote reader. However, with the right antenna, it wouldn't be impossible for someone to be able to read all the RFID information in a room of people from a distance.

Thumb Drives You Won't Believe

When law enforcement is executing a search warrant, they must be extremely broad about what they might possibly seize. Gone are the days when a search warrant was for "personal computers." These days, every possible electronic device—hard drives, routers, Wi-Fi-enabled systems, gaming systems, and any potential storage devices—must be included in the affidavit, just in case evidence resides on it. Imagine the frustration of a detective searching for child pornography images at a known distributor, only to be thwarted because the images are hidden on a covert device.

Figure A.2 shows one of these unexpected thumb drives that law enforcement is up against. Think about walking into someone's cluttered house trying to catch any storage media. Would you think to grab this up?

(Courtesy of bewineconnected.com)

FIGURE A.2

Wine bottle USB drive

Other devices, such as the Domino flash drive, pill thumb drive, and watch thumb drive, can be found at http://gizmodo.com/gadgets/thumb-drive/.

And while we're on the subject of thumb drives, be very careful where you get yours, especially if it is handed out for "free" at a convention. It could very well have malware installed on it that executes the moment you plug it into your computer.

B

CSI Versus Reality

We feel obligated to correct several misconceptions that have been perpetuated by Hollywood when it comes to law-enforcement work. Kristyn recently watched an episode of the television show *CSI: Miami*. (Even cops get a kick out of being entertained once in a while.) This particular episode centered around a vigilante murdering pedophiles who used the Internet to solicit sex from minors. As much as we enjoy viewing the fantasy facilities and resources these popular crime scene investigators have at their disposal, we feel the need to set the record straight on the reality of police work and what real-work conditions are like:

- First of all, police officers do not get Humvees assigned to them as unmarked police cars. Call her jealous, but Kristyn was saddled with an older Ford Taurus that was the color of a blue port-a-potty. The only commonality is that it is just as impossible to do any type of undercover surveillance in a platinum-colored Humvee as in a port-a-potty blue Taurus. That is where the similarities end.

- We have seen our share of dead bodies, and *none* of them was nicely laid out in the presidential suite of the Bellagio, in a stretch Lincoln limousine, or on the lanai of a multimillion-dollar mansion, complete with wave pool and sauna. Our dead bodies have always been several days old, stinky and bloated, leaking fluids, in an old trailer that is hotter than hell, stacked with pizza boxes, empty cans, and reeking of stale cigarette smoke and beer.

- No one, and we mean *no one*, wears all-white designer outfits with matching stiletto pumps to do police work unless she is working undercover as a hooker in a vice sting. Kristyn once made the mistake of wearing a cute little pair of black flats to work on a day she wound up in an old mobile home with a body she initially missed because of the several inches of raw sewage, rotting carpet, and piles of trash and cigarette butts that reached the ceiling. The resident had also been defecating in the bathtub, and therefore not bathing. Kristyn borrowed a pair of fireman's boots and threw out her entire ensemble upon returning home from work that day. She has never been to a glamorous crime scene.

- DNA results are not immediately accessible to the investigator. We recently received results back on a known suspect from the state lab on a case that is now almost *2 years old*. We also do not have immediate access to fingerprint analysis or ballistics—the wait time is often more than a year. If we need a license photo, we have to send a letter to our state DMV, and then wait for the mail to deliver a printed copy because license photos in our state cannot be sent via email.

- In this particular *CSI: Miami* episode, a suspect's IP address was immediately traced back to an Internet service provider (ISP), to the mailing address, and then to the suspect himself. It took approximately 10 seconds. We can assure you that in the real world of law enforcement, we have to manually locate the ISP, send them a preservation order to hold the information, write up a report and letter requesting an administrative subpoena, testify in front of a grand jury, and then wait a few weeks for the Internet service provider to mail or fax the information we are seeking. This often holds up a case for weeks.

- You won't see all that fancy equipment in most police departments. Take, for example, the computer monitor on *CSI: Miami* that looks like it is suspended in mid-air. The monitor is the size of a big-screen plasma TV—all touch screen-controlled so the users don't need a mouse to manipulate anything. They just move their hands around to go from view to view. The graphics are wild and colorful. We know that this type of technology actually exists, but this—along with the funky, high-style furniture, glass interview rooms, and wall-to-ceiling windows—makes us wonder what kind of budget the producers think the average police department has. Some of our computer monitors are still the old 15-inch monitors. Cubicles are gray and piled with papers, and our interview room is adjacent to the lunch room and has no air circulation. It is not uncommon to conduct a suspect interview with loud laughter and the smell of onions wafting from the room next door.

- On *CSI: Miami*, you never see the investigators write reports, fill out evidence tags, and photocopy their case files for court. We spend a ridiculous amount of time writing and reviewing reports, and if the case has a lot of evidence, filling out evidence tags and photo logs. This can be tedious and time consuming, and, we suppose, not very exciting to show to the primetime television audiences.

This is law enforcement's reality. Sometimes the most difficult task on a given day is trying to explain to 24 grand jurors why we can't solve crime like they do on television because of all the legal hurdles we'd face. (Come to think of it, we don't ever remember watching an episode where the investigators had to testify in front of the grand jury.) Search warrants, subpoenas, evidence testing, and access to confidential information require resources, manpower, and lots of time, which in turn slows down case investigation. The *CSI* series is a nice diversion from what is the reality in law enforcement in most jurisdictions, particularly in light of the fact that small- to mid-sized agencies are the norm in most states. Often people forget that crimes occur in smaller communities too.

We have a term for this phenomenon that biases juries and the public in general: "the *CSI* effect." At a recent law-enforcement convention, several lecturers addressed how law enforcement must take steps to combat "the *CSI* effect." They detailed how it has had an impact on the investigation and prosecution of cases, and even the trial of cases.

We can only hope that the stories we put forth will help you understand that the best way to prevent becoming a victim of crime is through awareness—of your personal space and your cyberspace. This is not a television show, it is reality.

Index

D

G

H

I

J

K

L

P

S

Y

Z

FREE Online Edition

Your purchase of **Cyber Crime Fighters: Tales from the Trenches** includes access to a free online edition for 45 days through the Safari Books Online subscription service. Nearly every Que book is available online through Safari Books Online, along with more than 5,000 other technical books and videos from publishers such as Addison-Wesley Professional, Cisco Press, Exam Cram, IBM Press, O'Reilly, Prentice Hall, and Sams.

SAFARI BOOKS ONLINE allows you to search for a specific answer, cut and paste code, download chapters, and stay current with emerging technologies.

Activate your FREE Online Edition at www.informit.com/safarifree

> **STEP 1:** Enter the coupon code: VJSSLZG.

> **STEP 2:** New Safari users, complete the brief registration form. Safari subscribers, just log in.

If you have difficulty registering on Safari or accessing the online edition, please e-mail customer-service@safaribooksonline.com